Harvest Heritage

Harvest Heritage

Agricultural Origins and Heirloom Crops of the Pacific Northwest

Richard D. Scheuerman and Alexander C. McGregor
With color plates by John Clement

Washington State University Press
Pullman, Washington

Washington State University Press
PO Box 645910
Pullman, Washington 99164-5910
Phone: 800-354-7360
Fax: 509-335-8568
E-mail: wsupress@wsu.edu
Web site: wsupress.wsu.edu

Library of Congress Cataloging-in-Publication Data

Scheuerman, Richard D.
    Harvest heritage : agricultural origins and heirloom crops of the Pacific Northwest / by Richard D. Scheuerman and Alexander C. McGregor ; with color plates by John Clement.
        p. cm.
    Other title: Agricultural origins and heirloom crops of the Pacific Northwest
    Includes bibliographical references and index.
    ISBN 978-0-87422-316-3 (alk. paper)
1. Agriculture—Economic aspects—Northwest, Pacific—History. 2. Agriculture—Northwest, Pacific—History. 3. Heirloom varieties (Plants)—Northwest, Pacific—History. I. McGregor, Alexander Campbell. II. Clement, John. III. Title. IV. Title: Agricultural origins and heirloom crops of the Pacific Northwest.
    HD1761.S218 2013
    338.109795—dc23

                                                                                            2013028189

Fine Quality Books from the Pacific Northwest

Front cover photograph: Bringing in the Sheaves, Wheat Harvest near Walla Walla, Washington, by John Clement. Chapter epigrams are from "Harvest Home" by Robert Herrick (c. 1645), unless otherwise noted.

For John Clement, our longtime companion
in many Northwest adventures;
and in memory of Dr. Orville Vogel,
scientist, humanitarian, and mentor.

Contents

The dreaming hills with their precious rustling wheat meant more than even a spirit could tell. Where had the wheat come from that had seeded these fields? Whence the first and original seeds, and where were the sowers? Back in the ages! The stars, the night, the dark blue of heaven hid the secret in their impenetrableness. Beyond them surely was the answer....

—Zane Grey, *The Desert of Wheat* (1919)

Preface

The idea for this work germinated from our opportunity to co-present the 2010 E. Paul Catts Lecture at Washington State University in Pullman through the kind invitation of Dr. John Brown of the College of Agricultural Sciences and Dr. Mary Collins, Director of the Columbia Plateau Center for American Indian Studies. We were asked to speak on the theme "Life on the Prairies: Indians, Farmers, and Ranchers," and the presentation prompted us to share related perspectives we have long formulated through experiences with area pioneer families, tribal elders, and professional associations in history and farming.

We greatly benefited from the goodwill, encouragement, and knowledge of Dr. Orville Vogel, Washington State University's world renowned plant geneticist from the 1930s to '70s and recipient of the National Medal of Science. Dr. Vogel was also deeply interested in regional agricultural history and introduced us to the research and writings of pioneering college, regional experiment station, and USDA "cerealists" who had preceded him in the Northwest. Notable among this group who published widely on landrace grains and other heritage varieties for both technical and popular readers were Mark Carleton, John Martin, Harry Harlan, and Carleton Ball.

We are grateful to members of many of these families for sharing knowledge that helped make this story possible. We thank Dick Nagamitsu of Lind, Washington, for sharing recollections of the historic Brevor-Norin cross made in Pullman in 1949 with Dr. Vogel that eventually led to the Green Revolution. The contributions of Stephen Jones, Steve Lyon, Gary Moulton, and Brook Brouwer of WSU's Northwestern Washington Research and Extension Center in Mt. Vernon, are also acknowledged, as are those by Robert Allan, Washington State University, Pullman; Robert Pelant of Coupeville's Pacific Rim Institute; and Stephen Reinertsen of The McGregor Company. These individuals have facilitated our efforts with Harold Brockelman, Curator of the USDA Small Grains Collection at Aberdeen, Idaho, to reintroduce Oregon White Winter, Pacific Bluestem, Scots Bere, and other nutritious heirloom grains to twenty-first-century residents of the land where they once ripened against summer skies.

Marc Marino and Cameron Schaefer also rendered essential assistance in this work. Other scholars whose work has significantly contributed to our understandings of these subjects include Palouse Country native Donald Meinig, Syracuse University, and author of Yale University Press's magisterial "Shaping of America" series; James Gibson, York University; Robert Carricker, Gonzaga University; ethnobotanist Sharon Rempel of Victoria's Vancouver Island Wheat Project; Mike Ambrose, John Innes Centre, Norwich, England; and Patrick Hayes and Andrew Ross, Oregon State University, Corvallis.

We are grateful for valued guidance provided by Bill Rhind and Mike McGuire at the Tacoma, Washington, Ft. Nisqually Living History Museum, where the fort's original granary of massive hewn timbers remains one of the oldest buildings in the Pacific Northwest. The museum's library and archives contain the area's largest primary source collection on Hudson's Bay Company fur trade operations. We have greatly benefited from the expertise of Ft. Nisqually and Cowlitz Farm historians including Bud McBride (a descendant of farm manager John McLeod), Steven Anderson, and George Dickey. A host of volunteers there have patiently transcribed a trove of journals and letters from employees of the fort, farm, and operations of their affiliated Puget Sound Agricultural Company.

Northwest tribal elders who have generously shared their knowledge of regional history and culture with us over the years include Andrew Joseph, Sr. (Colville-Lakes), Billy Frank, Jr. (Nisqually), Marvin and Michelle Kempf (Snoqualmie-Wenatchee), Jeffrey Thomas (Muckleshoot)—a descendant of Hudson's Bay Company middleman (paddler) Basil Courville; and Michael Finley, Colville Tribal Council Chair and a descendant of fur trader-guide Jaco Finlay. We also gratefully acknowledge the assistance of Adrienne Meier, Cindy Strong, David Wicks, Janiess Sallee, and Dominic Williams, Seattle Pacific University Library; Trevor Bond and Cheryl Gunselman, Washington State University Holland Library Archives, Pullman; Blynne Olivieri, University of Washington Suzzallo Library Archives, Seattle; Tim Wood, Champoeg State Park; Stephanie Lile, Shanna Stevenson, Maria Pascualy, and the late Winnifred Olson, Washington State Historical Society, Tacoma; Karin Clinesmith, Ritzville Public Library, and Kristie Kirkpatrick, Whitman County Library, Colfax.

We also thank Diane Wunsch, National Agricultural Library, Beltsville, Maryland; Gary Mitchell and Carolyn Weber, Royal British Columbia Archives, Provincial Museum, Victoria; Margaret Shields, Lewis County Historical Museum Archives, Centralia; and Gordon Grant, Island County Historical Society, Coupeville.

Area historians, farmers, and ranchers whose research significantly contributed to this work include Dick and Paula Coon, Benge; Harland Eastwood, Ritzville; Donald Schmick, Colfax; Valerie Sivertson, Pioneer Farm Living History Museum, Eatonville; David Pflugrath, Peshastin; Fred Schultz and Tom Henrich of Woodland's historic Cedar Creek Mill; Joanne Brown and Louise Mueller, Coupeville; and the late Martin Plamondon (a descendant of Simon Plamondon), of Toledo. We also thank Linda Becker, Arthur and Maria Ellis, Keith Merritt, Gary Schneidmiller, Chuck Eggert, Dan Birdsell, Scott and Jo Repp, Gerry and Lisa Bernhardt, Delores Mader, Naomi Mackey, Verne and Barbara Strader, Anita Deyneka, Dwight Gibson, David Anderson, Lena Hardt, Rene Featherstone, and Nina Wheatley. The abiding support of our spouses, Lois Scheuerman and Linda McGregor, has greatly facilitated our research and writing projects through the years.

Finally, we are grateful to Dr. David Stratton, Professor Emeritus of History at Washington State University; and the late Glen Adams, founder of Ye Galleon Press; for encouraging our research and writing through the years and for introducing a generation of young people to the Northwest's frontier era through compelling stories and lessons from that time with relevance for our own.

Richard D. Scheuerman
Seattle, Washington
Alexander C. McGregor
Colfax, Washington

Foreword

Richard Coon, Jr.
Benge, Washington

This work about the Pacific Northwest's agricultural heritage resulted from the collaboration of two longtime friends and lifelong residents of the region. Author-educator Richard Scheuerman of Seattle Pacific University, a native of southeastern Washington's Endicott-St. John area, teamed up with Alexander McGregor, historian and president of The McGregor Company, to present native and pioneer perspectives on Northwest geography and natural resources. Their work is accompanied by National Hall of Fame landscape photographer John Clement's masterful color images of the region as well as historical photographs from community and university archives. Reading this account and experiencing the accompanying illustrations is an experience at once pleasurable and informative.

The authors have their roots in the rolling hills and rugged basalt canyons of the Inland Northwest's legendary Palouse Country, and the remarkable story they have assembled from long-overlooked oral and written sources evokes personal memories in those of us who cherish our enduring regional heritage. Their regard for the Indian and European-American elders who shared their stories is evident in the many personal accounts that inform this telling. Alex reminds us that just a century ago ranchers and farmers comprised 40 percent of America's population versus one percent today. It is both an opportunity and an obligation to tell the larger public about frontier experiences that have so shaped our present world and contribute to the vitality of our cities.

In the 1870s there were just fifteen settlers living in Washington Territory's Adams County and they were all bachelors. One was colorful George Lucas, who ran a way station on the old Colville Trail near the mouth of Cow Creek, just down the road from our ranch west of Benge. The historic route was used by generations of migrating Indians and later, fur traders, who traveled between Ft. Walla Walla and Ft. Colvile. To the east on Rebel Flat, Georgia native and former Confederate soldier Alfred Holt wrote in 1872: "You'd love this Palouse Country. Our sheep, cattle, and horses will do splendid. But we would like some of your spare girls as they are rather scarce out here. Whenever you find a girl who is good looking, smart, agreeable and will furnish money for me, let me know."

Our family's roots go back to 1884, when William Snyder, my great-grandfather, took up a homestead and timber culture on Rattlesnake Flat south of Ritzville because "the bunch grass stood as high as a horse's belly." The four Snyder brothers were from Ohio and all took up homesteads to farm. My grandfather, Ralph W. Snyder, called our dry patch of land a cattleman's Garden of Eden. In the broad expanse that extends from Sprague Lake southward to the mouth of the Palouse River are three important things that made it so desirable to immigrants like my ancestors: mild winters, strong grass, and plenty of spring water.

Grandfather Snyder spent a lifetime developing his cattle herd and was careful in his management of the grass and crops. His goal was to return the rangeland to its former high state. He said, "There were a lot of fellows who took the attitude that with state land, the thing to do was to get every damned thing off of it... They didn't want it to get too good because if it did... their neighbors were liable to bid on it." He felt that was wrong. "The ideal way to take care of the range is to stay off of it, but if you pasture only in the winter time, after it is ripe, you really can't destroy it." Grandfather, my Uncle Bill Snyder, and my dad, Richard Coon, Sr., were named Washington State Cattlemen of the year in 1955.

Ralph also served as a director on the Washington Cattlemen's Association Range Management Committee for many years. His major goal was to leave the land in better condition than he found it, and he was proud of the ranch and the result of those efforts. Grandfather was devoted to his wife and his family. He thought it significant to be the first Snyder to welcome our daughter, Aisha, to the ranch. She was the first child to spend all of her first eighteen years here, and our son, Paul, was the second.

Richard Scheuerman has written extensively on Northwest Native American history and tells how Indian language and myth, artistic expression through baskets and clothes, and environmental knowledge offer moral and spiritual lessons for persons of all cultural backgrounds who seek to live in sustainable relationship with the land. I first met him when he took horse-drawn wagon loads of grade schoolers across portions of the Colville Trail and Mullan Road. Dick taught the students, community members, and others along for the ride what sustained Indians and pioneers as we dug camas root to eat, and shared Mullan teamster fare of smoked sardines, hardtack, and dried fruit.

We learned about how the region's First Peoples and frontier trappers and missionaries learned from each other to provision themselves with native foods like salmon and camas as well as crops like wheat and barley that grew abundantly on the virgin Columbia Plateau. It is an important story of mutual respect and cooperation tempered by subsequent political strife that led to an era of Northwest warfare in the 1850s. As teacher and administrator for St. John-Endicott Cooperative Schools, Dick was instrumental in giving an entire generation of young people new and fuller perspectives on their culture and history. He made history come alive.

Area farmers and ranchers who used their wagons and teams to carry students and community members on the trail reveled in the time-honored experience Dick terms "trans-generational learning" to share their knowledge with young people. Other gifted teachers came along who dressed and dined as pioneers. Aisha remembers Mr. Scheuerman rescuing a teacher's aide clad in a gingham

prairie dress and blue bonnet from a clutch of rattlesnakes she had surprised while walking in the old rock corral built by George Lucas along the trail. On other tours he brought university geologists to teach students about the Channeled Scablands and Missoula Floods, or arranged for fur trade reenactors to encounter the wagons en route to tell stories and give the kids a taste of frontier living. Our remote valley has been a well-used trail, and students read teenage frontiersman and diarist Ross Cox's vivid account of being accidentally left behind by a brigade traveling to Spokane country from the Snake River. Ross encountered wolves and rattlesnakes at every turn as he lumbered northward before being rescued several days later by local Indians and taken to Spokane House to meet his countryman—perhaps with a few words about their negligence.

Our forebears in this land encountered everything from frontier hardships and early-twentieth-century harvest disruptions organized by the International Workers of the World, to the devastating winter of 1924 and the difficult Depression years. Low prices, bad health, and oppressive bankers tested a whole generation. Maurice McGregor, the second generation leader of the McGregor Land and Livestock Company, and one of my grandfather's close friends, wrote during the Depression that "a good farmer is one who farms his land with full regard for duty to the soil." Growing up in our little rural communities with all the feverish postwar activity, we young people learned much from farm and ranch families about values that endured from frontier days.

Alex has written about my grandmother, Aimee Snyder, the first woman to graduate from the University of Washington with dual degrees in mathematics and engineering. She told us of her life on the family cattle and wheat ranch: "We just got up first thing in the morning and worked hard all day. It never occurred to us not to." She also spoke about Mary Ellen Milam, a neighbor who had agreed to let railroad crews use the family spring when building a new main line so long as they left the pump when they were done. When the crew sneaked back to her place at sunrise to get the pump, they found Mary Ellen sitting in her rocking chair, puffing a corn cob pipe with a shotgun across her lap. The pump stayed. Ralph remembered: "She was a wonderful woman. She was very dogmatic and knew who she was going to support. She was a very strong willed woman. Quite often you'd find a woman that was the head of a family that way."

Alex has observed that my grandfather taught how "the early settlers were workers. They wanted to be busy, doing something, creating something. To survive you had to be tough, frugal, sometimes daring. A man's word was important. So was a positive attitude. You never want to tell a man your troubles, because he wants to work for a winning outfit. I always said, 'we're getting things done, getting more acres, getting more range.' That's the spirit of work, and they liked it." We learned, too, of the remarkable legacy we owed to those who arrived so long before our grandparents. McGregor ranch records give evidence of close ties with area Native Americans: Sam Fisher's 1885 homestead certificate; a map of thirteen Indian homesteads; and records of the battles crusty Peter McGregor fought through Department of Interior hearings to help the Palouse keep their ancestral land. Etched into our memories are places like Sam's Spring where that heritage still resonates.

Beginning with a passionate agronomist and two store clerks, The McGregor Company farm supply business has grown over the years to serve nearly four dozen farm communities in Washington, Oregon, and Idaho, all within the bounds of the amber waves of grain and the fruited plains of our intermountain prairies. Alex's entrepreneurial father, Sherman, built the business around some bedrock agricultural principles: invest what you earn to help your farm neighbors, find dedicated people, and be willing to embrace change—the only constant we've known in a century and a quarter of agriculture on this remarkable land. The reinforcing traits that Alex's uncle, Archie McGregor, articulated back in 1885 would be keys to future success in agriculture—industry, work, character, honesty, and fair dealings—are etched on the walls of the company's headquarters, located a stone's throw from Alfred Holt's original homestead on Rebel Flat near Colfax. They still describe farm families and Northwest agriculture in the twenty-first century.

Much has changed since the frontier days profiled in this fascinating story that recounts how the first grains and livestock came to our region. Our footprints on the land are much different than those of the people who preceded us. But farm families' deep respect for the land endures, with passion for its wise care. I find it reassuring that places like the ancient rutted courses of the old Colville Trail and Mullan Road, where one can sit and think before a view in any direction that is substantially unchanged since the days of David Thompson and Chief Kamiakin, still exist. As Alex puts it, it should be no surprise that absentee corporations remain a rarity on Northwest ranches and farms—the risks are daunting, the returns too erratic to satisfy anyone looking for a robust quarterly dividend.

Agriculture here is a success story in so many ways—for consumers, for the environment, for the regional economy and, once in a while, for the farm and ranch families who have made it all possible. I am grateful to Richard Scheuerman and Alexander McGregor for the valued work that they have done to enrich the lives of the Northwest's urban, suburban, and rural residents through this work that poignantly grounds us in a treasured heritage.

Heirloom Grain Nursery
WSU-Mt. Vernon Research and Extension Center
R. Scheuerman Collection

Introduction

*"Gave all hands a holiday for Harvest Home, who enjoyed themselves
in the evening by a merry dance...."*
—Dr. William Tolmie, Fort Nisqually Chief Trader, September 4, 1846

On August 25, 1841, Governor George Simpson of the Hudson's Bay Company arrived at Ft. Vancouver after an arduous four-month journey from Montreal. Rarely betraying sign of exhaustion, Simpson set about to draft a lengthy report to the London Board of Directors about the company's various enterprises in its far-flung Columbia Department. During his visit, Simpson proudly reported that Archibald McDonald at Ft. Colvile had "an excellent farm, yielding bountiful harvests of maize, wheat, and other crops," while John McLoughlin's "grand depôt" at Ft. Vancouver hosted substantial grain fields, a grist mill, and 166 emigrants from Canada's Red River district en route to company farmlands on Cowlitz Prairie and surrounding Ft. Nisqually. Grain, cattle, and butter from these operations provisioned Russian-American outposts in Alaska, as well as Spanish and American settlements in California. Northwest wool, furs, and hides were shipped to China and England. The changes brought to the region by the global trading network that had emerged in scarcely a decade were sweeping indeed.

The story of agriculture in the Pacific Northwest includes the many groups that participated in these developments—frontier English, French, and American, Columbia Sahaptin and Coastal Salish Indians, pioneer Oregon Trail and European immigrants, and others. Relationships among these peoples in the context of agriculture inevitably led to considerations of geography and ecology. The Northwest is a highly diverse region environmentally, divided with the major division by the Cascade Mountains into the drier eastern plateau and coastal lowlands, and further characterized by locales with unique growing conditions and cultural histories. The foresight of nineteenth-century figures like Simpson, McLoughlin, and McDonald, who sought to promote farming and ranching, was enjoined by Native American leaders like Chief Kamiakin of the Yakama-Palouse and Columbia-Sinkiuse Chief Moses. Extensive agricultural development was widespread long before the Oregon Treaty of 1846 through which Great Britain ceded its interests to lands south of the 49th Parallel and which spurred significant overland American immigration to the region. The consequences in the Pacific Northwest of what historians sometimes call "the frontier process" have special agricultural significance regionally and globally that will be explored along with notable developments in the twentieth century.

Heritage Grains

For the purposes of this story, heritage—or heirloom—grains are ancient cereal landraces; nineteenth century "improved selections"; and hybridized crosses grown in the Pacific Northwest between 1825 and 1950. Landraces are ancient plant "land strains" of rich genetic integrity with similar appearance adapted over many centuries to a particular home area from which many derived their common names—Lancaster (England) wheat, Oderbrucher (Germany) barley, Sisoslk (Russia) rye, Strathallen (Ireland) oats, and countless others. Landrace wheats that predominated across the plains and valleys of the Pacific Northwest throughout nineteenth century included English "White Winter" and "Pacific Bluestem" Lammas, the hard red "Turkeys" from southwestern Russia and Ukraine, and Mediterranean soft yellow Sonora that migrated north from New Spain. Landrace Scotch and Manchurian barleys grew alongside Northwest fields of English Side and White Tartarian (Russian) oats.

In botany's late-eighteenth-century imperial age of global specimen naming, landrace grains were assigned various Latin designations as scientists grappled with their origins and relationships. But naturalists and farmers alike kept alive common names that enrich present understandings of place, people, and peculiarity associated with grain varieties. An 1889 *Journal of the Royal Agricultural Society* article cites some of these from Sir Joseph Banks' regional and global wheat collecting: Bland's Imperial Brown, Flanders White, Blue-Chaffed Rivet, Oxfordshire Duck's Bill, and Oregon Big Club.

ANCIENT GRAINS

The ancestor of modern domesticated grains, wild einkorn *(Triticum boeoticum)*, appeared among other ancient grasses some half-million years ago in the western apex of the Fertile Crescent. The word for this primitive patriarch is from Old German *einkorn* ("one grain") for its characteristic single kernel head row, although both single row *(T. aegilopoides)* and double grain *(T. urarutu)* subspecies exist. This ancient diploid species (fourteen chromosomes from two sets of seven contributed by each parent for about thirty thousand genes) fortuitously crossed during that era with a wild goat grass *(Aegilops speltoides)* to create tetraploid wild emmer, or farro *(T. dicoccoides, 4 x 7 = 28 chromosomes, or some sixty thousand genes)*. Archaeological evidence indicates that wild emmer was gathered as early as seventeen thousand years ago by Neolithic hunters and gatherers on the southwestern shore of the Sea of Galilee.

Free-threshing domestic emmer appeared about 8,000 to 9,000 BP in the foothills of southeastern Turkey's Karaca Dağ Mountains and elsewhere in the region. The nutritious kernel of this "naked" grain threshed free from the indigestible hull during harvesting and made possible the rise of modern wheats. Wild and domesticated populations likely grew together for several centuries and were cut by early agriculturalists using bone sickles embedded with sharp obsidian blades. This beginning of agriculture in the Fertile Crescent some ten thousand years ago represented a key breakthrough in civilization and led to the rise of settled, urban populations.

All modern tetraploid durum wheats *(T. d. durum)* descend from cultivated emmer, as have the more limited relict stands of Polish *(T. polonicum)*, Persian *(T. carthlicum)*, Khorasan *(T. turanicum)*, and English Pollard *(T. turgidum)* wheats. A subsequent natural hybridization of cultivated emmer with another wild grass *(A. tauschii)* about 7,500 BC then created spelt, the first hexaploid grain *(T. spelta)*, having forty-two chromosomes (28 + 14) with some ninety thousand genes. From this species emerged the progenitors of modern common soft white ("fine") and hard red bread wheats, and club wheats *(T. a. compactum)*. With sixteen billion base pairs of DNA, this complex set of triple-paired chromosomes represents the largest genome of any organism in the plant and animal kingdoms—including *Homo sapiens*.

Genetic research on molecular and cytological markers with wheat confirms that the ancestral range of the Triticeae tribe of grasses stretched over fertile foothills and uplands from Turkey east-

Simplified Wheat Species Chronology

```
Wild Einkorn
(T. boeoticum) \
            Emmer————————> Durum Wheats
              / (T. dicoccoides)    (T. durum)
Goat Grass 1        \
(A. speltoides)      Spelt———->Bread Wheats
                    / (T. spelta)   (T. aestivum)
      Goat Grass 2
      (A. tauschii)
```

ward across the southern Caucasus and Mesopotamia to Kashmir and south to Ethiopia. By about 3,000 BC landrace grains gained a foothold in central Europe and Scandinavia at a time when greater Eurasia likely hosted many thousands of varieties. The remains of Ötzi the Iceman, recently discovered in the Italian-Austrian alpine border region and estimated to have died around 3,300 BCE, indicated his consumption of unleavened bread from einkorn.

F. I. Meyer, drawing of Pyramid Barley,
White Emmer, and Pallidum Barley
F. Könicke, *Arten und Varietäten des Getreides* (1885)

Archaeobotanists theorize that humanity's original farmers—most of whom were likely women who tended hearth, home, and hoe while men ranged widely to hunt—first selected for large kernel size and shatter-resistant graminea (grass-related) heads. They also came to prefer "free-threshing" grains that better enabled separation of the kernels from their husks.

Successive choices led to early maturing selections to assure yield and prevent damage from pests and the elements, followed by choices for uniform ripening time to facilitate harvest. In this way, wheat genotypes gradually came to grow more uniformly around early settlements from the Anatolian Plain and Jordan River Valley to Mesopotamia and across the Eurasian steppe to Manchuria. But for millennia grains grew across these landscapes and dispersed to others amidst a mélange of irregular "off-types," wildflowers, grasses, and other plants. Yields improved significantly following the advent of the plow about two thousand years ago, and varieties that descended from these ancient landraces today supply nearly one third of humanity's nutritional needs.

EARLY GRAIN USE

The use of grain foods cannot be dated with precision, but archaeological evidence indicates humans mixed crushed grain with water to form gruel as early as one hundred thousand years ago. By about 10,000 BC in the Fertile Crescent of Mesopotamia, flatbreads and pancakes were being baked by the sun or fire from a paste of stone-ground flour. Yeast fermentation was added to this mortar of life some four thousand years ago in the Middle East, marking the beginning of the craft of modern bread-making using wheat varieties that possessed high levels of gluten. When combined with water, this complex protein enables flour and water to form a malleable dough, trapping the yeast gases that enable bread to rise. This discovery had great significance by providing civilizations with a nutritious food of flavorful variety and pleasing texture that was also easy to store and transport. Yeast's miracle-working properties soon led in turn to the art of brewing.

Ancient observers were well aware that specific grain varieties imparted distinct flavor and quality profiles. The third century BC philosopher Theophrastus, Aristotle's successor at the Lyceum and author of *Inquiry into Plants*, observed that triticum (wheat) differed "in color, size, form, and... as regards their capacities in general and especially in their value as food." Two centuries later, the Roman agriculturalist Varro further noted the grain farmer's obligations to conservation: "Agriculture is a science which teaches us what crops should be planted in each kind of soil, and what operations are to be performed, in order that the land may produce highest yields in perpetuity." Cereal grains contributed significantly to Greek and Roman diets that were generally high in plant protein and carbohydrates. The cultural significance of barley and wheat is evident in numerous copper, silver, and gold coins from the ancient world that depict these grains. Two-spiked Italian farro wheat was a staple of the legionnaires who made nutritious soups from the cracked grain and likely spread it and other Roman varieties throughout the empire.

CLASSES OF WHEAT

Wheat has been divided into eight general classes based on kernel texture (soft, hard), and kernel color (white, red), and seasonal habit (fall/winter, spring). Habit is related to the growing season as winter-habit wheats require vernalization—the impulse to shift to the reproduction phase following winter cold—so are typically sown and germinate in the fall. Spring-habit grains grow continuously without exposure to winter cold so are usually planted in the spring and harvested in mid- to late-summer after fall-sown wheat. Facultative grains may be sown in either season. Some nineteenth-century records also refer to yellow or amber kernel varieties which are usually classed today as whites.

Secondary wheat characteristics include such attributes as head shape (lax, mid-dense, and dense; bearded or bald), kernel nutritive composition (protein and gluten content), and milling and baking quality for preferred food products. Hard red spring wheats are highest in protein with medium-strong gluten, the protein that provides elasticity to dough, so are used for yeast breads and hard rolls. Hard red winters have the strongest gluten and are used primarily for pan breads and buns. Soft red winter wheats have medium protein and weak gluten for flat breads, pastries, and crackers; and low protein, weak gluten soft winter and springs are used for pastries, noodles, and batters. High protein and strong gluten durum wheats are preferred for pasta, macaroni, and spaghetti.

The wheat kernel is primarily composed of a the carbohydrate-rich white inner endosperm (83 percent) in a protein matrix, the fatty germ embryo (2 percent), and the outer bran layer (15 percent) rich with B-complex vitamins, trace minerals, and fibrous cellulose. To facilitate production of white flour, many early twentieth-century millers removed the bran and embryo from whole wheat flour, and induced early crop breeders to develop varieties with less bran.

F. I. Meyer, Summer White Club and California Chili Club Wheats
F. Könicke, *Arten und Varietäten des Getreides* (1885)

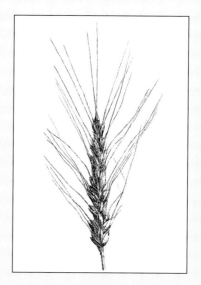

F. I. Meyer, Bearded Banat Wheat
F. Könicke, *Arten und Varietäten des Getreides* (1885)

The Latin term "gladiators," *hordearii*, literally means "barley men" since they heavily consumed high energy foods like barley, oatmeal, and legumes. The technology of water-powered gristmills remained virtually unchanged into the modern era from its first century BC description by the Roman engineer Vitruvius who explained the ingenious combination of the flume, wheel, axle, drive-gear, and millstone.

BARLEY

Wild barley, better adapted to dry and acidic soils than wheat, was gathered by humans along the Sea of Galilee as long as twenty thousand years ago. About 5,000 BC this primitive self-pollinating grain—capable of evolving more rapidly than any known organism—grew in southern Europe after dispersion along the Mediterranean coast. Most likely it reached central Europe by about 4,000 BC via the Danube, Rhine, and Dnieper valleys. Barley, with only fourteen chromosomes, is generally classed according to seasonal habit (fall/winter, spring), use (food, malt, feed), and head arrangement of kernels (two-row, four-row). Two-row barleys have a single row of seeds on each axis of the head spike while six-row varieties have three on each side. Although two-row spring grains have traditionally been preferred for brewing, some six-row barleys like Scots Bere and Trebi have been prized for imparting crisper flavors.

F. I. Meyer, Brachyatherum Barley and Common Rye
F. Könicke, *Arten und Varietäten des Getreides* (1885)

Crop	Wild Progenitor	Domesticated Form
Emmer wheat:	*Triticum dicoccoides*	*T. aestivum*
Barley:	*Hordeum spontaneum*	*H. vulgare*
Rye:	*Secale vavilovii*	*S. cereale*
Oats:	*Avena sterilis &*	*A. sativa*
	A. fatua	

Origins of Neolithic Cereal Founder Crops
(after B. Kilian, et al., 2009)

RYE

Rye (*Secale cereale*) probably arrived in Europe about 2,500 BC as a weed in stands of wheat and barley, but developed into useful varieties through natural hybridization and mutations. The earliest known cultivated ryes emerged about 1800 BC in Moldova and Ukraine and reached Scandinavia by the first century AD. Landrace grains then spread further throughout Europe after the third century along Roman military and trade routes, and often grew together in mixed stands known as maslin (wheat and rye) and dredge (barley and oats). These grains arrived in the New World in the late fifteenth century with Columbus and were transported across Mexico by Spanish conquistadors who followed in his wake. Juan Garrido, a West African freeman who traveled with Hernando Cortés' expeditionary force to Tenochtitlan, received property near the Aztec capital in 1522 and raised wheat and grapes. By the 1550s cultivation of grains had reached Oaxaca and Pacific coastal areas. A century later, Father Eusebius Kino introduced Sonora wheat to the Pima Indians of present New Mexico. Soft enough for stone grinding by hand, cultivation of this variety and six-row Mediterranean "Coast" barley spread across the American Southwest via Jesuit and Franciscan missions.

NEW WORLD GRAINS

The only grains native to the Western Hemisphere are maize, wild rice, and quinoa. When European colonization commenced, the Great Plains of North America were devoid of any cereal grain in spite of hosting prodigious fertile soils and stands of prairie grasses. James Fenimore Cooper's *The Prairie* (1827) presages this "vast country" at the dawn of its transformation into the world's breadbasket just as Northwest fur trade era visionaries like Sir George Simpson endeavored to introduce agriculture to the far-flung outposts of the Hudson's Bay Company (HBC). However, a number of pseudograins such as blue wildrye (*Elymus glaucus*) and grain amaranth (*Amaranthus* spp.) were in use by Native Americans at the time of colonization. Russian-American Company fur traders at Ft. Ross described the practice of some California Indians to gather the seeds of blue wildrye and other grasses. These were winnowed with special baskets, parched, and pounded into a kind of pinole flour used to make bread and gruel, but such plants were not domesticated. Far to the south in present-day Arizona, the Sonoran Hohokum people may have cultivated small patches of grass-like little barley (*Hordeum pusillum*) as long as a thousand years ago.

Hudson's Bay Company trading posts had been involved in grain production from the earliest years of the company's founding in the seventeenth century. A 1674 directive from London headquarters instructed officials to send the company's James Bay posts "a bushel of wheate & of rye, barley & oats, or a barrel of each in caske, Such sorts of garden Seed as the governour Shall advise...." Detailed instructions for cultivation of grains continued as HBC operations expanded along the west shore of Hudson's Bay where Governor George Geyer of York Factory received the following communication from London in June 1693: "We recommend to you the sowing of Corne we have sent you of all grains some as for wheat you may sow a Gallon in one place and a Gallon in another as soone as the ships come in must be sowed under furrow as Termed in England.... Then in Spring as soon as you can get the spade into the ground sow againe of wheat Barley Oates Beans and pease but must not be soe deep in the Earth.... If all be lost the loss is to us & noe body else. But if it should take, what comfort will it be to those that inhabit there...."

Early Hudson's Bay Company post manuals recommended consumption of whole grain foods to maintain the health of employees who labored under challenging conditions. Landrace grains had more bran and protein than many modern varieties, as well as higher levels of micronutrients, especially iron, magnesium, phosphorus, selenium, and zinc.

INTO THE MODERN ERA

By 1800, tens of thousands of landrace grains grew throughout Eurasia, with the most significant factor in adaption to a locality being flowering time of the plant. This key attribute is determined by an organism's response to day length, soil composition, and vernalization. Landraces may undergo physical variation when grown somewhere else due to genetic, climatic, and soil variations, as well as cultivation practices. During the twentieth century, approximately 75 percent of global crop plant genetic diversity was lost, and most European landraces disappeared entirely. This was due to improved "plant selections" undertaken by farmers and seed providers and from artificial hybridization. Therefore, all modern grains are kernels atop a vast expanse of ripened stalks deeply rooted in the ancient past. The pioneering work of Russian agronomist Nicholai I. Vavilov to determine core prehistoric grain "centers of origin" contributed to a global effort led by the USDA and other world agricultural agencies to locate remnant stands and systematically collect and preserve seed samples in remote areas of Scandinavia, Scotland, Spain, Italy, and Russia. But the pace of climate change, alternative land use, and other factors further threaten to fragment these centers of dynamic meta-population diversity.

Modern scientist-humanitarians like Norman Borlaug, Orville Vogel, and Stephen Jones have worked in close partnership with Northwest farmers to forge beneficial relationships envisioned by the framers of the Morrill Land-Grant Acts, who sought to apply education and research for practical benefit. The mission conjures up images of Morrill's champion, Abraham Lincoln, eloquently urging a Congress preoccupied with wartime measures to establish a national system of agricultural schools. One early beneficiary of such an education, University of Missouri graduate and pioneering Northwest agronomist William J. Spillman, exemplified this ethic. Spillman was equally at home tying grain bundles with farmers and students in Pullman area wheat fields or addressing scholarly audiences in the East on the world class breakthroughs in crop improvement for which he was substantially responsible.

Agronomist José Esquinas-Alcázar points out the twenty-first-century relevance of heritage grains to biodiversity: "The heterogeneous varieties of the past have been and still are the plant breeder's raw material. They have been a fruitful, sometimes the sole, source of genes for resistance, adaptable to different environments, and with other traits like the dwarf-type in grains that have contributed to the Green Revolution." Such observations underscore an underlying tension between conservationists and developers regarding contemporary needs to feed a burgeoning world population while averting the threats to cereal monocultures as experienced in the Irish Great Potato Famine of the 1840s. (Resistance to blight was eventually found in the tubers of a Mexican landrace.) Similar disease threats recurrently arise as with the present epidemic of UG 99 wheat stem rust in east Africa and the Middle East which crop breeders seek to confront by hybridizing for new varieties using landrace germ plasm. Over three thousand seed accessions for this international effort have been supplied by the USDA Small Grains Research Unit in Aberdeen, Idaho. As Cary Fowler of the Svalbard Global Seed Vault observes, "Yesterday's crop diversity is tomorrow's food security."

Success in producing bountiful crops in this day of advanced technologies is often taken for granted, or thought to be of little consequence. For example, in *The World is Flat*, best-selling author Thomas Friedman writes of globally interconnected corporations and supply chains in a future where natural resources will be irrelevant. The strongest countries, Friedman opined, would be those with few natural resources at all. University of California, Davis Professor Steven Blank in *The End of Agriculture in the American Portfolio* states, "American agriculture is headed for the last roundup. America doing agriculture is like a PhD doing child's work—we can do it, but it is a waste." Yet agriculture today is the largest employer in the Pacific Northwest and

remains the last bastion of family business among all commercial endeavors with over 95 percent of the region's farms and rangelands under the management of individual families.

Farm families have achieved much along the way. Demographers report that today's "average" farmer of the Inland Northwest is just over fifty-seven years of age. During that period, yields have increased 250 percent, waterborne soil erosion has been reduced 85 percent, stubble burning has been cut by over 95 percent, and windblown dust has been reduced six-fold—the biggest gains in stewardship and productivity of any generation since cereal crops were first grown eleven thousand years ago.

Throughout the Pacific Northwest, thousands of families still farm in a region where their predecessors sank deep roots a century or more ago. During a 1980s "Centennial Families" television program, Palouse Country farmer-stockman William McGregor suggested that pioneer settlers had two traits that helped them succeed: dyed-in-the-wool optimism, and tenacity that verged on stubbornness—traits that he felt were useful then, useful today, and would be just as useful in the future. Northwest farm families are a remarkable lot who battle the vagaries of weather, global markets, operating costs, and political wrangling that can throw sudden roadblocks to success. Their ranks have been winnowed by tough times and uncertainties, but they persevere with hope that the next crop will be an extraordinary one. Returns are erratic, sometimes less than could be received for entry level urban employment, and the risks are great. But there is satisfaction in renewed appreciation for stewardship that seeks to leave the land in better condition for generations to come. Such spirit is captured in lines from William Cullen Bryant:

> Honor waits, o'er all the earth,
>   Through endless generations,
> The art that calls her harvest forth,
>   And feeds th'expectant nations.

L. L. Fitzgerald, "Governor George Simpson on a Tour of Inspection"
(after a painting by Cyrus C. Cuneo)
Hudson's Bay Company Archives, Provincial Archives of Manitoba
(HBCA, PAM P-390/N9370)

CHAPTER I

Fur Trade Farming

Come, sons of summer, by whose toil
We are the lords of wine and oil:
By whose tough labours, and rough hands,
We till up first, then reap our lands.
Crowned with the ears of grain, now come;
And to the pipe sing Harvest Home.

Hudson's Bay Company officials commissioned a series of paintings in the 1920s to commemorate Governor George Simpson's historic first journey to North America in 1825. Mindful of their distinction as stewards of the continent's longest continuously operating commercial enterprise, the company sought to memorialize notable events of their past. One of these grandiose works, L. L. Fitzgerald's vibrant "Sir George Simpson on a Tour of Inspection," depicts the iron-fisted visionary seated amidst a cadre of voyageurs who lustily row along some unnamed river of the Far West. Although the company had been founded in the seventeenth century, not until Simpson's reign did its operations extend beyond the Rockies, and he meant to fully utilize the region's vast resources, including its fertile soil.

Simpson's formal attire and accompanying bagpiper shown in Fitzgerald's impressionistic rendering are not fanciful. The governor often arranged ceremonial entries for his entourage all along their transcontinental route. But safeguarded in the canoe's cargo was something more enduring than top hats and woolen toques, for Simpson also brought seed grain for crops that would transform the Northwest into one of world's most agriculturally productive regions. Many company employees expressed skepticism at the prospect of exchanging traps and trade beads for harvest cradles and seed wheat, but the determined Englishman would prevail in his vision of economic and cultural transformation a generation before American pioneers ventured west on the Oregon Trail.

The Pacific Northwest's earliest fur traders explored commercial opportunities in the region because US–British rivalry after the Revolutionary War had disrupted traditional trans-Atlantic trading routes. Although British culture continued to strongly influence the new nation, Americans were forging their own identity through experience in democratic government and expansion westward. Captain James Cook's 1784 account, *Voyage to the North Pacific Ocean*, reported fabulous prices for Northwest otter pelts in Asian-Pacific markets and sparked an international rush to capitalize on the trade. Later in the same decade top hats made from the luxurious pelts of North American beavers became fashionable in Europe, which encouraged greater commercial interest in the continent's fur-bearing animals and the scenic lands they inhabited.

In 1789, Spanish explorer Esteban José Martinez established the settlement of Santa Cruz de Nuca at Nootka Sound on Vancouver Island for trade and to deter Russian expansion into areas claimed by Spain. Martinez planted wheat on the last day of October "to try the land, if anyone returns next year," and then departed for further coastal exploration. Captain Pedro Alberni was placed in charge of the post the following spring, and though no mention was made of Martinez's experiment, Alberni planted a variety of grains and vegetables week by week to determine the best seeding times in case of long-term occupation. He found that barley, potatoes, squash, and beans thrived under coastal conditions but wheat, corn, chickpeas, and tomatoes failed to sufficiently ripen. The Spanish also introduced the first livestock to the island—black cattle, sheep, goats, and pigs—but Alberni's efforts were "useless in successfully cultivating the grains." Although the barley "gave some hope," the wheat never formed heads.

In the spring of 1792, the Spanish viceroy of New Spain dispatched Sálvador Fidalgo and a crew of eighty-seven to establish the outpost of Núñez Gaona on Neah Bay on the northwestern tip of present Washington State. This location became the first European settlement on the Pacific Coast between California and Alaska. Fidalgo's men erected a palisaded fort enclosing dwellings, a chapel, and a bakery; and raised cattle, sheep, goats, and chickens. The Spaniards also established a vegetable garden with transplanted seedlings brought from San Blas, their pestilential coastal headquarters west of Guadalajara. Although the garden fared well during the summer, the Spanish abandoned Núñez Gaona in the fall to avoid potential conflicts with American and British traders and to consolidate their hold at Nootka, which possessed the most favorable harbor on the coast. A Spanish presence remained there until the Nootka Convention of 1793 with Great Britain, by which Madrid agreed to withdraw southward to present California.

During a Pacific trading expedition aboard the *Columbia Rediviva* in May 1792, Boston explorer-trader Robert Gray discovered the Columbia River, giving the United States its first firm claim to the region. America's position was further strengthened by the 1804–06 overland journey of Lewis and Clark, who wintered at Ft. Clatsop along the Netul River (now called the Lewis and Clark River) near the mouth of the Columbia River. In 1811, personnel of John Jacob Astor's American Fur Company established Ft. Astoria several miles to the northeast on the south bank of the Columbia. Astorian Gabriel Franchère described the area as a Garden of Eden where plantings of Indian corn, potatoes, and other vegetables yielded well.[1]

The North West Company (also known as the Nor'Westers) had been organized in 1783 by Montreal merchants of Scottish ancestry who employed brigades of French Canadians to exploit the rich fur-bearing districts of the interior. The company also sought to capitalize on the Pacific Slope's fur trade possibilities and dispatched the intrepid explorer-trader David Thompson to find the Columbia River's source. He crossed the Continental Divide into present British Columbia via Athabasca Pass in 1807 to successfully complete his mission and established Kootanae House, the Nor'Westers' first outpost in the region, on the headwaters of the Columbia in today's British Columbia. On a visit to the place the following April, Thompson planted a small garden of vegetables and grain to which he returned the following summer. That August he noted disappointing results with the peas and turnips ("only in leaves"), but that "5 or 6 grains of barley that were sowed have thriven well." In this humble way the first cereal grain momentarily ripened on the fertile lands of the Inland Pacific Northwest.[2]

Spokane House was founded in 1810 near the mouth of the Little Spokane River by Thompson's mixed-blood Chippewa Indian guide, Jacques Raphael "Jaco" Finlay, and Finan McDonald. Thompson's historic "journey of a summer moon" followed in 1812 during which he made the first recorded trip from the upper Columbia to the Pacific. Astor's response to Nor'Wester activity east of the Cascades was to establish Ft. Okanogan the following year near the mouth of the river that also bears this tribal name, and Ft. Spokane near

Spokane House on the Spokane River in 1812. Two intrepid teens involved this work, Ross Cox and Joseph Laroque, had come to the Northwest on the Astorian supply ship *Beaver* in 1811 and followed in the wake of Thompson's upper Columbia explorations. The *Beaver* brought the first hogs to the region the following year. The crew also attempted to carry cattle from the Sandwich Islands, but the creatures proved too wild to round up. During the War of 1812, a British warship threatened Ft. Astoria so the Americans surrendered inventory, livestock, and post to the British who renamed it Ft. George. By 1817 workers there raised twenty acres of potatoes and other vegetables on a nearby field. The Nor'Westers also first brought cattle to the region in 1814 when two young bulls and two heifers arrived at Ft. George from California—probably the tough, bony "Spanish cattle" from the Russian's Ft. Ross and described by Puget Sound pioneer Ezra Meeker as "slim, active, hardy, long-horned, vicious, and poor milkers."

The belated entry of the British Hudson's Bay Company into the Northwest fur trade marked the genesis of an enduring Euro-American presence and agriculture on both sides of the Cascade Mountains. After merging with the North West Company in 1821, the new leadership moved with monopolistic power to form "regular establishments" that would serve as more than mere exchange points for beaver and other peltries. Early in the long career of Sir George Simpson as the Honourable Company's visionary if autocratic governor, he evidenced as much interest in grain and growing seasons as in furs and supply routes.[3]

An ambitious plan to provision the company's substantial chain of inland fur trading operations had been launched in 1811 with the formation of the Selkirk Settlement on the Red River south of Lake Winnipeg. Lord Thomas Selkirk recruited young Archibald McDonald, a sturdy Scot from Argyllshire just twenty-three years old, to head his vast agricultural domain. The service provided valuable experience for McDonald's later roles as Chief Trader at forts Nisqually and Colvile in the Pacific Northwest. Colonists may have been supplied with British and Norwegian winter wheats—

about twenty-five bushels were harvested in 1814 and milled with a hand-quern (a primitive mill consisting of two circular stones with the upper one being turned by hand). But raids from area Métis, insect plagues, and winterkill on the Canadian grasslands threatened the viability of the settlement. Yields finally improved after the Selkirk settlers obtained 250 bushels of seed wheat in 1820 following an arduous journey to the American settlement of Prairie du Chien in present Wisconsin. The grain was taken in flat-bottomed boats back to the Red River Colony and planted in June. The Prairie du Chien variety is not specified in period accounts, but some Canadian historians conclude it may have been soft Red May, the Yellow (Red) Lammas widely raised in Colonial America.

Soon after the 1821 merger of the two British fur trading companies, directors of the new London-based enterprise directed Simpson to inspect the far-flung Pacific empire. On his first trip to the region in the fall of 1825—an epic three-month transit commencing in August on which the voyageur brigade carried seed grain—Simpson observed while camped at the mouth of the Okanogan that, "Grain in any quantity might be raised here, but cultivation to any extent has never been attempted, indeed throughout the Columbia no pains have been taken to meet the demands of the trade." The far-seeing Simpson lamented this "oversight" and added, "It has been said that Farming is no branch of the Fur Trade but I consider that every pursuit tending the leighten the Expence of the Trade is a branch thereof...." After reaching the Pacific, he recommended that the center of the company's newly formed Columbia Department be relocated from Ft. George near the mouth of the Columbia River to an inland site more favorable to agriculture. Simpson's intentions were facilitated by Great Britain and Russia's 1825 Treaty of St. Petersburg to divide their claims to the North Pacific coast at 54°40'.[4]

In April 1826, Simpson directed construction of Ft. Vancouver on a verdant plain north of the Columbia River some ninety miles inland and appointed former Nor'Wester Dr. John McLoughlin to serve as the region's Chief Factor. Within two years, the ambitious doctor-manager transformed the company's misman- aged chain of thirteen interior posts into an expanded and profitable operation of twenty-two, and worked to attain Simpson's goal of agricultural self-sufficiency. Also relocating from Ft. George to the new outpost were seven cows and one bull—possi- bly McLoughlin's Durham "English cattle"—to form the the nucleus of the company's prosperous livestock herd. The Northwest's oldest apple tree— probably an Antonovka from England still producing in the twenty-first century—was likely planted from seed in 1825 at Ft. Vancouver—to form the nucleus of a substantial orchard. The large, green-skinned fruit is sometimes called the "Simpson apple." The first peach starts were planted in 1829.

On Simpson's spring 1826 return eastward with the annual "Columbia Express"—the HBC's 2,600- mile fur brigade connecting York Factory with Ft. Vancouver—he also directed the relocation of Spo- kane House northward to the vicinity of the great Indian fishery on the upper Columbia at present Kettle Falls, Washington. He named the new post Ft. Colvile in honor of Hudson's Bay Company director Andrew Colvile (distinct from Ft. Colville, a U.S. military fort later built nearby). Simpson noted, "We selected a beautiful point on the south side, an excellent Farm can be made at this place where as much Grain and potatoes may be raised as well would feed all the Natives of the Columbia and sufficient numbers of Cattle and Hogs to sup- ply his Majesty's Navy with Beef and Pork."

Governor Simpson supplied McLoughlin with seed potatoes and peas in the spring of 1825. A bushel each of wheat, barley, oats, and corn arrived from York Factory in the fall, which McLoughlin planted "in proper time"—likely the following spring. Former Astorian and millwright William Cannon fashioned a primitive mill for the fort by

Dr. John McLoughlin
Washington State History Research Center,
Washington State Historical Society
(2009.0.470)

gouging a deep mortar-shaped impres- sion in a fir stump. A rounded wooden log suspended from a "spring-pole device" served as the pestle that ground the Northwest's first flour. Fifteen bushels of bar- ley, the first grain substantially grown in the Inland North- west, was raised at Ft. Col- vile in 1826 with seed from McLoughlin. Horses, cattle, and hogs from Ft. Vancouver and the abandoned Spokane House also flourished on Big Prairie near the fort. Wheat was likely planted the following year as grain production rose to two hundred bushels in 1827. By the fall of 1828, Simpson proudly reported to London that with a season of "very abundant" crops his goal of agricultural self-suf- ficiency had been achieved. But English landraces adapted to European maritime climates fared better in the milder climes west of the Cascades than inland, and further experimen- tation would be needed to determine which grain varieties were best suited to the regional Northwest environments.

Following the closure of Astor's Pacific oper- ation, young Joseph Laroque had remained in the region as a free trapper and in 1824 married into the family of the prominent Walla Walla Chief Piyópyo Maksmáks (Peopeo Moxmox). The couple first settled in the Willamette Valley but returned east of the Cascades in 1823 to his wife's people, where Laroque was hired by the Hudson's Bay Company to tend horse and cattle herds that could range year-round on the sheltered meadows surrounding "Hudson Bay Farm" several miles west of present Umapine, Oregon. The area provided luxuriant pasturage, fertile land for gardens, and shelter for company and free-trapper passers-by. Spring trapping expeditions that came up the Columbia obtained horses from Laroque before heading into the rugged Rockies for the seasonal trade, and animals were also moved north to outfit

Fort Colvile Granary and Trader's House
Special Collections, University of Washington Libraries (UW 35768)

the annual express, whose members often traded paddles for saddles at Ft. Colvile to ride across the inland prairies to Ft. Vancouver. The Laroque's homesite in the Walla Walla Valley became the nucleus of Frenchtown, a substantial farming community clustered near present Lowden, where retired Métis trappers and their families began settling in the 1830s.[5]

Ft. Vancouver's farms, dairies, and pasture lands developed in these years along the fertile parkland prairies that flanked the fort. Fort Plain to the east of the palisade covered some five hundred acres with substantial barns, stables, and outbuildings, while the smaller West (Cox's) Plain acreage commenced just beyond the northwest bastion and included workers' cabins, gardens, pasture, and an orchard. The First and Second (North) Back plains rose on the higher uplands north of the post beginning three to six miles inland, and the expansive Camas (Vancouver) Plain began downstream below the West Plain and stretched for nearly fif-

teen miles. A thousand acres, gristmill, sawmill, and other buildings comprised Mill Plain about six miles upstream from the post. Open acreage amidst copses of Oregon oak and berry bushes were also farmed on nearby islands including Sauvie's (Wappatoo) Island at the mouth of the Willamette River, named for McLoughlin's French Canadian dairyman, Laurent Sauvé, who supervised the island's four dairies. Ft. Vancouver's 1833 harvest yielded three thousand bushels of wheat; three thousand of peas; fifteen hundred of barley; and one thousand bushels each of oats and buckwheat. In September 1834, naturalist John Kirk Townshend arrived with American fur trader Nathaniel Wyeth and wrote that the surrounding company farms "…produce abundant crops, particularly of grain, without requiring manure. Wheat thrives astonishingly; I never saw better in any country." By the end of the decade, however, manure was regularly applied to area fields, and crops sometimes suffered from drought.[6]

Gustavus Sohon, "Fort Vancouver" (1853)
I. Stevens, *Narrative of Explorations for a Route for a Pacific Railroad* (1860)

As early as 1830, McLoughlin surrendered to persistent requests by some French Canadian and Métis freemen who lived seasonally in the Willamette Valley to provide help in establishing their farms. The shift in mentality was significant. Having reached the Pacific Slope on the back of the fur trade, the mountain men began exchanging that exploitive regime for a sustainable economy based on agriculture. McLoughlin had come to respect veteran Astorians and Nor'Westers like Joseph Gervais and Etienne Lucier who had chosen to remain in the region as free trappers. In the late 1820s Gervais and Lucier decided to stake claims on the rich alluvial bottomland of the Willamette Valley in the Champoeg (sham-poó-ee) or Campment du Sable area. McLoughlin knew from personal inspection that the arcadian environs of the prairie and adjacent Tualatin Plains had great agricultural potential.

The "White-Headed Eagle" had first opposed the idea of outfitting prospective farmers for fear their claims might jeopardize The Honorable Company's claims to regional sovereignty, but by 1830 his goodwill could no longer resist the pleas of the frontiersmen and McLoughlin began advancing seed wheat, lending livestock, and selling implements to the Oregon Country's first independent farmers who began living permanently on what became known as French Prairie. Gervais built a "substantial" two-story home with square-hewed Eastern Canadian post-in-sill construction and a forty-by-fifty-foot barn, and by 1832 visitors commented on his fine crops of wheat, barley, corn, potatoes, pumpkins, and melons.[7]

New Hampshire native John Ball straggled into Ft. Vancouver in October 1832 with the Nathaniel Wyeth expedition, and McLoughlin recruited the erstwhile Dartmouth graduate to establish a fort school for a lively group of children speaking English, French, Gaelic, Cree, and Klickitat. Following the winter term and unlike most of his fellow American adventurers, Ball resolved to make "a long stay." He wrote his parents in February, "I am going to the trade you taught me—farming—from which more comforts can be obtained with less labor, and it is more healthy than most others." He relocated to prairie land above Willamette Falls (present Oregon City) in March 1833 with tools and twenty-five bushels of seed wheat, corn, and potatoes supplied by McLoughlin, to become the first American farmer in the area.

Ball plowed "quite a large field" which he fenced and seeded with twenty bushels of the grain. He subsisted on the remaining grain and supplemented his diet with venison and salmon, vegetables obtained from neighboring French Canadians, and meal for bread from Ft. Vancouver. Two other veterans of the Wyeth expedition, John Sinclair and perhaps Calvin Tibbetts, are believed to have later joined Ball, but by fall Ball and Sinclair had tired of their "primitive lonely life." They sold their wheat to McLoughlin and arranged passage on the Company's brig *Dryad* never to return to the Northwest. Departure was not without regret, however, as Ball observed, "The grandeur of these beautiful mountains, Hood and Jefferson, were the hardest to leave." Tibbetts remained to farm in the vicinity of Chemaway (near present Salem, Oregon), and

Wyeth himself established a short-lived farm in the area.

Brooklyn Quaker Webley John Hauxhurst contracted "Oregon Fever" from frontier entrepreneurs Ewing Young and Hall Jackson Kelly during their 1834 stay in California. The Americans arrived at Ft. Vancouver in the fall and Hauxhurst took up land near Champoeg where he completed construction of Willamette Valley's first gristmill, possibly on Champoeg Creek, in the fall of 1835. Noting their dependence on crude wooden mortars to hull barley and a small cast-iron corn cracker to grind wheat "after a fashion," one of the area's Methodist missionaries commented that the new operation "greatly added to the comfort of the inhabitants." About 1839, Hauxhurst sold his interest in the mill to Dr. McLoughlin's stepson, Thomas McKay.[8]

Donald Manson Barn
Champoeg State Heritage Area, St. Paul, Oregon
R. Scheuerman Collection

Ft. Colvile Grist Mill on Myer's Creek
Robert Smith

Following Ft. Colvile's construction and management under John Work and Francis Heron, Red River Colony veteran Archibald McDonald was placed in charge of local operations in 1835. "Every Post can and must provide for itself," Simpson declared, and therefore free employees from dependence on "country produce" of traded salmon, venison, roots, and berries. McDonald took Simpson's directives to heart, and within a decade local operations grew to employ twenty men at the company store, gristmill, four-hundred-acre grain farm, and hay lands twelve miles east near present Colville. Trader McDonald wrote of being "a considerable sort of Canadian farmer" as local fields grew wheat, barley, potatoes, turnips, and garden vegetables.

Writing in September 1838, American missionary Elkanah Walker praised McDonald's "great crops" and the fort for having "more the appearance of civilized life…than any place" in the Northwest,

and "more than you see in some of the new places in the States." The intrepid British botanist David Douglas visited Ft. Colvile soon after its founding and observed, "The scenery from this place is sublime high, well-wooded hills, mountains covered with perpetual snow, extensive meadows and plains of deep fertile alluvial deposit covered with a rich sward of grass and a profusion of flowering plants."[9]

Even languid Ft. Nez Perces (later Ft. Walla Walla at present Wallula) showed progress under McLoughlin's attentive guidance. Surrounded by "treeless sandy desert," the post was built entirely of driftwood and personnel came to specialize in horse-breeding. However, in the spring of 1831 Chief Trader William Kittson experimented with a small "kitchen garden" of corn, potatoes, onions, radishes, and pumpkins on a patch of loam near the river. Weary of a steady diet of parched corn and dried peas supplied from Ft. Colvile with an occasional Indian salmon, Kittson was gleeful when the plants sprouted in April. In early June he directed workers to clear a broader area of "the farm" by scythe and prepare the seedbed with plow and harrow. They planted forty-one quarts of corn seed and a keg of potatoes which were harvested in September. Simon McGillivray, who arrived from York Factory with the annual in-bound Columbia Express in July 1831 to replace Kittson, hired Indian women to clean and hang the corn. Some potatoes were salvaged, but most vegetables not flooded by the Columbia's periodic high waters withered in the late summer sun.

Cayuse, Palouse, Columbia-Sinkiuse, and other Columbia Plateau Indians often visited Ft. Nez Perces and soon began growing grains and vegetables near their villages. Their words for various crops indicate the influence of French-speaking traders and missionaries as potatoes were called *lapatát*, peas *lipwá*, and barley and oats were *láwen*. Chinook Jargon for barley was *lolshr*, likely derived from French *l'orge*. (Wheat and bread in both Plateau Sahaptin and Puget Sound Salish is *sap'olil*, from an indigenous Chinook word, *tsápolil*.)[10]

Genesis of Western Grains

The region's first wheat yields were fifteen to twenty bushels an acre, which McLoughlin attributed to poor seed sown both in spring and fall, though the latter usually yielded more heavily. What did ripen, however, he reported being "the finest I ever saw in any country." Within ten years approximately a thousand acres near Ft. Vancouver were in production. "Red" and "white" seed wheat as well as barley came by ship in 1827 from the prominent British nursery Gordon, Forsyth & Company, which also supplied the post with European seed for an array of vegetables including Welsh and Strasbourg onions, French and Hungarian beans, Dutch turnips, melons, squash, and herbs.

The principal British bread wheats of the period were Red and White Lammas landraces (*T. a. vulgare*) from England and Scotland. Early Northwest accounts indicate that White Lammas, or "White Winter" wheat, was the region's first widely grown variety. This stiff, late-maturing soft white grain

was ideal for the cool summers of the Willamette Valley. It became synonymous with fur trade-era farming and was sometimes called "Hudson Bay" wheat by Northwest farmers. The most common British barleys of the period were the two-row late maturing Archer and stiff-strawed Spratt landraces (*H. distichum*). A Suffolk farmer's selection about 1820 from a field of Archer gave rise to English Chevalier, an excellent malting grain widely raised in England and the United States and Canada later in the century for production of beer and spirits. Although Chevalier came from a single plant, its landrace genetic diversity led to the appearance of several types.[11]

The Gordon, Forsyth company was among the first seed nurseries established in Europe. Such firms emerged in England and on the continent at this time due to economic pressures from industrialization, population growth, and emerging techniques of "improved" plant types through specimen selections by farmers and horticulturalists for yield, threshability, time of maturity, milling quality, and other preferred characteristics. Cereal grains are self-pollinating plants that do not typically cross with another variety that might grow in close proximity. Natural hybridization took place, therefore, under rare conditions or through infrequent genetic mutation.

By 1829 workers at Ft. Vancouver had established a small maltery using local barley for the brewing of beer and distilling spirits from three stills. Company clerk George Roberts judged the product "good whiskey" but noted "it was given up due to the bad effect on the men." The hardy six-row landrace Scots Bere was raised at the time on the Orkney and Shetland islands for brewing and, when hulled, to make barley bread and pot barley for the national dish—Scotch broth. Not as susceptible to lodging (downed and tangled stems) as some other varieties, Bere was also acclimated to cooler climates and most strains were early-maturing "Ninety-Day" spring barleys. These were cultivated as early as the eighth century by Viking colonizers in the northern British Isles where their word for the grain was the Old Norse *bygg*. That landrace barley seed from Scotland found its way to the Northwest is evident in reference to locally grown "Scotch two-rowed and six-rowed barley" in early Willamette Valley press accounts and pioneer reminiscences. Commonly raised early nineteenth-century oat varieties in Great Britain—all probably native to Northern Europe—included the "common" white, black, and grey landraces widely raised in the British Isles and later in the Pacific Northwest. The most widely grown English ryes were St. John's Day (Midsummer) and Winter (Common).[12]

This period witnessed the genesis of scientific plant breeding. In 1819, horticulturalist Patrick Shirreff of Hopetoun, Scotland, began selecting "pure line" wheat and oat "sports" or "off-types," or exceptional individual plants, from "old form" landraces in order to determine if successive generations exhibited patterns of desired agronomic traits like yield and milling quality. Shirreff's groundbreaking work led to his release of the Shirreff and Hopetoun varieties widely raised on the British Isles in the nineteenth century. Shirreff's successes contributed to the Isle of Jersey experimenter John Le Couteur's development of the "isolation method" in the 1830s by which a particular line was grown over several generations in order to establish pure strains of a preferred variety. The work of these horticulturalists laid the foundation for advances made later in the century by agricultural scientists like William Spillman at Washington State College.

CHAPTER II

The British-Russian Contract

The horses, mares, and frisking fillies,
Clad all in linen white as lilies.
The harvest swains and maidens bound
For joy, to see the hock-cart crowned.

In an age before plant genetics and area land-grant college experiment stations, Northwest farmers depended on field selection of exemplary plants, fortuitous accidental crosses, and international connections to provide grain strains adapted to the region's distinct environmental conditions. A contributor to the popular nineteenth century periodical *American Agriculturalist* contrasted the science of selective livestock breeding with prevailing folk traditions of grain selection: "When it comes to plants, the same laws hold with equal force and importance, but a pedigree is rarely insisted upon. If the wheat is plump…that is sufficient, and questions are seldom asked as to the method by which the plumpness has been obtained. Pure seed should mean that which has resulted from in-breeding of a variety for a sufficient length of time, so the qualities become fixed and will be perpetuated."[1]

In May 1828, John Work delivered eight bales of Ft. Colvile barley meal to the company's northern posts in the Fraser River district of New Caledonia, today's British Columbia. Laborers at Ft. Langley, which was established by McLoughlin in 1827 near present Vancouver, British Columbia, were soon raising wheat, barley, Indian corn, and peas nearby for local consumption. Hand-burr (buhr) milling equipment was used to produce the first flour at Ft. Colvile until a water-powered grist-mill using a pair of millstones chiseled from local granite was built in 1830 several miles south of the fort at Myers Falls on the Colville River. Early mills used two granite grinding stones with canted grooves cut in the rock so grist would be crushed rather than smashed between the stationary nether (bottom) and runner (top). As the runner turned, the grain gradually moved out more finely in the furrows to be thrown out at the edge as flour. This crude milling required considerable time and produced an oily, starchy germ (which causes flour to become rancid), and whole wheat mixture of protein-rich gluten, fibrous bran, and vitamins. Other

Quern (Hand-Burr) Milling

19

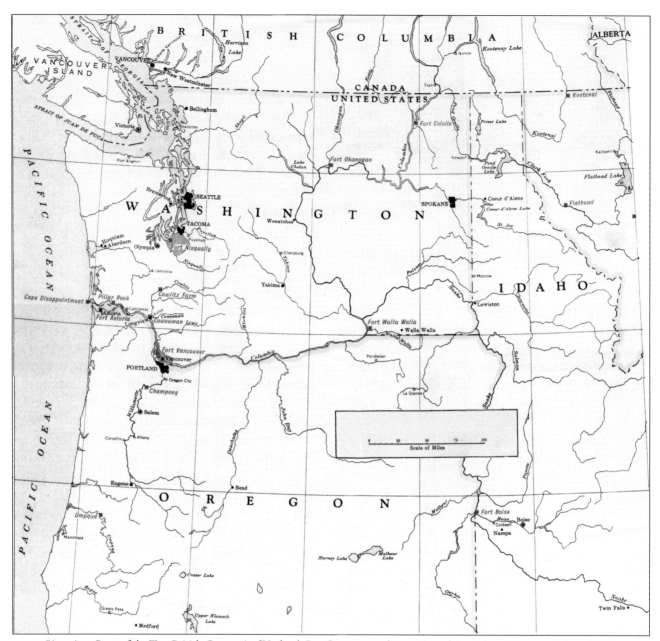

"American Posts of the Two British Companies [Hudson's Bay Company and Puget Sound Agricultural Company] from 1846"
H. Miller, ed., *Treaties and Other International Acts of the United States of America, Vol. 8* (1948)

products used for "flours" and cereal included brans (outer skins or husks), shorts (bran and germ), and middlings (endosperm and bran). Five bushels of wheat weighing about sixty pounds per bushel typically yielded one two-hundred-pound barrel of flour.[2]

Larger areas were soon under cultivation at two nearby company farms that in 1832 yielded three thousand bushels of wheat, corn, barley, oats, buckwheat, and peas. A second, more efficient gristmill was constructed near the original Ft. Colvile structure in the late 1840s and became operational in 1850 to enable substantial distribution of company flour to New Caledonia and the Snake River country.

Ft. Vancouver's first mill used a small hand-turned stone and was apparently located near the sawmill about 1828. A larger mill made of locally quarried stone was operating in 1834. Powered by slow-moving oxen or horses, the mill provided

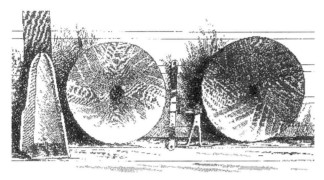

Northwest Millstones Imported from Europe

barely enough flour for local needs, though Rev. Samuel Parker considered the flour "of excellent quality." Millwright William Crate's water-powered gristmill was completed in the spring of 1839 on Mill Creek. It could grind and bolt about sixty bushels of wheat per day, or ten thousand bushels annually. The sound of rotating stones accompanied by the rhythmic clacking and splashing from the enormous wheel played pleasantly throughout the valley. A visitor to the fort wrote that the mill's "deep music is heard daily and nightly half the year" as it processed the previous year's harvest, which also came via wheat bateaux and barges from farms of Willamette Valley settlers. Rev. Samuel Parker noted in 1836 that the French Prairie "hunters turned farmers" aided by McLoughlin were producing "first quality" wheat and found a ready market at the fort where it was traded for imported molasses, cocoa, salt, rum, claret, and Chinese tea.

Ft. Vancouver, Ft. Nez Perces, Ft. Okanogan, and Ft. Colvile soon came to employ a host of voyageurs, farmers, herdsmen, carpenters, blacksmiths, tinsmiths, tailors, and other laborers who regularly worked from 6:00 A.M. to 6:00 P.M., six days a week. Ohio native and wagon train leader Lansford Hastings described bustling Ft. Vancouver in the 1840s as a place of "diligent and incessant plying of the hammer, sledges and axes, and the confused toiling and ringing of bells, present all the impetuous commotion, rustling, tumultuous din of a city life in the oriental world."[3]

Company officials like McLoughlin and Peter Skene Ogden recorded that anticipation of the semi-annual Columbia Express from York Factory on Hudson's Bay and yearly "London Packet" ship arrivals provided the main topic of fort conversation for weeks. Regular provisioning by HBC trading ships began in the 1830s. Their substantial deliveries of Indian trade goods, tea, sugar, tools, and other supplies transformed Ft. Vancouver into the Pacific Northwest's "Grand Emporium," and kept clerks working long hours under the "Great Tyee" McLoughlin to carefully record inventories and sell to Indians who often traveled vast distances to trade at the region's posts. But as early as 1830, Simpson urged establishment of an outpost on the southern shore of Puget Sound where deeper draft, ocean-going vessels could more easily navigate.[4]

COWLITZ AND NISQUALLY FARMING

Diminished European demand for fur in the 1830s, combined with a decline in pelts due to extensive trapping, spurred interest by the Honourable Company's leadership in the region's proven agricultural potential. Overtures had been made during the decade by HBC Governor John Pelly and Simpson to Russian-American Company representatives in St. Petersburg to establish spheres of influence on the Pacific Slope and to provision their distant outposts. The expense and limited availability of foodstuffs from eastern Russia contributed to recurrent shortages for the Russian *promyshlenikii* (fur trapper-traders) who traded as far south as Ft. Ross in Alta California. Simpson had long considered the prospects of trade with the Russians and in 1828 wrote to London headquarters, "We could…furnish them with Provisions, say Grain, Beef & Pork, as the Farm at Vancouver can be made to produce, much more." Russian-American Governor Arvid Adolf Etholén characterized yields in California as "precarious" due to periodic drought which forced them to venture as far as Chile to procure grain.

The Russian government was initially wary of British intentions, but in February 1839 Simpson and Baron Ferdinand von Wrangell, former governor and now a director of Russian-American Company, met and reached agreement in Hamburg on a ten-year "Russia Contract." The British would provide up to 8,400 bushels of wheat, eight tons of flour, six and one-half tons of barley groats, six and one-half tons of peas, butter, cheese, and other

Fort Nisqually, 1843
Special Collections, University of Washington Libraries (NA 4132)

provisions at negotiated prices. The agreement further stipulated that the British would lease the coastal lisiére between Cape Spencer and 54°40′ N. which the Russians considered less productive in furs. Simpson then joined Pelly and Andrew Colvile in London to incorporate the Puget Sound Agricultural Company (PSAC) for developing tracts of farmland at Ft. Nisqually and Cowlitz Farm between the Cowlitz and Chehalis rivers northeast of present Toledo, Washington. The Hudson's Bay Company Governing Committee felt "quite sure that the Fur trade and farming pursuits, branches of business so foreign to each other, will be done more justice to and be much more likely to prosper under distinct managements...." The HBC formally transferred title to Ft. Nisqually and Cowlitz Farm to the Puget Sound Agricultural Company in December 1840, but in actual practice operations of both enterprises would be highly interrelated and mutually beneficial.[5]

Simpson traveled to the Pacific Northwest for a second time in 1841 as the first leg on a journey around the world, and worked out details of the agreement with Russian officials in New Archangel, "the great depôt of the Russian-American Company," where Governor Etholén led an amalgam of workers including Russians, Finns, and Baltic Germans. Company officials there expressed a preference for Columbia wheat over grain from California or Russia. British traders transported provisions northward via their growing fleet of Pacific vessels that included the barques *Columbia* and *Vancouver*,

schooner *Cadboro*, and the first steamship to operate in the Pacific Northwest, the brigantine-rigged, twin sidewheeler *Beaver*. The Russian vessels *Alexander*, *Okhotsk*, and *Constantine* plied the coast-southward to California.

A related favorable consequence of the British-Russian arrangement was expansion of the Russian-American trade the following year to include an additional ten thousand bushels of Columbia wheat to New Archangel—now called Sitka—so the Russians could provision Kamchatka more cheaply than if the grain had been shipped from European Russia. With Ft. Vancouver and the Puget Sound Agricultural Company expanding production in the early 1840s, Russian ships were soon unloading tons of Columbia grain at the harbor of St. Peter and Paul (present Petropavlovsk), administrative center of the Russian Far East. The arrangement continued for a decade until the Oregon Treaty of 1846 deprived the Hudson's Bay Company of its Columbia farming operations. About the same time, wheat production in California had recovered, which enabled Yankee traders to reenter the Russian-American market.[6]

British settlement on Puget Sound had begun in 1833 when McLoughlin directed Archibald McDonald to establish Ft. Nisqually on the shore southwest of present DuPont and Nisqually Plain's twenty-by-thirty-mile scenic "Grand Prairie." The area's first wheat was sown the following fall. McDonald was appointed Chief Trader and built a small log enclosure for his young family—the first

Fort Nisqually Granary
Robert Smith

step in opening the strategic area on Puget Sound to agriculture and the fur trade. McDonald's wife, Jane, had grown up in the Northwest as daughter of the Nor'Wester Dutch-Canadian, Michel Klyne, and his Indian wife.

Just weeks after McDonald had commenced operations, twenty-one-year-old William Fraser Tolmie, Glasgow University graduate and newly enlisted company physician from Inverness, Scotland, arrived at "Nesqually" en route from Ft. Vancouver to serve at Ft. Simpson north of Vancouver Island. Soon after his arrival at Ft. Nisqually, however, an axe-wielding worker seriously injured himself, and Dr. Tolmie remained to treat the wound. The incident, combined with subsequent reassignments of Nisqually per-

Dr. William Tolmie
Special Collections, University of Washington Libraries
(PC 482.59953)

sonnel, eventually led to Tolmie's appointment as "commander of a trading post in this remote corner of the New World." Tolmie's wide-ranging scientific, geographic, and commercial interests led to excursions throughout the region, and while aboard the *Cadboro* in December 1833 he was allowed to briefly explore "the much admired plain on Whidbey's island," noting its fertile "black loamy soil." Simpson characterized the island and surrounding mainland areas as "in every way adapted for tillage and pasture, and perfectly healthy," and recommended to Pelly and Colvile that "attention ought to be directed particularly to this quarter."

The hardworking, temperate Tolmie also pursued studies in linguistics and literature, and

Fort Nisqually Granary Farm Tools
R. Scheuerman Collection

By the mid-1840s Tolmie was supervising operations at a dozen farming and ranching stations around Ft. Nisqually that employed from fifty to seventy-five workers. Clusters of evergreens and Garry oak dotted the pastoral prairies providing abundant habitat to grouse and partridges, deer and elk. Annual yields were generally ample but not assured given the vagaries of coastal growing conditions. Ft. Vancouver's 1840 grain yields were reduced by mild blight, the 1842 crop at Ft. Colvile suffered from severe drought, and in 1843 Nisqually's winter wheat was damaged by a hard spring frost. Despite these setbacks, Tolmie oversaw the farms, including herds of some ten thousand head of sheep, cattle, and horses from Ft. Nisqually. McLoughlin was selling up to fifteen thousand bushels of grain, butter, and cheese annually to Russian America from area company operations and Willamette Valley settlers, and exporting fur, hides, tallow, and wool to England. The Puget Sound Agricultural Company turned a profit in 1844 and in the following year paid its first dividend to shareholders. But following withdrawal of British interests following the Oregon Treaty of 1846, McLoughlin retired to Oregon City with his family to a spacious two-story home, and PSAC operations were largely confined to southern Vancouver Island.

Most of the cattle and sheep owned by the Hudson's Bay Company on the lower Columbia in the 1840s had descended from stock herded north from California. But Governor Simpson also arranged to send Sussexdown, Leicester, Cheviot, Merino, and Southdown purebred sheep from England in order to improve "the degenerate stock of the country" and remedy the coarseness of the wool. Ft. Vancouver also maintained a substantial herd of goats as early as 1828. Since Ft. Nisqually came to specialize in sheep-raising, as many as fifteen thousand animals were divided into bands of about five hundred which were regularly moved from the southern Nisqually prairies to the northern Puyallup ranges to prevent overgrazing and provide manure for crops. Several Scotch shepherds tended the herds, which were at risk from wolves, eagles, and other predators; while English, Indian,

corresponded extensively as a member of the Royal Horticultural Society with Sir William Jackson Hooker, later director of London's famed Royal Botanic (Kew) Gardens. Through perseverance and skillful diplomacy with area tribal leaders, Tolmie soon transformed Ft. Nisqually into a successful agricultural enterprise and regional trade center of European culture. A substantial post-and-sill granary was built in 1850 to replace an earlier structure, and remains the oldest building in the state. Tolmie married Jane Work, daughter of longtime HBC trader John Work, and the couple raised a large family at Nisqually. Dr. Tolmie's medical and botanical interests significantly contributed to the company's success on the south Sound's marginal soils.

Hawaiian (Kanaka), and other shepherds worked year-round in a half-dozen surrounding farm "stations." Many resided in huts placed on wheeled frames so they could be moved among the stations.

The company's Tlithlow (or Tithlow) farming headquarters was located seven miles east of the fort along the head of present Murray Creek. Other company farms in the vicinity included Spanueh (Spanaway), Old and New Muck, and Wyatchie. Spanueh was near Spanaway Lake, and its name was derived from the native Lushootseed word *spáduwe*, meaning "dug roots," for the abundant and nutritious camas (*Camassia quamash*) that once abounded in vast stands of ultramarine blue throughout vicinity. Old and New Muck, located north of present Roy, were named for the British Isle of Muck. Bands of sheep were routinely pastured on these farmlands following harvest of wheat, barley, and rye to manure the fields and control weeds. The crops and livestock at Wyatchie were capably managed around the shores of present Gravelly Lake in the late 1840s by Hebredian John McLeod (1815-1905), who married T'lalquodote (Mary), daughter of the influential Cowlitz Chief Skanáwuh.[8]

In 1833 two retired company employees, French Canadians Simon Plamondon (Plamondeau) and Francois Failland (Faignant), had begun farming operations on fertile Cowlitz Prairie that stretched for four miles above the east portage of the Cowlitz River. Plamondon was a highly regarded, self-reliant frontiersman variously listed in early Hudson's Bay accounts as a trapper, trader, and "independent scout." He first came to the Pacific Northwest in 1815 with the North West Company and remained in the region after the British firms merged in 1821. Family accounts suggest Plamondon first spied Cowlitz country on a journey upstream during the winter of 1818–19. He met Chief Skanáwuh and eventually wed his daughter,

Merino Sheep
Report of the Commissioner of Agriculture (1862)

Thasemuth (Veronica). The couple lived seasonally among her people and after Thasemuth's death about 1827, Plamondon remarried Emilie Finlay Bercier, the Métisse daughter of legendary Northwest pathfinder, Jaco Finlay. The family established a productive farm on Cowlitz (Grand) Prairie that Plamondon called "The Highlands."

Simpson described Cowlitz Prairie soil as "the best quality for growing wheat, consisting of a fine rich loam, running at the depth of fifteen inches, into a subsoil of stiff clay" and judged the area as "probably the finest tract of tillable land in the Indian Country." In 1839 McLoughlin dispatched young John Tod to superintend construction of a substantial dwelling, barns, and an enormous sixty-by-one-hundred-and-twenty-foot, two-story granary built of six-inch squared fir beams. A small trading post located near the river was dubbed Cowlitz House. The first company fields were planted that year with disappointing results, but persistent efforts under the capable leadership of Tod and Charles Forest soon led to abundant harvests. In the fall of 1841, Simpson reported that eight thousand bushels of "wheat of excellent quality" was produced from 729 bushels of seed, two hundred bushels of seed oats yielded two thousand bushels, and four hundred bushels of barley was harvested from twenty bushels of seed. American explorer Charles Wilkes visited the farm in May of that year and found it "covered with a luxuriant crop of wheat" with orchards planted among the trees. "Nature," Wilkes observed, "seems as it were to invite the husbandman to his labors."

Before completion of a gristmill in 1840, local Cowlitz Indians used stone mortar and pestles to grind grain and carried the grist in coiled cedar root burden baskets exquisitely imbricated with geometric designs. By 1842, PSAC employees farmed nearly 1,500 acres of the 3,600-acre tract,

Puget Sound Salish Winnowing Basket
R. Scheuerman Collection

with other land apportioned to scattered settlers and St. Francis Xavier's Cowlitz Indian Mission, founded by Father Modeste Demers (1809-1871) during the winter of 1838-39. The mission's substantial farm was tended by Augustin Rochon, one of the voyageurs who had brought the missionary from Montreal. Rochon harvested a small crop of spring wheat and peas in the summer of 1839 and erected a sixty-by-thirty-foot barn as well as the area's first church, known as Wolf's Head Chapel for the peculiar shape of its roof.[9]

Some two dozen HBC workers were regularly employed at Cowlitz Prairie, including a principal farmer, shepherd, and carpenter, as well as laborers to operate eight to ten plows and harrows. [See map in Appendix 1] The ranks of cradlers swelled to forty during harvest. Company lands were carefully divided by Tod and his successor, George Roberts, into twenty-nine fields ranging in size from ten to 120 acres that also included oats, buckwheat, and flax. Grain and other produce was first conveyed in planked bateaux all the way to Ft. Vancouver until 1845 when McLoughlin authorized construction of a granary at the mouth of the Cowlitz River near present Longview.[10]

A typical Old Oregon Country grain rotation reflecting British influence might include White Winter wheat, followed by Scotch Two-Row barley or English Gray oats. In accordance with the Old World model, many Northwest farmers enriched their soils with a third-year rotation crop of green manure with green clover, native to the region, or introduced varieties like white and red clover. Livestock typically grazed on nearby grasslands and harvested stubble. Cowlitz's Roberts records an enigmatic reference to Champoeg "Anent wheat and flour" that McLoughlin sent him to purchase in the fall of 1842, perhaps to meet company obligations for that year's Russian contract. "Annat" was an obscure Scottish red club wheat from which the more commonly known Browick was developed as a Norfolk field selection in 1844. But neither name appears elsewhere in extant Northwest records of the period. Expanding global grain trade and improved selections from landraces a generation later would add such varieties to the mix as White Chile Club (South America) and Pacific Bluestem (Australia) wheats, Oderbrucher (German) and Chinese Manshury (Manchurian) six-row barleys, and Norway White, Black (Russian) Tartarian, and Angus (Scotch) oats.[11]

GRANARY GOVERNMENT

Much of the grain from the Willamette Valley was transported by boat to present Oregon City and then transferred to barges for delivery to Ft. Vancouver. The company also built a twenty-by-forty-foot warehouse on the western shore of the Champoeg townsite about 1843 to stockpile additional wheat purchased for the Russian contract from French Prairie farmers who had also established the rural hamlets of St. Paul, Gervais, St. Louis, and Butteville. McLoughlin and Simpson's schemes for marketing grain to Russian America and the Sandwich Islands led to annual purchases in the 1840s of ten to twenty thousand bushels of the Willamette Valley farmers' wheat. The profit margin on sales in Hawaii and Alaska, however, amounted to the equivalent of just pennies on the dollar. Considerable expense accrued from storage at the company's

Champoeg, Oregon City, and Linton warehouses, transportation by boat to Ft. Vancouver, milling operations, and subsequent delivery of barreled flour by ship.

When Methodist missionary Jason Lee arrived in the area with other Americans in 1834—with the first pair of cattle to cross the Oregon Trail—he found the best farmlands on French Prairie already claimed. Lee decided to establish his headquarters at present-day Salem. His entrepreneurial co-worker, George Abernathy, joined with pioneer merchant Francis William Pettygrove to build a store, granary, and warehouse for trading grain, furs, and other commodities a short distance downstream at Portland, which he named for the port city in his native Maine. Settler concerns about marauding wolves, cougars, and other predators prompted organization of area "Wolf Meetings" in February and March 1843 by Abernathy and his associates. These gatherings, combined with concern about means to probate the considerable estate of trader-rancher Ewing Young, led area settlers to recommend organization of Oregon's Provisional Government, a move long feared by McLoughlin.

Young had been one of the founders of the Willamette Cattle Company who had driven livestock from California to Oregon in order to break the Hudson's Bay Company's monopoly on cattle in the valley. He had settled near Champoeg with Webley John Hauxhurst, but died in 1841 with no heirs or will. By that time the Tualatin Plains had become home to a substantial rural settlement of independent American ex-trappers including Joseph Meek, William Doughty, and others like Congregational missionary-farmer John S. Griffin. Meek helped Doughty plant wheat from Ft. Vancouver in the spring of 1842 and the colony's success and available land in the north plains area attracted other American wayfarers wanting to settle down. They called their popular gathering place at the famed "Five Oaks" near Hillsboro the "Rocky Mountain Retreat" for the region's first substantial American enclave west of the Rockies. Here amidst the stand of centuries-old trees, veterans of the old Rocky Mountain Fur Company's annual rendezvous gathered again for horse-racing and celebrations, picnics, and revival camp meetings.

Many of the French Prairie Métis who participated in the proceedings opposed the American settlers' push for US sovereignty. The matter was resolved, however, when the two men who were probably the first permanent settlers there—Joseph Gervais and Etienne Lucier—voted in favor of the historic measure calling for a provisional government at a May 2 Champoeg meeting where the issue was decided by a vote of 52-50. The group then appointed a committee led by Abernathy to draft a constitution. The group convened in May and June in the Methodist Mission granary, where school and worship services were also held, and on July 5, 1843, they announced completion of the "Organic Act of the Provisional Government in Oregon." Nine years later Americans living north of the Columbia gathered at the settlement that had sprouted around the Hudson's Bay granary at the mouth of the Cowlitz River, named Monticello for Jefferson's home, to petition Congress for creation of a territory separate from Oregon. Congress responded favorably to the request although the proposed territorial name "Columbia" was changed to Washington, and in 1853 the measure was approved.[12]

The Northwest Farm Year

Hudson's Bay Company farm workers at Ft. Vancouver followed a planting schedule gleaned from experience to ensure crops would ripen sequentially to prevent sprout damage and "shake," or kernel loss from dislodging. Peas were seeded before March 20, oats before April 10, followed by spring wheat (May 10), barley (June 20), and winter wheat (before October 20). The general sowing sequence at Ft. Nisqually was slightly earlier and began with oats, rye, and wheat in late February and March followed by peas (March), and buckwheat and barley in May (see Appendix I). For field operations, one Puget Sound frontiersman recommended advice from the ancient Roman writer and farmer Virgil: "Plow early, plow deep, cross furrow, harrow well, manure and fallow your land, and change your crops."

The ripe grain was typically cut in July and August using scythe and cradle with stalks deftly

Flailing Wheat
T. Michell, *Russian Pictures Drawn with Pen and Pencil* (1889)

tied into a half-dozen sheaf bundles for shocking to prevent lodging. The long handles of the first "turkey-wing" scythes were almost straight and soon replaced by slightly crooked "muleys." Eventually the considerably bent "grapevine" model prevailed by providing better leverage for cutting, and these remained in use throughout the Northwest for decades. Grain was first threshed by hand with wooden flails made of thorn, yew, or other tough wood; or by leading horses in a circle around a hard threshing floor, often inside a barn during winter, to "tread" or "tramp" out the kernels from the golden mass of piled stalks.

The method was described by legendary Oregon pioneer Jesse Applegate who came west with Marcus Whitman in 1843: "[A] clayey spot is made smooth and hard by being dampened and beaten with maul, or tramped with animals. Around it a high, strong fence is made, and over it those fond of shade throw a few bushes. On this 'floor' the grain is laid out regularly, the heads pointing obliquely upward. A wild, skittish band of horses are turned in and driven against the bristling heads of the grain, and by their scampering, in a very short time the wheat is threshed from the straw, and much of the straw itself broken to pieces, much more time being required to separate and remove it from the grain than is occupied in the threshing. Leaving the bottom undisturbed to the last, as it is sometimes dirty, the threshed grain is pushed to the center,

and another floor laid down; and so on until the crop is threshed."

Before hand-powered fanning mills came available in the late 1840s, workers waited for a stiff wind or a pair waved a blanket between them, as wooden spades full of harvested wheat were tossed five to six feet into the air to winnow grain from chaff. The kernels were then scooped into barrels or imported burlap sacks that smelled of old Calcutta. Grain yielded up to thirty or more bushels an acre in the 1840s, and much of the surplus was transported on company vessels to Ft. Vancouver for milling and shipment to Russian Alaska. Wheat soon became legal tender to British authorities in the Northwest with one bushel equaling one dollar.[13]

RED RIVER COLONISTS

Simpson was wary of growing Yankee influence in the region from both Willamette Valley American farmers and the "Great Reinforcement" of the Methodist Mission in Salem in 1839. In 1841 he commenced a colonization campaign to lure settlers from Canada "with the view of gradually forming a European Agricultural Settlement" along the lower Columbia River. The company offered leases to prospective settlers on thousand-acre parcels, each with a house, barn, livestock, and seed grain. Simpson's program brought mixed results. The British managed to recruit some colonist families from Canada's Red River district (Assiniboia) where the Hudson's Bay Company's troubled attempts to establish an agricultural area finally brought a measure of prosperity to some residents by the 1830s. However, British sovereignty in Canada protected private interests, so settlers there were more willing to enter into long-term lease agreements on farmland.[14]

Such security did not extend to the disputed lands jointly occupied with the Americans in the Oregon Country. Simpson found prospective colonists from Red River reluctant to risk an arduous journey and the demands of frontier living on leased lands with an uncertain future. But the prospects of a new start in the West appealed to some, and twenty-one mostly young families—one hundred and sixteen individuals—many of whom were Métis, assembled on June 5, 1841, for the three-month overland trek, bringing fifty Red River carts laden with furniture, tools, pots and pans, chests, and other household goods.

The group was capably led by HBC trader-explorer James Sinclair, and included some families who would play leading roles in agricultural development west of the Cascades—those of brothers William, James, John, and David Flett, and Joseph Klyne, Charles McKay, and Pierre and Louis Larocque. They crossed the Rockies at Whiteman Pass in August 1841 and after a harrowing descent of the rugged slopes, the group emerged onto the Kootenay Plain and continued west to the Colville Trail. The time-worn route descended south across smooth but rocky terrain through the Channeled Scablands to the Snake River and Ft. Nez Perces on the Columbia. The trail-weary travelers paused only briefly before pressing along the river to Ft. Vancouver where they finally arrived on October 12, 1841, after a 130-day journey across seventeen hundred miles. The distance covered was about the same as the Oregon Trail—crossed that same year by the first substantial wagon train, the Bidwell-Bartleson party.

At Ft. Vancouver McLoughlin shared the disappointing news that the company was not yet prepared to honor terms of the settlement agreement in the Willamette-Vancouver area as effusively promoted by Simpson. He encouraged them to continue north where arrangements had been more fully made, so seven French Canadian families settled at Cowlitz Farm with some reluctance, while fourteen nearly destitute English and Scot families located on lands near Ft. Nisqually. But conditions on Puget Sound were scarcely more favorable than at Ft. Vancouver: houses were not completed and farm implements were in short supply. Blacksmith James Flett fashioned hardware and farm implements and after a difficult winter slowly began building up a dairy herd that would eventually become one of the area's most thriving enterprises.[15]

The greatest problem hindering Simpson's scheme, however, was the lure of life south of the Columbia in the fertile Willamette Valley where the Euro-American settlement had been prospering for nearly a decade, and where rights to patented land were guaranteed. For these reasons, most of the families that had settled in the vicinity of Ft. Nisqually drifted to Oregon by late 1843, although more favorable growing conditions at Cowlitz brought an expansion of the colony there to sixty-four people by that time. Englishman Joseph Heath arrived at Ft. Nisqually in June 1844 looking to revive his sagging fortunes and arranged through Tolmie to lease a farm abandoned by one of the Red River colonists north of the fort on the prairie above Steilacoom Bay.

Heath erected several log buildings and raised wheat, peas, potatoes, and livestock on about thirty acres. Encroachments by American settlers on the substantial two-hundred-fifty-square-mile Puget Sound Agricultural Company claim around Ft. Nisqually began soon after terms of the Oregon Treaty of 1846 were announced, settling the border between British possessions and the United States at the forty-ninth parallel. The agreement led to a settlement of claims and withdrawal of the Hudson's Bay Company from the Oregon Territory to British Columbia, although compensation claims to Ft. Nisqually and its surrounding network of valuable farms continued in litigation for over a decade. After Joseph Heath's death in the spring of 1849, the U.S. Army leased the Heath farm which became the site of Ft. Steilacoom.

As negotiations continued in Europe on the US-Canada boundary in Puget Sound, Hudson's Bay Company officials sought to further secure British claims to these strategic waters by establishing farms on the San Juan Islands. In 1853, Ft. Victoria Chief Factor James Simpson directed Irishman Charles J. Griffin to manage PSAC livestock and grain operations on San Juan Island. Its headquarters station, named Belle Vue Farm for the splendid view of the ocean and snow-clad Olympics, was established on the southeastern side of the island near Eagle Cove. Within several years Griffin supervised a team of several dozen British, Hawaiian, and Native American workers who tended eighty acres of wheat, oat, peas, potatoes, fruit trees, and 4,500 sheep divided into four separate flocks that ranged at stations clustered near the Friday Harbor, Kanaka Bay, Mitchel Bay, and Belle Vue. A company wharf was also constructed to the north in sheltered San Juan Bay. Orkneyman Robert Firth assumed management of the enterprise in 1862 and leased the farm after 1864 when the islands passed into American possession.[16]

British Columbia Farms and Grains

Hudson's Bay Company workers at posts in British Columbia continued to manage substantial agricultural operations in the 1860s. About two thousand acres were cultivated on the "Great Prairie" near Ft. Langley, and about an equal area of hayfields were tended near Ft. Kamloops at the Thompson River forks as well as a two-hundred-acre dairy six miles north. Longtime Métis interpreter Jean Baptist Lolo (Shuswap Chief St. Paul) had raised horses and hay since 1843 on nearby lands at the Nor'Westers' old Thompson's River Post, which had been located along North Thompson's eastern shore at the confluence. The HBC purchased additional farmland between 1870 and 1900 at Similkameen Post, Ft. Simpson, Ft. McLoughlin, Bella Coola Post, and Ft. Shepherd. British government land grants provided additional HBC farms at Chilcotin River Post, Fraser Lake, Ft. George, Stuart Lake, McLeod Lake, Babine Lake, Ft. Berens at present Lillooet, and Ft. Alexander's Hudson Bay Meadows.[17]

Ft. Victoria served as headquarters of Hudson Bay Company regional operations and the PSAC from 1849 under the leadership of new HBC Governor James Douglas. After relocating to the island in 1859, Dr. Tolmie and a team of bailiff-managers supervised the organization's four Victoria area farms—Viewfield and adjacent Kanaka Ranch, Colwood (Esquimalt), Constance Cove (Oaklands), and Craigflower (Maplebank, Maple Point). As Chief Factor, Tolmie was also appointed to the HBC's Western Department Board of Management and established his own eleven-hundred-acre Cloverdale Farm near Saanich. From the splendor of the family's three-story mansion of sandstone and redwood, Tolmie superintended purebred livestock breeding and grain production there until his death in 1870. Founded in 1850, Viewfield was the first PSAC farm on the island and was located on its southeastern tip along several small bays north to Old Esquimalt Road where substantial numbers of sheep and cattle grazed. Sandwich Islanders recruited to labor at HBC posts and farms resided at nearby Kanaka Ranch, and in 1850 Viewfield workers constructed a gristmill near the mouth of Mill Creek.

Colwood and Constance Cove farms joined each other along Mill Creek and Esquimalt Harbor where livestock were raised as well as crops of wheat, oats, and peas. Englishman James Skinner and Kenneth McKenzie, a Scot, arrived with a group of twenty-five British colonist families aboard the HBC's annual supply ship, the barque *Norman Morrison*, in January 1853 to serve as bailiffs for area PSAG farms. (An 1850 arrival was John Helmcken who afterward served as HBC trader, company doctor, and prominent Victoria political leader.) Influenced by Edward Gibbon Wakefield's colonization strategy involving artisans, laborers, and investors, the group included farmers, carpenters, bricklayers, a baker, teacher, and servants. Wakefield's paternalistic scheme would prove impractical given the availability of lands on the Canadian frontier, and the penchant of some bailiffs for self-indulgence. But prospective farmers faced the challenge of frontier speculators whose transactions inflated the cost of area real estate.

The immigrant newcomers anticipated comfortable cottages awaiting them in a nascent frontier farming community, but their hopes were soon dashed. Arriving amidst bitter coastal winter winds, they found that construction had hardly begun on the promised residences. The group was compelled to spend their first months in storehouses, barns, and shacks in and around Ft. Victoria. McKenzie and Skinner supervised planting of grain fields and vegetable gardens in the spring of 1853 as work continued on homes and outbuildings built for both farms. McKenzie brought a seven-horsepower steam engine to power a small gristmill and sawmill that were both operational by late October.

Lines composed that year by James Deans, one of several PSAC young men working on five-year labor contracts, provided release from the profound homesickness experienced by many of the colonists:

Cheer up, sad heart and while I stray,
Sadly o'er Craigflower woody brae
Come fancy paint each glade and glen,
With waving grain and homes of men.
Then lay aside, your hopes and fears,
A change shall come with passing years
A time will come when you will say,
This is my home, here I will stay.[18]

Craigflower, a 760-acre farm named for HBC Governor Andrew Colvile's Scottish estate, became the crown jewel of the company's Vancouver Island agricultural colonies. By 1855, the manorial estate two miles west of the fort on Victoria Arm consisted of twenty-one dwellings, a carpenter shop, blacksmith shop, slaughterhouse, brick kiln, and flour mill surrounding an imposing Georgian two-story house built for McKenzie, his wife, and their five children. The McKenzie farm household came to serve as one of the area's most popular social centers throughout the 1850s and '60s, as Craigflower hosted gatherings of local government officials, company personnel, and visiting naval officers who danced and played croquet to the lively music of ships' bands. Craigflower personnel and area friends regularly gathered to hear lectures from each other on topics ranging from "Phases of the Moon" and "Immortality of the Soul" to recitations of Scottish poetry.

With lighter soils and cooler growing season temperatures than the Willamette Valley, southern Vancouver Island farmers sought crops adapted to the

Craigflower Farm Manor House; Victoria, British Columbia
R. Scheuerman Collection

local environment. Four kinds of wheat emerged as most favorable including Velvet Chaff, a semi-hard red winter wheat; the Spanish soft spring landrace selection Talavera, a "smooth chaff white"—possibly the beardless Essex mentioned by McKenzie—and an unidentified bearded red wheat. McKenzie's daybooks also mention Chevalier barley and oats which yielded well on acreage that had been cleared from dense stands of maple, oak, and evergreen trees. German mangle beet was also raised in the area principally as livestock fodder.

McKenzie's mill and brick ovens contributed significantly to company revenue during the Crimean War (1853-56) between Great Britain and Russia. British warships in the Pacific frequented Victoria Harbor to obtain bread, hardtack, and other provisions, and government orders required grain from all four company farms as well as imports from Oregon. By 1860, "Craigflower Mills" was also marketing Scotch oatmeal and pearl barley. Area residents petitioned the provincial Legislative Council in 1864 to fund a larger gristmill to process area grain for domestic markets and export. Three years later the island's first large-scale operation, the Victoria Gristmill, was processing some fifty bushels of grain per day.[19]

Chapter III

Missions and Migrations

Some bless the cart, some kiss the sheaves,
Some prank them up with oaken leaves:
Some cross the draft-horse, some with great
Devotion stroke the home-borne wheat:
While other rustics, less attent
To prayers than to merriment.

Waiilatpu Mission was established among the Cayuse Indians in 1836 by Presbyterian missionaries Marcus and Narcissa Whitman near present Walla Walla. The location served for ten years both as a center for religious work among the surrounding tribes and as a way station for Oregon Trail travelers. Both the Whitmans and their co-workers, Henry and Eliza Spalding, who established the Nez Perce Mission the Clearwater River near present Lapwai, Idaho, had planted grain and fruit in 1837 at their missions. Some accounts mention a jar of seed wheat the missionaries brought from the East, and that their limited supply was likely augmented by Hudson Bay Company traders. That same year Nez Perce headman Red Wolf planted apple seeds that he had obtained from Mrs. Spalding to begin an orchard at the mouth of Alpowa Creek on the Snake River.

At first the Whitmans tub-milled wheat into flour with iron "millstone" plates, but a small open-air gristmill was operating at Waiilatpu by 1841 using millstones two feet in diameter hewn from local granite. That summer, members of the United States Exploring Expedition, commissioned by naval officials in 1838 for a cartographic world tour and under the command of Charles Wilkes, visited

the area and reported on Spalding's forty acres of "fine wheat" in addition to potatoes, corn, beans, and melons. They also noted that area Indians had plots of five to twelve acres of fenced wheat, corn, potatoes, and melons. The following summer, Narcissa Whitman wrote, "The Kayuses almost to a man have their little farms now in every direction in this valley & are adding to it as their means & experience increases."

An iconic photograph of Reverend Spalding holding a Bible in one hand and a hoe in the other conveys Protestant missionary strategy of the era that held cultivation of the soil as synonymous with that of the heart. In March 1838, the Whitmans and Spaldings were joined by missionaries Elkanah and Mary Walker and Cushing and Myra Eells. The Walkers and the Eellses established a mission among the Spokane Indians in 1839 at Tshimakain near present Ford, Washington. Within a month of their arrival in the area, Elkanah began plowing with "a homely looking thing…to sow our wheat" which supplemented grain raised for the mission on lands adjacent to Chief Trader McDonald's gristmill near Ft. Colvile. To Reverend Walker, the fort was "a rich sight… after so long without seeing anything that indicated that the hand of indus-

Kamiakin's Ditch, Ahtanum Valley near Tampico, Washington
R. Scheuerman Collection

try had been there. To see fields well fenced, large stacks of all kinds of grain, cattle & hogs in large droves in the country so far removed from the civilized world, was a feast to my eyes."[1]

While the Presbyterian missionaries were planting and building, Indians of the region, as Narcissa Whitman noted, were embarking on their own agricultural pursuits. The name of renowned Yakama-Palouse Chief Kamiakin first appears in an 1841 travel account by American military explorer Lt. Robert E. Johnson and Ft. Nisqually journals of the period. Johnson's group had been dispatched from Nisqually to Ft. Colvile by Charles Wilkes, departing Puget Sound in May and reaching the Kittitas Valley by the first of June via the precarious Indian trail across Naches Pass. On June 2, the men found a camp of twenty Indians near present Ellensburg. "The chief, Kamaiyah, was the son-in-law of old Tidias [Teias], and one of the most handsome and perfectly-formed Indians they had met with."

The Yakamas traveled widely and Kamiakin acquired cattle and horses from the Willamette Valley and likely journeyed as far as California. The black, long-horned "Spanish" beef cattle and milk cows he brought home are believed to have been the first in the valley. In the spring of 1845, Rev. Alvan Waller, along with fellow missionary Jason Lee, rode north from The Dalles to the Yakima Valley where he noted small herds of livestock belonging to Chief Kamiakin and his brothers, Showaway and Skloom.

The Yakama leaders also introduced potatoes, peas, and other crops to the area. During Waller's visit, Kamiakin showed the circuit-rider a few sacks of crib corn remaining from the previous year's harvest. In the Ahtanum Valley, Kamiakin raised potatoes, squash, pumpkins, and corn in substantial garden plots irrigated by the waters of a spring below the principal fork in the stream. The half-mile-long canal, later dubbed "Kamiakin's Ditch" by white settlers, snaked along the contour just north of his camp from the spring to the gardens. Building it was a monumental undertaking given the rocky terrain and primitive tools available to the workers, and it remains clearly visible to this day.

Territorial frontiersman Francis Chenowith and three friends encountered Kamiakin in late June 1851 while on an excursion from The Dalles to the Simcoe Valley, where Chenowith noted that Indians were raising bountiful fields of ripening wheat and flax. They also raised wheat in the vicinities of present Ephrata and Douglas, and wheat, corn, peas, and vine crops in Moses Coulee. Chenowith judged the inland Northwest's climate "perhaps as near perfect as any in the world," and marveled at the "large bands of fat horses and cattle that rove unmolested upon the rich pastures." Years later, naturalist John Muir described the "treeless" Columbia Plateau as "green and flowery in the spring, but grey, dusty, and forbidding in summer." But he also observed valleys that "have proved fertile and produce large crops of wheat, barley, hay and other products." Oblate missionary Charles Marie Pandosy established St. Joseph's "Ahtanum" Mission in 1852 a short distance downstream from Chief Kamiakin's streamside camp. The Catholic

"black robes" raised large gardens, likely with seed provided by Kamiakin. "We get everything from him," Pandosy wrote appreciatively, and in appreciation, Jesuit successors at the mission planted a substantial apple orchard in 1867.[2]

TENDING SOUL AND SOIL

Catholic missionaries, while more tolerant than the Protestants of native cultural beliefs and practices that valued sustenance through traditional hunting, fishing, and gathering, also encouraged agriculture. The first Catholic black robes entered the region in the summer of 1841 led by Father Pierre De Smet. Father De Smet's humility and tenacity won the admiration of whites and Indians alike in an era when the interests of both groups frequently collided. The peripatetic Belgian priest led a group of two other Jesuit priests—Nicholas Point and Gregory Mengarini—and three lay brothers on a four-month journey to the Salish Indians' main village in the Bitterroot Valley near present Stevensville,

Nicholas Point, S.J., "St. Mary's Mission" (showing grain fields), c. 1841
Manuscripts, Archives, and Special Collections,
Washington State University Libraries (537.7.14.25)

Montana. They arrived in August 1841 to establish St. Mary's Mission, the first of a dozen Northwest centers established by Jesuits in the 1840s.

The missionaries envisioned the creation of a Jesuit Reduction, or settlement, akin to the self-sustaining agricultural communities developed by the order in the seventeenth century among the Guaraní Indians of Paraguay until brutal commercial interests of Spanish officials led to the expulsion of the Indians' missionary defenders. De Smet and his co-workers sought an enduring paradise for the Northwest tribes' spiritual wellbeing in the pristine wilderness of the northern Rockies far away from exploitive Americans. En route to their destination, Father Point drew plans for the first reduction with huts and fields arranged in a broad crescent fanning out from the new mission center. Chiefs Pierre, Victor, and other Salish leaders welcomed the black robes to the valley, and within weeks of their arrival erected a chapel and outbuildings.

In the fall of 1841, De Smet set out from St. Mary's to Ft. Colvile on an arduous six-week journey to procure wheat, oats, and potatoes from Archibald McDonald, who kindly obliged his request. In spite of De Smet's characterization of his reception as "warm hospitable," his gregarious host privately expressed doubts about missionary prospects for success. McDonald wrote about cultural obstacles inhibiting the native peoples' conversion "to the habits of civilized life." But De Smet already anticipated Euro-American colonization in the wake of the fur trade's decline, and understood the Jesuit mission to be one of promoting cultural change through farming so area tribes could better subsist when freedom to inhabit their vast traditional lands inevitably diminished.[3]

McDonald had no cattle to spare the ambitious black robe, but managed to stow a generous supply of sugar, chocolate, tea, flour, and other provisions in his packs. The Jesuits planted grain and vegetables the following spring to provide the region's first harvest "to the delight of the natives." The grain was both roasted and boiled for consumption, and some was roughly milled in a coffee grinder and by mortar and pestle. De Smet undertook extensive travels in the region in 1842 to establish missions among the Coeur d'Alenes and the Pend Oreilles. Two years later De Smet founded St. Ignatius mission where Father Adrian Hoecken soon supervised cultivation on three hundred acres and raised cattle and chickens. St. Paul and St. Francis Regis missions opened in 1845 near Ft. Colvile. Mission locations were strongly influenced by proximity to potential farmland and De Smet obtained plows, spades, hoes, scythes and "every sort of implement" to foster agricultural success.

Father De Smet returned to St. Louis in 1843 and journeyed to Rome to seek new recruits to reinforce his far-flung field. Several dedicated missionaries responded, including the young Italian priest Anthony Ravalli, who arrived at Ft. Vancouver in 1844. Father Ravalli was a Renaissance thinker also trained as a physician, sculptor, and naturalist, who applied his many interests in ways that promoted agriculture at Northwest Jesuit missions. He traveled to St. Mary's with two fifteen-inch-diameter millstones given to him by an Irish merchant in Antwerp, and fashioned a small water-powered gristmill and sawmill. In 1845 the black robes and Indians harvested a thousand bushels of wheat under the pleasant summer skies of the Bitterroot Valley. With Ravalli and Mengarini's guidance, the mission became a "terrestrial paradise" producing "abundant crops" of wheat, oats, and potatoes, as well as cattle, hogs, and chickens.[4]

Northwest Stars and Stripes

America's "Great Migration" of 1843 brought nearly nine hundred emigrants across the Oregon Trail to the sparsely settled Willamette Valley. Amidst all the supplies carefully packed for journeys lasting from four to six months, there may well have been wooden boxes with precious seed wheat to be planted in the New Canaan. But pioneer accounts of such special provision are rare, while many reference the purchase of crop seed on credit from McLoughlin at Ft. Vancouver soon after arriving in the Northwest. (The Chief Factor would later be criticized by Hudson's Bay Company officials for his beneficence toward the American settlers.)

If the emigrants managed to safeguard grain seed from the Midwest or East, the wheat varieties were likely those commonly grown in those areas like Red May (Yellow Lammas) and Genesee Giant. But such grains were not well adapted to Northwest environmental conditions and never rivaled other wheats commonly mentioned in 1850s newspaper and government reports like Colonial Spanish Sonora Spring, Little Club, and White Chili (Chile) Club; and the old English Lammas landrace selections White Winter and Pacific Bluestem. (Oregon farmer Joseph Watt exhibited a stool—or plant crown—of the latter grown from a single seed at the 1854 Yamhill County Fair—the Northwest's first, claiming that it had ninety-six "full large heads.") The docile Shorthorn and Durham cattle that accompanied the overlanders on the Oregon Trail in the 1840s significantly improved Northwest livestock herds.

Most emigrants in the 1840s settled in the Willamette Valley. A few of the twelve hundred who arrived in 1844, however, found conditions north of the Columbia River more favorable. These included Samuel Crockett, Reuben Crowder, and Jesse Ferguson; a Kentuckian of Irish descent, Michael T. Simmons, his wife and seven children; a fellow Kentuckian of Scottish background, James McAllister, his wife and children; and, from Missouri, former fur trapper George Washington Bush, his wife and six sons. Bush, the first black settler in what would become Washington State, was barred from owning land in Oregon Territory. This group spent the winter of 1844–45 near Ft. Vancouver where McLoughlin hired several of the men, including Simmons, Bush, and Crockett, to make cedar shingles for export to the Sandwich Islands. The following summer several of these Americans undertook a series of exploring expeditions to Cowlitz (Grand) Prairie and south Puget Sound. The Simmons and Bush families found good prospects in the lower Deschutes Valley near present Tumwater, originally named New Market

Owen Bush Family Farm, c. 1890
Henderson House Museum; Tumwater, Washington

(versus the Hudson's Bay Company's "old market"), where they finally arrived in early November 1845, each claiming 640 acres of land along the Cowlitz-Nisqually Trail. McLoughlin supplied a letter of recommendation to Dr. Tolmie at Ft. Nisqually that enabled Simmons to obtain two hundred bushels of wheat, three hundred bushels of potatoes, ten head of cattle, and other provisions on credit for use during the difficult months of settlement on the Puget Sound frontier.[5]

Other American families soon settled throughout the area that became known as Bush Prairie, and in the fall of 1846 Levi Smith and Edmund Sylvester settled at present Olympia. These farms fostered Washington Territory's first American settlement and during the winter of 1846–47 Simmons and Bush constructed a small gristmill on the former's land claim at Deschutes Falls using millstones chiseled from Eld Inlet granite. The operation was the region's first American-owned milling venture. By the end of the decade the Bushes were raising substantial crops of wheat, oats, rye, potatoes, and hops, and had planted apple and pear trees from seeds brought with them over the Oregon Trail. In 1852 Samuel Crockett relocated to Whidbey Island and was followed by the family of his father, Virginia native and War of 1812 veteran Colonel Walter Crockett, Sr.

The amiable Tolmies established friendly relations with area Nisqually, Puyallup, Cowlitz, and other area Indians, as well as parties of Yakamas and Klickitats who frequently traded at the fort. Dr. Tolmie hosted such prominent Euro-Americans as David Douglas, John Townshend, and Charles Wilkes, and regularly met with Northwest tribal leaders like Quiemuth, Owhi, and Leschi—who Owen Bush characterized as "the best friend we ever had." Flower gardens and orchards flourished around the fort where the Tolmies' genial hospitality promoted widespread goodwill over tea served with colorful Spode-Copeland earthenware and news from the annual Columbia Express from York Factory.

Tolmie and fellow company trader Donald Manson also contributed significantly to the region's intellectual climate by persuading McLoughlin to expand the Ft. Vancouver library into a circulating "Columbia Library." Funds received from company subscribers were used to purchase additional works from British booksellers, and Tolmie contributed a number of his own medical and other volumes. The collection grew to include literary, religious, scientific, and other books as well as periodicals that were distributed to Northwest posts from Ft. Vancouver.[6] A new surge of immigration in 1846 brought more Americans to the area that led to brisk business at Simmons's gristmill and construction of a brick kiln at Simon Plamondon's farm in the Cowlitz Valley.

With the extension of US sovereignty over the Oregon Country in 1846, many Americans expressed renewed interest in the lands north of the Columbia River. The Tolmies remained at Ft. Nisqually to protect company interests until their relocation to Victoria in 1859, and Puget Sound Agricultural Company claims were not adjudicated for another decade. On both sides of the Cascades, Hudson's Bay Company outposts provided the nucleus for a series of small agricultural settlements. About thirty-two employees were working at the three interior locations in 1846 and many, like Angus McDonald at Ft. Colvile and Pierre Pambrum at Ft. Walla Walla, chose to remain and continue similar livelihoods among the Indians and nascent Euro-American populace.

In the late 1840s, a settlement also appeared about eighteen miles east of Ft. Nez Perces on the Columbia where the families of Eduard Beauchemin, Amable Lacourse, and others began raising livestock and farming along the grassy banks of the Walla Walla River. Later arrivals including the Bergevin, Gagnon, and Poirer families would remain for generations to come. Appropriately, the place became known as Frenchtown. Others like James Birnie, a native of Aberdeen, Scotland, chose to retire from the HBC and acquire land for themselves in the unspoiled wilderness west of the Cascades. In 1846 Birnie moved with his family to found the Columbia River hamlet of Cathlamet, where he opened a store provisioned with Hudson's Bay Company stock, local produce, and trade goods procured from visiting ships.

Fruit Nurseries and Orchards

In 1847 two wagons of a most peculiar appearance traced the Oregon Trail, and they marked the genesis of what would become the most Northwest's most prominent frontier fruit nursery enterprise. That year Henderson (Luelling) Lewelling set out with his wife and eight children from their home Iowa for new opportunities in Oregon Territory. Lewelling and his younger brother, John, had established a substantial nursery business near Salem, Iowa, where Henderson became an "enthusiastic admirer of Oregon" after reading the travel accounts of Lewis and Clark and John Fremont. In preparation for the 1847 migration, Henderson spread a foot of mixed compost and charcoal in two box wagons. He and his family carefully planted some eight hundred two- to four-feet high grafted apple, pear, plum, cherry, and other trees, as well as Isabella grape vines and gooseberry bushes. Four yoke of oxen were needed to pull the heavy wagons with the precious cargo. They did not reach the Willamette Valley until November 17—exactly seven months after leaving Iowa.

After several weeks of searching, Lewelling found a suitable location for their orchard near the mouth of Johnson Creek at present Milwaukee, Oregon, and established the Pacific Coast's first nursery of grafted fruit stock. The following year he formed a partnership with his future son-in-law, William Meek, and Henderson's brother, Seth, joined the business in 1850. The men maintained the original scions until fruit stocks mostly grown from other settlers' seedlings and Ft. Vancouver transplants were ready for 18,000 graftings in 1850. These were then available for sale the following year. Apples soon fetched $1.50 per pound in Portland with San Francisco buyers paying two dollars or more. The Lewelling brothers and Meek responded to demand by expanding in 1853 to four branch nurseries in the Willamette Valley. Trees from these locations provided foundation stock for numerous home orchards in the Willamette Valley and across the Pacific Northwest including nurseries established in 1854 at Cowlitz Landing, Olympia, and Steilacoom, and in 1859 by Ransom Clark

and J. W. Foster in Walla Walla. Pioneer Walla Walla entrepreneur Phillip Ritz established the first nursery in the valley in 1861 with stock procured from Glen Dale near Corvallis. He would take offspring from these starts far and wide—delivering by mule team over the Mullan Road as far as Hell Gate Valley in present western Montana.

Among Lewellings' original stock were the summer apple varieties Pearmain, Golden Sweet, and Red Astrachan; fall apples included Gravenstein, Westfield, and Tompkins King; and winters were most represented with Yellow Bellflower, Baldwin, Lady, Northern Spy, Esopus Spitzenberg, Winesap, and Newtown Pippin among others. They also brought pears including the summer-ripening Bartlett (William Bon Crétien), fall Seckel and Flemish Beauty, and the Winter Nellis; as well as the Crawford peach and freestone Cling—Chinese progenitor of the popular yellow-fleshed Elberta. Their original cherry stock included Black Bigarreau, Napolean Bigarreau (Oxheart)—famously named Royal Anne by Henderson Lewelling, and disease-resistant Black Tartarian. An accidental cross from Seth's garden in 1860, likely Royal Anne with Black Tartarian, produced the flavorful Black Republican (from a Black Eagle seedling). In the following decade he introduced the improved Republican cultivar, Bing, named for the Chinese foreman of his Milwaukee property, Ah Bing. Indiana native Joseph Lambert acquired an interest in the Lewelling-Meek orchard in the late 1850s and his grafting of a May Duke to a Napoleon cherry resulted in the large, dark, and flavorful Lambert.[7]

Seth Lewelling and Meek along with other prominent Willamette Valley farmers and horticulturalists were also prime movers in the organization of the Oregon State Agricultural Society in 1860 to promote education and exhibitions. Yamhill County farmers organized the state's first county fair in 1854 in order to promote what Salem's *Oregon Statesman* termed "interchange of opinions and experience" to improve productivity. "The experience and experiments of 'the States' are of little or no service here," the editor observed. "Our climate, seasons and soil differ from those from all of them, and agriculture here must be conducted on different systems. New experiments must be tried, and new modes adopted."

Enthused with such spirit, members of the new society organized the Northwest's first state fair, which was held along the Clackamas River near Oregon City in October 1861. Fair premium lists indicate popular livestock breeds of the era (Shorthorn, Devonshire, and Hereford beef cattle; Holstein, Ayrshire, and Aldernay dairy cattle; Merino, Southdown, and Cotswold sheep; and Berkshire, Chester White, and Poland China swine) as well as silver medal recipients for such products and arts of pioneer self-sufficiency as bee-keeping and honey, cheese, soap, stocking yarn, lager beer, and quilting.[8]

PUGET SOUND FARMING AND MILLING

The quest for farmland, gold, and business opportunities attracted emigrants to the Pacific Northwest in unprecedented numbers during the 1850s. Disgruntled farmers who had sought gold in California a year or two earlier were now moving north in their continuing search for the precious metal. In the summer of 1850, Henry Spalding wrote, "Great nos. went from the country last June to explore the Spokane and Nez Perce countries…" Further incentive for travel to the region came in the fall of 1850 when Congress passed the Oregon Donation Land Law five years before Indian treaties extinguishing tribal titles to vast areas of the Pacific Northwest. This legislation granted every eligible citizen who had settled prior to 1852 a half-section (320 acres) while those occupying lands before 1855 could obtain quarter sections. News of these liberal provisions led to an influx of pioneers across the Oregon Trail, and the population above and below the Columbia River rose from approximately five thousand in 1850 to some thirty thousand five years later.

Seattle was founded in 1851 by Arthur Denny, Dr. D. S. Maynard, and others who were determined to create a regional supply center adjacent to the deep waters of Elliott Bay. Two years later Henry Yesler established a sawmill at the base of Seattle's Mill Street, adding a gristmill to his operation in 1864. A native of Holland, Henry Van Asselt, settled in 1851 on the lower Duwamish River where

he cleared farmland and squared timber and pilings for the San Francisco market. Swedish immigrant Nicholas Delin selected a homesite that same year on Commencement Bay at present Tacoma. However, neither Seattle nor Tacoma experienced significant growth until the following decade when coal was discovered at Issaquah and explorations were undertaken for bituminous deposits along the Cedar and Puyallup rivers. By that time Tacoma had emerged as the principal contender for the western terminus of the first northern transcontinental line, the Northern Pacific Railroad.

The onslaught of American settlers north of the Columbia after the 1846 boundary settlement with Great Britain led to the emergence of the most extensive west side grain district in Washington Territory after the Vancouver, Nisqually, and Cowlitz areas. Colonization of Whidbey Island and adjacent mainland vicinities began in October 1850 after an adventurous Missouri native, Colonel Isaac Ebey, filed a Donation Land Claim on the sweeping prairie overlooking the Sound southwest of present Coupeville. Ebey's wife, Rebecca, her three brothers, and the Samuel Crockett family followed in the spring of 1852 to his "paradise of nature" where they found resident Skagit Indians already cultivating potatoes likely obtained from Hudson's Bay Company traders. William Robertson arrived the following year to stake a claim nearby and assigned his young son, John, to tend the property while he continued to operate a shipping business out of San Francisco. The newcomers raised wheat, potatoes, and other vegetables, many supplied by Dr. Tolmie who periodically visited while on trips to Ft. Victoria. He transferred there in 1859 to manage Puget Sound Agricultural Company (PSAC) properties on Vancouver Island. Tolmie also generously shared grape slips with the Whidbey settlers from his Ft. Nisqually plantings—likely from Ft. Vancouver plantings of Catawba and Concord grapes. In March 1853, the Ebeys planted an orchard that included a Sweet Jane apple tree, a nectarine, and several peach varieties—Admirable, Ernest's Favorite, Avery's Early, and Rare-Ripe.

Barstow Trading Post at Coveland, Whidbey Island
Robert Smith

A narrow band of fertile coastal lands extended northeast from the Olympic Mountains in a dramatic rain shadow from Port Townsend across the sound to the Skagit Valley. Average precipitation of seventeen to nineteen inches in this swath renders a peculiar semi-arid climate along the shoreline ideally suited to dryland grain production. Hudson Bay Company officials had earlier considered establishing operations on Whidbey Island but reconsidered for logistical reasons and after encountering resistance from area Indians. Ebey himself fell victim to inter-tribal violence in 1857 when he was beheaded by a Canadian Salish raiding party. However, other family members and neighbors like the Crocketts remained on the island to establish an enduring presence. Two years later, Ebey's brother, Winfield, wrote of their progress: "The crops here have been abundant. It is the best country for wheat I ever saw as well as for all the small grains and vegetables. The grass is as green now as in summer…. The farmers are busy sowing wheat and will be until the first of April." But not all Whidbey pioneers could boast of such fortune. Drought and diseases like smut also led to crop failures on many farms in the district as farmers needed experience to determine appropriate planting times and preferred varieties.[9]

In 1852 frontier entrepreneur Benjamin P. Barstow opened a trading post, Barstow & Co., at the western head of Penn Cove (Coveland) and stocked it with Hudson's Bay Company inventory and other wares delivered by sailing vessels that began frequenting the fledgling settlement and nearby Coupeville and Oak Harbor. The following year, he was joined in the venture by his brother-in-law, Samuel Libbey, whose wife, Sarah, was Barstow's

Robertson Storehouse at Coupeville, Whidbey Island
Robert Smith

sister, and George Kingsbury. The frontier store-keepers served the needs of local families who claimed the island's fertile prairies and conducted a brisk trade throughout Puget Sound. Barstow's two packet ships, the barque *Mary Melville* and brig *Kingsbury*, regularly plied the waters to supply burgeoning markets from San Francisco to Whidbey Island. Following Barstow's drowning in 1854, his pioneering Coveland enterprise continued for some years under the management of Kingsbury and the Libbeys. Whidbey Island became home to families of many seafaring captains like Captain Howard Lovejoy who carried Hudson's Bay Company cargo. Lovejoy first arrived in Penn Cove in 1853 to load fir spars for San Francisco docks and built one of the first frame houses in the hamlet of Coupeville where he resided when not making coastal runs from California to Sitka.

William Robertson received an appointment from President Buchanan in 1860 to serve as the first keeper of Admiralty Head Lighthouse—the first on Puget Sound—while his son, John, acquired property to develop along the Coupeville waterfront. In 1864 the Robertsons built a residence and gristmill—possibly a steam-powered portable model—across the street from the Penn Cove wharf. John Robertson also built an adjacent storehouse and began shipping island grain, vegetables, and other commodities to Seattle and San Francisco on vessels like his father's Whidbey registered brig, *Tarquinia*. In 1869, New Jersey native James Buzby opened a larger gristmill near Barstow's trading post that was powered by boilers salvaged from a steamboat. The equipment was relocated to Seattle about two years later, and in the late 1870s Friend Wilson erected a substantial two-story mill near the neck of nearby Kennedy Lagoon on the northwest corner of the Barstow-Libbey property. The unique tide-powered affair with a six-foot reservoir gate could power the operation with a steady flow of impounded water for eight to ten hours, sufficient time to produce a ton of flour or feed. Splintered crib wharf pilings still mark the location of the grain warehouse and historic mill. It remained in operation until 1882 when it was reassembled on Chimacum Creek near Port Townsend.[10]

AGRICULTURE EAST OF THE CASCADES

Flour milling operations also expanded in western Montana during this time. Recurrent threats from Blackfoot raiders led to the Jesuits' difficult decision to relocate the headquarters of the Rocky Mountain mission in 1850 from St. Mary's in the Bitterroot Valley to St. Francis Borgia near Flathead Lake, and frontiersman John Owen purchased the building including the gristmill. Owen transformed the mission into Ft. Owen, which became the valley's principal trading and farming center. With the able partnership of his diminutive Shoshone wife, Nancy, the heavy-set trader expanded area grain and fruit production and experimented with other crops. The industrious couple built substantial gristmills in 1857 and 1865 to meet increasing local demand and to provision area mining communities. Mining activity surged in 1862 with gold discoveries in the Alder Gulch–Virginia City district where wheat sold for five dollars a bushel and flour for as much as a dollar per pound. Some fourteen thousand fortune seekers lived there in 1864 when bitter winter conditions prevented freighters from reaching the mining camps, prompting the Virginia City "Bread Riot." Residents hoarded supplies and the price of flour skyrocketed to $1.50 per pound, with a single loaf of bread fetching a dollar. Prices eventually returned to reasonable levels after the exodus of miners to other Western strikes.

A veteran Walla Walla packer recalled that preparations for transport were labor intensive: "It was some work, I'll tell you. The average time was 1½ to 2 minutes for two experienced men to pack a mule…. If it was 400 pounds of flour…each man had to swing his half of the heavy pack up from the ground on the animal's back, and hold it there on one side of the pack saddle with one arm, despite the kicks and bites and protesting lunges of the mule, until he and his partner had it securely lashed there by means of a 'diamond' or other hitch. To round up, saddle and load twenty five such packs a day and to meet all the emergencies of the trail was a real man's job…. We penetrated into the most remote and inaccessible places; over all kinds of country and in all kinds of weather conditions." As many as a dozen pack trains with forty to fifty animals each departed Walla Walla weekly in the spring and fall packing seasons laden with flour, whiskey, and general merchandise.[11]

The 1853 division of the Pacific Northwest into Oregon and Washington territories also brought into focus contrasting perspectives on land use by the region's First Peoples and Euro-Americans. Territorial Governor Isaac Stevens crossed the Rockies onto the Columbia Plateau in that year on his inaugural traverse to the Far West, and made frequent reference to the region's agricultural potential. He reached Ft. Colvile in mid-October and noted "a line of settlements twenty-eight miles long" in the valley that was inhabited by Hudson's Bay Company retirees. "They farm extensively," he noted, "and raise a great deal of wheat." Chief Trader Angus McDonald treated the Americans to "a great variety of dishes, roasted beef, bouillon, steaks, and an abundance of hot bread, coffee, [and] sugar." But Stevens reserved his greatest culinary praise upon a beef's head "cooked in Texas fashion" by baking in the ground for five to six hours.

After reaching the Walla Walla Valley on November 1, the governor penned a rare description of the Hudson Bay Farm and neighboring Frenchtown vicinity: "Arriving at the Hudson Bay farm, we exchanged [our horses] for fresh ones. This farm… is a fine tract of land, well adapted to grazing or cultivation. It is naturally bounded by streams, and is equivalent to a square mile. There is the richest grass there that we have seen since leaving St. Mary's [Flathead Mission]. We…returned to the fort by way of the Whitman Mission now occupied by [George] Bumford and [Lloyd] Brooke. They were harvesting, and I saw as many fine potatoes as I have ever beheld, many weighing two pounds, and one five and one-half. Their carrots and beets, too, were of extraordinary size. From Bumford's to the mouth of the Touchet are many farms, mostly occupied by retired employees of the Hudson's Bay Company."[12]

Yakama-Palouse Chief Kamiakin and Leschi of the Puyallup had been willing to make substantial accommodation with government officials and the emigrants. But Stevens' ambitious 1855 treaty councils among the Plateau and Coastal tribes pressed them and other tribal leaders to forfeit vast ancestral areas in return for reservations and pledges of perpetual hunting and fishing rights. The land and its bounty were sacred to the Indians and could no more be bought or sold than the air and water in their view. Chief Owhi of the Yakama explained that the Earth was the mother of mankind. "Shall I steal this land and sell it?" he asked Stevens. "Shall I give the lands that are part of my body?" While negotiations and threats led to agreements ceding tribal lands throughout the Pacific Northwest, they did not prevent the 1855-58 era of warfare on the Columbia Plateau and Puget Sound. Most Indians were then forced to occupy reservations where traditional hunting and gathering combined with farming and ranching for cultural and economic sustenance. Nevertheless, some traditionalists refused to relocate and secured occupancy rights to ancestral homelands through the Indian Homestead (Dawes) Act.[13]

Lincoln's "Soils, Seeds, and Seasons"

Legislation enabling Native Americans to obtain patented title to ancestral lands was based on the landmark Homestead Act which had been enacted in 1862 at the urging of President Abraham Lincoln. The law was one in a series of laws that were unprecedented for their significance to American agriculture and the pace by which they were approved by Congress. On May 15, 1862, Lincoln signed a bill creating the Department of Agriculture; on May 20 he signed the Homestead Act; on July 1 he approved the Pacific Railway Bill making possible the nation's first transcontinental line; and on July 2 he signed the Land-Grant College (Morrill) Act. This legislation would transform American agriculture by fostering Western settlement and increasing productivity nationwide, and had especially favorable outcomes in the Pacific Northwest.

Each of the four bills brought together an array of constituents whose causes found sympathy with a president from subsistence farming origins. Lincoln was acquainted with the challenges and opportunities of rural life known to few other chief executives. Aptly titling his vignette on Lincoln's early years as "Barefoot in Yellow Clay," biographer Carl Sandburg wrote that his youth was spent "plowing, hoeing, cutting…his bare feet spoke with the clay of the earth; it was in his toenails and stuck on the skin.… In the short and simple annals of the poor, it seems there are people who breathe with the earth and take into their lungs and blood some of

the hard and dark strength of its mystery." Lincoln experienced a succession of boyhood moves from Kentucky to Indiana and Illinois where the family eked out a living raising corn, wheat, oats, potatoes, and livestock. As a young man at New Salem, Illinois, in the 1830's, Lincoln worked at Denton Offutt's grist mill hauling sacks of grain and flour. In later life, Lincoln never expressed desire to return to these hardscrabble origins, but they fostered lifelong sympathies for European immigrants seeking new homelands on the western prairies, improved transportation to market agricultural produce, and practical education and scientific study to improve productivity.

In spite of legislators' preoccupation with wartime affairs, Lincoln knew that Congress in the 1850s had made little progress in these matters due to strong Southern objections to efforts that would promote settlement and economic development in the new Free states of the West. For this reason, his administration sought to harness constituencies soon after his 1861 election to approve the long-stalled measures. Lincoln had been offered the governorship of Oregon in 1849, but declined due to concerns about the popularity of Democrats in the Northwest, and because his wife opposed frontier life. He remained interested in happenings in the Far West and in agricultural development generally, which he termed "the largest interest of the nation" in his first annual message to Congress.[14]

The fullest expression of Lincoln's thoughts on farming is found in his September 1859 speech to the Wisconsin Agricultural Society at the state fair in Milwaukee in which he expounded on four practical themes that would guide his policies when in office. American farmers first would benefit from credible analysis of tillage techniques, soils, seed varieties, and other factors that had led to widely ranging yields of wheat, corn, and other crops. Furthermore, "successful application of steam power to farm work" was needed in a time when farm work was still largely being done by hand in spite of recent technological innovations. He further favored measures that would transform subsistence "mudsill" tenancy to the "free labor" of small farm ownership and prosperity. This would be possible, however, only through the "companionship" of an essential fourth element—education. "Every blade of grass is a study…. And not grass alone, but soils, seeds, and seasons" in order to improving crop and livestock production. In these ways, Lincoln reasoned, "book-learning" served as a powerful "remedy against oppression" by fostering self-reliance among rural folk.

Lincoln's advocacy of the Homestead Act, Department of Agriculture, Morrill Act, and related legislation, therefore, brought to fruition a range of ideas he had long contemplated. Although wartime responsibilities further diverted his attention after the rapid implementation of these measures in 1862, Lincoln kept

Abraham Lincoln
Washington State Historical Society
(CN 1920.8.1)

abreast throughout his administration of agricultural policy nationally and circumstances in the Pacific Northwest where he appointed over two dozen federal officials. Lincoln specifically instructed the USDA's first commissioner, Isaac Newton, to procure seed grain from Europe in order to improve US production and reported on the matter in his annual address to Congress in 1862. At the president's urging the following year, Congress approved a treaty with Great Britain to settle claims of the Puget Sound Agricultural Company for Ft. Nisqually and adjacent farmlands long under PSAC jurisdiction and in 1864 Lincoln appointed commissioners to fairly adjudicate PSAC losses.[15]

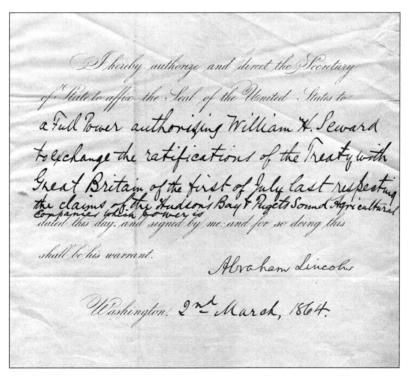

Presidential Memorandum to Settle Puget Sound Agricultural Company Claims (1864)
Washington State Historical Society (CN 1917.27.2)

The bread loaf, in an unobtrusive place,
Displays its cheerful, honest featured face,
A coin of triumpf, from the mintage struck,
Of chemistry, skill, faithfulness, and luck.
What statesman, moulding laws, can understand
The far-eyed cunning of a housewife's hand?

—Will Carleton, "The County Fair" (1881)

CHAPTER IV

Frontier Farming to Global Trade

Well, on, brave boys, to your lord's hearth,
Glitt'ring with fire, where, for your mirth,
With sev'ral dishes standing by,
As here a custard, there a pie,
And here all-tempting frumenty.

In his popular travelogue, *The Emigrant's Guide to Oregon and California,* emigration promoter Lansford Hastings, who traveled overland to the Willamette Valley in 1842, described the region's emerging farming enterprises:

> "Wheat is the principal grain grown in this section as yet, the greatest quantities of which are produced at the Willamette Valley, Tualatin Plains, and the farms of the Hudson's Bay Company at Vancouver, Nisqually, and the Cowlitz. The average crop is about fifteen bushels to the acre, yet, I have no doubt, but that portions of this section, which lies south of the Columbia River, and which is susceptible of cultivation, may, with proper agricultural skill, be made to produce twenty-five or thirty bushels to the acre."

Canadian settlement along French Prairie (Campment du Sable) had steadily grown throughout the 1830s and by 1840 some sixty "fine farms" of ten to forty acres dotted the arcadian landscape from St. Paul's to the Methodist mission. Throughout the region, farmers were experimenting with different varieties of wheat to find those best-suited to the soil and climate.

According to the most reliable accounts, a boatload of "Ukrainian wheat," likely a hard red spring Galician grain from the fertile *chernozem* ("black earth") Polish-Ukraine steppe borderlands, was shipped in 1842 from Danzig (Gdansk, Poland) via Glasgow to Peterborough, Ontario. Selections from this hardy, high quality bread wheat became the progenitor of Red ("Scotch") Fife, the rust-resistant Northern Plains grain that was also grown widely in the Northwest by the 1880s.

Red May, a soft red winter wheat popular since Colonial times but not widely raised on the cooler Pacific Slope, was derived from Red (English) Lammas, the ancient Celtic grain of the Roman era. In the warmer west, May wheat typically headed out in mid-April, ripened up to three weeks earlier than an early Northwest cultivar from South America, Chili (Chile) Club, and produced flour of high quality.

Chili Club, a soft yellow winter wheat also probably of southern European origin, was introduced along the Duwamish River on Puget Sound by Hudson's Bay Company workers as early as 1854, and reported on Crab Creek in eastern Washington in the 1870s where it was popularly known as

47

Big Club. With heavy hanging heads often holding more than one hundred fifty grains, Big Club yielded well in the region. Because hard reds contained more gluten than white wheat, bakers came to prize their flours which had more "rising" capacity and less bran, making a lighter bread. But the "plump and round" kernels of Northwest white wheats so favorably compared with the best grains in England and Russia that premiums were paid for it on the Liverpool exchange. Other wheat varieties raised in the region in the 1870s included White Velvet, White Russian, Golden Crown Club, Golden Amber, Sonora, and Odessa.

Yields in the Willamette Valley, Walla Walla, and Palouse regions generally ranged from twenty to thirty bushels per acre—about twice the average yield nationally in the 1870s. Soft white spring Little Club, likely derived from a southern European variety of Mediterranean (*T. s. compactum*), was raised widely in Mexico and Spanish California throughout the eighteenth century, and arrived in the Northwest about 1859 from California.[1]

That same year frontier road builder John Mullan reported that three- to four-hundred acres of "corn and wheat" in seven tracts were being raised by Nez Perce and Palouse Indians on fertile bottomlands along the lower Snake River. After explorations of the rolling bunchgrass-covered prairies of the Palouse hills, Mullan recorded that "the soil is mostly a black loam and will doubtless produce cereals and vegetables."

Other nascent enclaves of grain production at the time along Mullan's route from Ft. Walla Walla to Ft. Benton included ferryman Antoine Plante's farm on the north bank of the Spokane River; Coeur d'Alene Chief Seltice's "several acres" and other Indian farms near Lake Coeur d'Alene; and the nearby Sacred Heart (Cataldo) Mission, where several hundred acres of wheat, barley, oats,

Sacred Heart "Cataldo" Mission
John Clement

peas, and potatoes were "raised in rich abundance." Plante was a former voyageur and trapper who settled at present Dishman with his Coeur d'Alene wife, Mary, in 1852. Farther east across the Bitterroots, about fifteen farms had recently been established at Frenchtown along the Clark Fork River several miles downstream from present Missoula. A dozen others were spread out along small tributaries at Hell Gate Ronde, above Flint Creek, and at Deer Lodge. Ft. Walla Walla wagon master Charles Russell planted the first fields of oats and barley in the vicinity of the fort in the spring of 1858.[2] Early Northwest farmers also experimented with flax and spelt, a primitive grain generally used at the time for livestock feed. An early rye variety popular in the Willamette Valley was German Giant White, introduced from Europe about 1873 by a miller in Golden, Oregon, and lauded for being "as white as the purest white winter wheat, and [kernels] twice the size."

Pioneer Northwest oat varieties—principally used for fodder, included Hopetoun, Norway White, White Russian, English Side, Scotch Dunn, and Brown Winter. Prominent Oregon Country promoter John Minto, who raised substantial sheep herds in the Salem area, wrote that his English Side oats substantially outperformed Excelsior and Surprise. But an Oregon reporter observed that "wheat is the one crop that is more certain in yield as well as compensation." In addition, the frontier saying, "Wherever grass grows, wheat will grow" encouraged regional prospects. Minto, a proud singer of his native Scottish songs, credited the celebrated Highland author Robert Burns with his own "education," and reveled in long recitations of such poems as "Scotch Drink" that celebrated the distinctly satisfying benefits of distilled Scots Bere barley: "I sing the juice Scotch Bear can mak us, In glass or jug...."

Sufficient moisture in Northwest bottomlands usually allowed two cuttings of alfalfa and such grasses as clover and meadow fescue in June and September. Small cleared patches were seeded in the spring by hand broadcast to wheat, barley, oats, and rye. Pioneer farmers paid premium prices for good seed wheat, which was often in short supply. Necessity sometimes fostered creative solutions as noted in a late 1850s letter from Steilacoom area farmer James Patterson to his brother in Iowa. Patterson recounted the removal of a handful of spring wheat from the crop of a downed wild goose, and described the quality of the increase (seed) as "equal to the best fall wheat."[3]

The Frontier Larder

The early settlers of the Willamette Valley and Puget Sound Lowlands were subsistence farmers who also raised cattle, sheep, and hogs. They planted orchards and large gardens, and gathered wild black currants, huckleberries, gooseberries, and serviceberries for canning. The virgin sod of dense bunchgrass crowning a fibrous root system was broken in heavy, wet bottom lands by long-sheared breaking plows, primitive disks, and harrows fashioned from brush or wooden teeth. A two-horse team pulling a single shear plow could turn a half-acre per day while a larger three-horse triple shear gang could cover two acres in the same time. These laborious tasks required strong, steady hands and a cooperative horse. Dense stands of hawthorn and wild rose in many areas stubbornly resisted the pioneers' attempts to burn them out and plow through the sod and roots.

Meeting the physical needs of large frontier families was a substantial undertaking that required considerable planning, planting, and processing. Provisions "laid by" for winter and early spring were substantially home-grown or traded locally since trips to the few city markets, such as Oregon City or Walla Walla, for supplies meant paying premium prices that many families could not afford. A family with six children commonly required the annual butchering, then canning or smoking, of five hogs, plus five hundred pounds of flour, and a ton of potatoes—about twenty burlap gunny sacks or the product of one to two acres. The pioneer diet also included dried beef, salted venison, smoked salmon, and wild fowl.

Pioneer Methodist Episcopal missionary Margaret Jewett Bailey's *The Grains or Passages in the Life of Ruth Rover* expresses the frontier experience with details from a woman's perspective. With honest depiction of delight and depression, Bailey's 1854 account is considered the Pacific Northwest's first published literary work. The author's alter ego, Ruth Rover, includes a letter sent to her mother from their Willamette Valley home in 1839 that describes the family's garden and a typical meal:

> "We have a little patch of garden with onions, turnips, cucumbers, cabbage and corn, all growing heterogeneously together in as much confusion as if they blown from the skies in a gale of wind. This has been occasioned by my inserting a new plant or seed where the chickens had picked up the first.... Last eve we had for our meal some hasty pudding, a small bit of butter, some molasses and a cup of tea. This evening some more pudding, remains of a pea soup, some fried cakes, with blue berries, tea,

& c. Our staple dishes have been, this summer, salt pork and coarse wheat bread…. Poor as you may think this living is, we never repine for better, as with this we can satisfy hunger, and from it obtain strength to do our work."[4]

Henry and Maria Cutting, in-laws of Cowlitz Farm manager George Roberts and fellow natives of England, settled on a donation land claim in present Lewis County and recalled the challenges of life in the first year of settlement: "I assure you we had many privations and Hardships to endure and oh such makeouts sometimes having to use shorts [a by-product of wheat milling that includes the germ, bran, and only a small amount of flour] instead of flour, sometimes Sugar sometimes none, very very few vegetables or fruit till we could grow them except Blackberries and wild strawberries in there season. There were no luxuries to be had even if we had had even so much money."

Earthenware crockery ranging in size from five to ten gallons held cucumbers brined with salt, vinegar, and dill; tomatoes in water with herbs; or peaches with sugar and cloves. Potatoes, carrots, and beets were stored in root cellars that were often dug into an adjacent side-hill and connected to the house by a porch. Most families also pastured one or two dairy cows to supply milk, cream, and butter; farmyard chickens and eggs were also readily available. These needs required farmsteads with barns, chicken houses, hog sheds, root cellars, smokehouses, granaries, and other out-buildings for pioneer self-sufficiency. A typical day's menu, often served at all three meals, might consist of fried salted pork, mutton, or venison, mashed potatoes with thick white gravy, boiled white beans, stewed apples or applesauce, and hot rolls with peach preserves or blackberry jam.

Two coffee grinders were commonly used in pioneer Northwest households. Since coffee beans were usually green when purchased, they were oven-roasted for grinding with highly variable results depending on time and technique. Some recommended a one-to-four mixture of coffee with chicory root, which could be grown in Northwest gardens. Those for whom coffee and tea were luxuries often roasted kernels of wheat or rye until

dark brown to brew a flavorful substitute. Chehalis area pioneer homemaker Melissa Givens combined roasted oats and barley, and the Hunter family of Thurston County mixed a gallon of parched grain with two tablespoons of molasses to make "a very tasty drink." Volga and Black Sea Germans who settled throughout the Columbia Plateau adapted their popular Russian "steppe tea" ingredients of squeezed lemon, peppermint, basil, clove, cinnamon, and honey with citrus flavorings available in America like oranges. They were also familiar with coffee brewed from roasted wheat or barley grits and sweetened with beet sugar.

After a visit to the Pend Oreilles' (Kalispel) St. Francis Borgia Mission, Father De Smet commented that a non-fermented drink made by Fathers Ravalli and Mengarini from barley and native roots was "as pleasant and nutritious as the pale beer of Europe." The concoction was likely akin to the fabled Eleusian beverage *kykeôn*, with which the pair was likely familiar. Area Indians made extensive use of sweet-tasting camas, De Smet's "queen root of this clime," which yielded over a third of its weight as fructose when cooked. The grain and root infusion was a pleasant and healthy tea-like beverage enjoyed hot or cold. British settlers were familiar with wholesome barley tea or barley water, served hot or cold and sometimes flavored with currants, apples, or other fruit. Frontier residents also made "Hudson's Bay tea" from sprigs of the Cascade wetland shrub *Ledum groenlandicum* (Labrador tea), a traditional Indian sore throat remedy.[5]

The household's second grinder was often used for crushing wheat berries to mix with rolled oats or dried fruit for a boiled breakfast "mush," or for a rough whole grain bread flour described by Ellensburg pioneer Clarence Houser as containing "everything but the stalks." To immigrant English and Scots, the breakfast mixture was called porridge, while pioneering Germans knew it as *Hirsche*, from the Hessian term for millet. European immigrant women also improvised with available grains to make distinctive blended flours legendary for their flavor and variety. One favored combination, German *Veissmischa* ("white-mixed"), combined fine white flour made from hard wheats with smaller amounts from rye and barley, or both.

Another Northwest pioneer dish was hulled wheat hominy fried in butter or eaten with syrup, milk, and sugar. Pioneer women created a range of flavorful "flummeries" derived from the famed Welsh oatmeal-based pudding. The Hudson's Bay Company version of Anne Clarke's *The Dominion Cookbook* listed basic flummery ingredients as white oatmeal, sugar, cream, and orange flower water (egg yolks were traditionally added), into which resourceful Northwest cooks often mixed fruits and berries.

Mrs. Clarke's popular cookbook debuted in 1883 and included recipes for several mixed flour brown breads including combinations of whole wheat, rye, and Indian (corn) meal, with frontier Western ingredients like huckleberries and currants. This and other recipe books of the period also featured grain teas (tisanes) and coffees, oatmeal muffins, buckwheat pancakes, and hearty hulled barley-based soups with beef and winter root vegetables that were common dinner fare in Northwest frontier households.[6]

REGIONAL MILLING

While grinder and quern grain crushings were acceptable for gruels, flummeries, and biscuits, pioneers craved milled flour for good bread. High protein hard red wheats, prized for their "rising" qual-

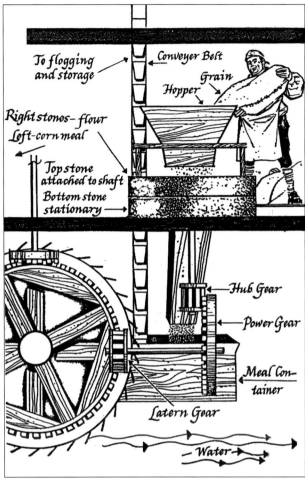

Gristmill Interior Workings
Commonwealth of Virginia Parks Division

ities, were difficult to mill with stone burrs. Steel rollers introduced after mid-century century more effectively separated the middling germ, endosperm, and bran, and greatly speeded up the tedious milling process, which in turn increased production. Tumwater pioneers George and Isabella Bush obtained one of the first hand-crank steel models.

In 1852 American entrepreneur E. D. Warbass built a gristmill and sawmill at the thriving settlement of Warbassport (Cowlitz Landing), and in the spring of 1856 Oregon Territorial Militia Volunteer Francis Goff oversaw construction of a blockhouse granary on the Chehalis River at present Chehalis. One of the

Fort Borst Blockhouse & Granary
Special Collections, University of Washington Libraries (UW 35769)

builders, area pioneer Joseph Borst, acquired the structure the following year and continued using it to store sacked grain. In 1859 gristmills had been established in the Walla Walla Valley, at the Coeur d'Alene and Pend Oreille missions, and at French-town and Ft. Owen in the Bitterroot Valley. A. H. Reynolds, John Sims, and Captain Frederick T. Dent—brother-in-law of Ulysses S. Grant—established the Walla Walla operation along Yellowhawk Creek south of the army post. Their enterprise expanded within two years to include a distillery using bran and shorts from the mill, and a brisk business in both flour and spirits followed to mining towns and farming communities from Lewiston to Boise. The Northwest's first commercial breweries also appeared in the 1850s. Henry Saxer founded Portland's Liberty Brewery in 1852, followed by others in Steilacoom (1854), Walla Walla (1855), and Ft. Vancouver (1856). Immigrant entrepreneurs Henry Weinhard and George Bottler established Portland's second brewery in 1856, and in the following decade Weinhard acquired Saxer's and Bottler's interests to launch one of the region's most successful and enduring businesses.

By 1860, about a dozen other grist mills were operating along water sources in present Clark, Lewis, and Pierce counties. The first Okanagan Valley gristmill in British Columbia was built at Lillooet near Kamloops in 1864. Increased demand for milled grain products and a burgeoning population west of the Cascades developed markets that encouraged eastside farmers and stimulated settlement. In 1865 the first flour mill in eastern Oregon was established by Martin Hazeltine and Alec McCallum in John Day City. Two years later a Walla Walla miller ventured to ship fifteen barrels of flour to Portland and received orders for five thousand more within two weeks.

Commercial millers installed corrugated steel rollers and bolting equipment by the 1870s to better separate bran from germ. Rollers were designed with canted steep grooves to peel away the outer layer of kernels that passed through several grindings. The crushings then went through a series of siftings with fabric sieves (usually cotton, linen, or silk) and screens. This process yielded several grades of flour from white, or light "superfine" flour, to brown. Mark Carleton, a late-nineteenth century USDA cerealist, recommended a ratio of 80 percent hard red wheat flour and 20 percent durum. Nineteenth-century "patent flours" were distinct company blends of various varieties and grades.

Millers were keenly aware of baking characteristics, flavor profiles, and milling qualities of various grains. As Northwest wheat production boomed in the 1870s with widespread settlement throughout the Willamette Valley and Puget Sound lowlands, millers also sought new domestic and foreign markets for Northwest flour, and these efforts sometimes contributed to the introduction of new varieties to the region. In 1876, Salem Flouring Mills founder R. C. Kinney sent his son, Albert, on a trip to France to explore European markets for Oregon flour. Kinney returned with an unnamed sample of hard red French bread wheat which the pair grew

Foos Grain Mill
R. Scheuerman Collection

North Star Grist Mill; Thorp, Washington
John Clement

for increase to spawn Kinney wheat, which was primarily raised across the Northwest for several decades. But the bargain could work both ways. Salem resident J. D. Pettyman gathered screenings from the Kinney mill in 1879 and sent them to a friend in Kansas who responded, "Send me one hundred bushels of those screenings and I will forward in return $100." Pettyman complied and also sent samples of other Oregon grains.[7]

FRUIT, FARMS, AND IRRIGATION

The Columbia River orchard industry entered a new era in the 1860s. By then, the region's original frontier-era plantings at places like Ft. Vancouver, Ft. Nisqually, and the Whitman Mission had become relic curiosities, while the efforts of pioneer nurserymen like Henderson and Seth Lewelling and Phillip Ritz had spawned productive home orchards throughout the region. In 1861 frontier packer and merchant Hiram "Okanogan" Smith set out twelve hundred fruit scions and vines on land along eastern Osoyoos Lake near the international border about ten miles north of present Oroville. He obtained the plantings from Ft. Hope, a Hudson's Bay Company post on British Columbia's Fraser River. Among Smith's apple varieties still producing a century later were Winesap, Pippin, Schwaan, and Gloria Mundi. A Beurre d'Anjou pear may also have been among his earliest plantings.

Smith acquired a substantial portion of his property from Okanogan Chief Tonasket, who later relocated east to the Toroda Creek district west of present Curlew. Smith established a flourishing ranch near present Curlew where he raised hay and oats for his considerable herds of horses, cattle, and sheep. The enterprising family also raised wheat for markets in Marcus and Spokane, which they threshed by leading horses around a small circular corral. Chief Tonasket also urged area Indian agency officials to more effectively promote agricultural development on the Colville Indian Reservation for the livelihood of area tribes. In the early 1880s, Army scout Henry Pierce visited four villages in the vicinity of Kettle Falls under Colville-Lakes Chief Edward and pronounced their grain "the best in the Colville country."

Prussian immigrant Frederick Brent [Brandt] joined Hiram Smith in 1864 after serving at Ft. Colville as a scout with the U. S. Army, and the following year relocated to Duck Lake near the Oblate Okanagan Mission (present Kelowna) in British Columbia, where he constructed the area's first flour mill near the mouth of Pion (Mill) Creek. Brent purchased the small steel grinding equipment from the Hudson's Bay Company at Ft. Hope and fashioned a sieve from finely woven horse hair. With wheat flour selling at ten pounds for a dollar, Brent's enterprise flourished and in 1870 he built a larger mill using quarried stones imported from Chalons, France, shipped via San Francisco and Victoria. Sacks of "Brent Mills Family Flour" sold throughout the Okanagan Valley until others took over the operation in the 1890s.[9]

Jesuit priests planted apples at St. Joseph's Mission in the Ahtanum Valley in 1867, and in the following year German immigrant "Dutch John"

Galler relocated from the Kittitas country to the Wenatchee Valley. A year or two later, Galler and his Wenatchi Indian wife, Mary, established a small orchard and vineyard of Malaga grapes at the mouth of Squillchuk Creek near present Wenatchee. Pioneer rancher-merchants Samuel Miller and brothers Frank and David Freer established a trading post in 1871 and laid out an orchard the following year to give birth to the settlement of Wenatchee. Early commercial orchards were established in 1872 at Almota, Washington, on the Snake River; along the Columbia at Hood River, Oregon, in 1876; and in the 1880s in the Wenatchee, Okanogan, and Yakima valleys. Availability of irrigation water from mountain lakes, streams, and rivers transformed the sandy valley soils of central Washington and Oregon into the world's most productive fruit-raising districts.

By 1890, approximately fifty thousand acres were being irrigated in central Washington, mostly in Kittitas and Yakima counties where substantial crops of alfalfa, clover, and timothy hay were raised as well as grain, potatoes, and fruit. Some enterprising families earned extra income by raising tomatoes, strawberries, and other crops between rows of fruit trees. Early apple varieties grown by central Washington pioneers around the turn of the century included Rome Beauty, Yellow Banana, Arkansas Black, and King David. Early ripening Yellow Transparents were introduced by the USDA from Russia in 1870 and grown throughout the Northwest. But the apple varieties grown after the turn of the century that would establish the region's "apple capital" reputation would be the sweet Red Delicious, originally the red and yellow striped Hawkeye, and Golden Delicious.

PALOUSE AND BASIN GOLD

The inland Pacific Northwest's fertile Palouse region, where annual rainfall ranges eastward from twelve to twenty-nine inches, became synonymous with wheat production in the late nineteenth century. The varied landscape is a tousled tapestry of contrasts with valleys, hills, and mountains woven together by the twisted course of the Palouse River and its tributaries. The Colville Trail and other fur trade era routes that crossed the western Palouse

Delong Heirloom Orchard Apples
R. Scheuerman Collection

rangelands remain visible for considerable distances where Indian horses foraged for generations. The first settler in the Palouse hills was George Pangburn, a twenty-seven-year-old bachelor from Walla Walla, who visited the area as early as 1862. He squatted on unsurveyed land along lower Union Flat Creek south of present Endicott, Washington, to farm, plant a small orchard, and raise hogs for the boomtown Lewiston mining markets. Pangburn lived in an earthen dugout south of the stream and in 1867 was raising wheat, corn, and oats.

Moving to the vicinity of present Central Ferry on the Snake River in 1865 was Joseph Delong, who had crossed the plains three years earlier and settled on the Tucannon River north of Walla Walla. Delong soon joined Pangburn on Union Flat but relocated in 1867 to the scenic bottomland where the Kentuck Trail crossed the Palouse River after finding his errant cow grazing contently near the water. Delong built a log cabin on a knoll of wild sunflowers that protruded from the northern bluffs and sold provisions to immigrants traveling along the ancient Palouse thoroughfare.

The account books kept by Delong at his Palouse River ranch and store provide a rare glimpse of life on the Palouse frontier during its earliest years of settlement. Entries record information essential to pioneer self-sufficiency under such scribbled headlines as "Smallpox Cure" (a concoction of sugar, foxtail, and zinc sulfate), "Recipe for Preserving

Green Fruit," and "Grasshopper Poison." Articles clipped from early issues of the *Walla Walla Statesman* and Colfax's *Palouse Gazette* were safeguarded between small, lined pages of hardboard-bound books, providing such useful information as the mathematical formula "To Measure Hay in Ricks," stories about President Lincoln and General Grant, and favored verse: "Let live and forever grow, and banish wrath and strife; So shall we witness here below, the joys of social life."

Most folks with whom Delong shared company were families of those who later settled near him along the pine-covered slopes and bottomlands of the Palouse River. Names frequently appearing in his account books include Ben Davis, Steve Cutler, Link Ballaine, and E. E. Huntley. These families came to Delong's store to socialize, collect mail, and procure staples, often on credit. His inventory included eggs, onions, coffee, sugar, and baking powder; soap, sarsaparilla, and tobacco. He also stocked hardware supplies like nails and wire, and such curatives as oils of anise and bergamot, and sulfuric of ether.

Delong and his neighbors spent considerable time building and repairing split rail fences to safeguard livestock, and also experimented with a number of grains and fruits to determine those best suited to Palouse soils and climate. The frontier bachelor planted hundreds of apple trees obtained from Walla Walla Valley nurseries as well as pear, cherry, plum, and prune stock, grape vines, and currant bushes. Summer visitors to Delong's farm could always expect a good supply of Newtown Pippin, Yellow Bellflower, Northern Spy, and other apples. He also traded produce with area Indians for their salmon. Ben Scissom, who settled a short distance upstream from Delong in 1867, was credited with seeding the first wheat along the Palouse River.

Delong was fond of rural verse and stories that he clipped from early Northwest newspapers. Naturalist poet Liberty H. Bailey, whose horticultural efforts at Cornell University would soon help launch the nation's Cooperative Extension Service, penned lines in "Apple-Year" with which farmers like Delong and his neighbors could readily identify:

Kentuck Trail Palouse River Ford near Delong Farmstead
John Clement

I planted these orchard trees myself
   On hillside slopes that belong to me
   Where visions are wide and winds are few
That all the round year might come to my shelf
And there on thy shelves the white winter through
   Pippin and Newtown, Rambo and Spy,
   Greening and Swaar and Spitzenberg lie
With remarkable tense of sun and the dew.[10]

In November 1867, a substantial wagon train of German Catholic emigrant farmers following the Kentuck Trail stopped at Delong's store. They had been traveling since late June from St. Cloud, Minnesota, en route to the Willamette Valley. Henry Lueg, a diarist with the column of twenty-one wagons, described the Palouse River valley as "very romantic" and noted the region's "soft hills" were composed of soil "very rich and

not in the slightest rocky." Members of the group included brothers Frank, Michael, and George Niebler, Michael Schultheis, J. B. Wittman, and Peter Jacobs. All continued on to St. Louis, Oregon, a small farming community on French Prairie, where most of the area's best farming tracts had been claimed by the late 1860s. In 1873 Schultheis returned east of the Cascades to the Walla Walla Valley. Two years later he relocated to upper Union Flat near present Uniontown and Colton in the Palouse hills.

Within a year other members of the original emigrant group joined Schultheis to form the nucleus of what would become a vibrant farming community. The pioneers raised wheat, barley, flax, and other crops and followed the Old World practice of manuring their fields. Grain was marketed to Grief's Distillery and Jacobs's Brewery, and via a torturous descent into the Snake River Valley, to the muddy boomtown of Lewiston, Idaho. The Palouse Country's first flour mill was established in 1875 by W. O. Breeding in the town of Palouse and within two decades some twenty-eight mills were operating in small farming communities throughout the area.

Volga Germans who had established farming colonies in Russia's southwestern Saratov-Samara region a century earlier during the reign of Catherine the Great emigrated in significant numbers to Kansas and Nebraska in the 1870s in search of religious freedom and economic prosperity. They were heavy consumers of inexpensive rye bread flour and yellow millet, and had grown hard red Saxonka in Russia for pastry and bread flours, as well as the Saratov and Beloturk durums. A major Volga export to western Europe, bald spring Saxonka was also known as Colonist wheat since the German landrace was brought to Russia in the eighteenth century to be raised by the immigrant farmers. As with the Uniontown-Colton Catholics in the 1860s, Midwestern colonies of these people relocated to Oregon in 1881 searching for available farmland. Some were directed to the Palouse a year later by representatives of Henry Villard's Northern Pacific Railroad, which had just organized the Oregon Improvement Company to promote sales of the railroad's 150,000-acre Palouse tract of "the finest agricultural lands in the northwest" and other land-grant properties to the west in present Adams and Lincoln counties.[11]

The Kansas group, including the families of Phillip Green, Peter Ochs, Henry Litzenberger, Henry Repp, Conrad Schierman, and John Helm, traveled by rail and wagon in 1882 from Portland to the vicinity of present Endicott and St. John, Washington, where they settled along the Palouse River downstream from Delong and also on Rebel Flat Creek. In later years Helm often reminisced about the vanguard's first glimpse of the area's steeply rolling prairies. His grandson, Palouse Country native Harry Helm, rendered those memories into verse.

Grandpa said:
The grass was like Europe's grass,
Soft and waving like a sea.
It hissed and whispered like a friend
In well-known German words to me.

The hills were like German hills,
Green plumed against a feckless sky.
As I went riding bunchgrass trails,
Where the prairie chickens fly.
Clear waters tumbled through the trees
In every golden, sun-swept vale.
While flowers tipped their hats to me,
As they touched my prancing pinto's tail.[12]

A Nebraska colony of Volga Germans led by Frederick Rosenoff, Henry Kanzler, Jacob Schoessler, George Dewald, and Jacob Thiel journeyed in the spring of 1881 from Hitchcock County to Ogden, Utah, by rail. There they joined with others to form a train of forty wagons for the trek northward. The column lumbered along the Oregon Trail to Walla Walla where some remained to scout the area for settlement prospects while the others continued on to Portland. Jacob Thiel was among the Walla Walla contingent and found employment with pioneer developer and horticulturalist Phillip Ritz, who had recently acquired five thousand acres from the railroad in the vicinity of present Ritzville. The promoter encouraged Thiel and his kinsmen to settle in the area, which led to the genesis of significant Russian-German immigration to the fertile Ritzville-Odessa grain districts. Volga Germans from the Endicott area resettled on prairie farmlands in the Calgary and Edmonton, Alberta, areas beginning in 1891. The son of one Calgary family, Samuel Litzenberger, became a pioneer in crop breeding and plant pathology who worked extensively with the USDA and universities in Montana, Alaska, and Colorado.

Black Sea German farmers familiar with Russian Ukraine's famed high quality Turkey Red bread wheats began settling in Washington's Big Bend grain belt from Lind northeast to Ritzville and Odessa following Gottlieb Pflugrath's exploration of the region in 1887. Their Mennonite kinsmen had introduced drought-resistant, winter-hardy Turkey Reds to Kansas in 1874, which transformed

Henry and Mary Repp and Henry and Anna Litzenberger Families, Palouse River Ranch, c. 1885
R. Scheuerman Collection

the Midwest wheat industry. Russian-German farmers from the Beresan colonies settled in near Eugene, Oregon, beginning in 1891, while Bessarabian German families settled soon afterward near the Marlin, Ruff, and Warden, Washington, areas. Leaders of some Midwest Mennonite colonies like Cornelius Jantz, J. R. Schrag, and Adolf Gering relocated to the Ritzville-Odessa area to establish the first Mennonite colonies on the Columbia Plateau around the turn of the century. The names of several Adams County rural districts like Batum, Moscow, and Tiflis (Tbilisi) testify to the area's original South Russia immigrant origins. "Wherever wheat is grown you'll find Mennonites," observed Jantz's son and colony historian, John Jantz. Skagit Valley farmer J. W. Wiley may have been the first in the region to raise hard red Odessa wheat, but the seed had not come directly from the Ukraine. As often happened during this time of farmer self-reliance, he procured four pounds of seed in the spring of 1878 from a friend in southern California.[13]

GRAIN BREEDERS AND FARMER EXPERIMENTERS

Completion of the Northern Pacific transcontinental and subsidiary lines in the 1880s and '90s coincided with a surge in regional grain production. A revolution in agricultural mechanization enabled more extensive farming across the country, as the one hundred and fifty man-hours needed to plant, cultivate, and harvest an acre of cropland in 1840 had been reduced to about forty hours by 1890. More lands had come into production with wheat varieties farmers found more suitable to Northwest growing conditions like Little Club, Red Chaff, and Pacific Bluestem (White Australian)—a West Coast White Lammas landrace descendant introduced via Australia. French Touselle (Touse), the legendary Languedoc white winter wheat prized by King Louis XI for restoring his health, was an early maturing soft variety also raised on a limited basis in the region. A field of red winter Fultz, an 1862 scion from a field of Lancaster Red in Pennsylvania, was grown with timothy and clover forage in the 1870s in the Tualco Valley near present Monroe, Washington; and in 1881 Canby, Oregon, farmer Aaron Wait reported on his "choice variety" winter wheat test plots of White Velvet, Defiance, Clawson, Chester-Headed, Molds, and familiar White Winter. The latter outperformed the others but all yielded well. Wait's highest yielding oat varieties in order of performance were White Zealand, White Probsteier (likely of Baltic ancestry), Sommerset, and White Russian.[14]

The late nineteenth century also witnessed a proliferation of work by European grain breeders that built on the discoveries of Shirreff and Hallett and eventually brought significant benefit to farmers in the American West. In the 1850s, British cerealist Frederick Hallett formulated the era's classical method of patient "continuous selection" in order to improve progenies by seeding kernels only from the best heads of preferred wheats. The "wheat pedigrees" charted by Hallett were famously noted by Charles Darwin in his 1868 book, *The Variation of Plants and Animals under Domestication*, as evidence of selection processes similar to those taking place over longer periods of time in nature. Hallett released over a dozen improved commercial wheat varieties with Talavera, likely descended from a Spanish landrace, the most successful. The pioneering research done in the 1860s by Austrian monk Gregor Mendel on the genetics of peas was not widely published until the end of the century, so the Mendelian Laws of Inheritance were little understood by Hallett and his contemporaries. But the exchange of ideas by European plant scientists throughout Europe through publications and conferences led to a globalization of grain improvement methods and varieties.

An American student of Hallett and his continental colleagues, USDA cerealist Mark Carleton, explained the "improved selection" process for developing better varieties from parent stock:

> Just before harvest go through a field of a good, hardy, standard variety that has given the best results in the locality, and mark plants that exhibit to the highest degree the special quality which it is desired to increase, such as freedom

from [fungal] rust, fertility of head, or otherwise.... At harvest time cut with a sickle enough of these marked plants for sowing the plat and, after thrashing them, select the largest and most vigorous seed for this purpose, by means of a screen or even by hand picking. Sow the plat early, drilling it at the average rate of about 1 ¼ bushels per acre. Next season use none of the field crop for seed, but select in the same manner enough of the best plants from the breeding plat for reseeding...."[15]

While the work of those like Hallett had focused on spontaneous improvement within individual strains, the French botanist Henri de Vilmorin transformed grain breeding by applying scientific principles to the development of the first commercial grain hybrids. Vilmorin benefited from his prominent Paris grain trader family's experience in the vegetable and flower seed supply business. He began experiments in 1873 that demonstrated how a wider range of desirable traits could emerge by the combination of different wheat varieties, rather than from recurrent selections within the same strain. He also disdained the "pompous praise" recurrently heaped upon grains entered in national and international exhibitions that had not undergone long-term study for regional adaptability. American grain breeder Cyrus Pringle undertook a similar approach in Vermont between 1870 and 1877 and released four hybrids including two soft white wheats later raised in the Northwest—Defiance and Surprise. Vilmorin primarily used selections of Ukrainian wheats that had long grown in Aquitaine, as well as Squarehead, an English red derived from an 1868 selection in Yorkshire. The French innovator described methods of hybridization in *Les Meilleurs Blés* (*The Best Wheats*), a prodigious 1880 work that also surveyed nineteenth century European crop improvement efforts. The book featured artist Eugene Graff's lavish series of sixty-six color lithographs of wheat landraces and improved varieties collected as early as 1820. The Vilmorins worked zealously to analyze grains scientifically in order to determine geographic suitability.

Henri de Vilmorin's 1887 edition of the company's *Catalogue Méthodique et Synonymique des*

Taber Family Home and Orchard at Almota, Washington
F. A. Shaver, *An Illustrated History of Southeastern Washington* (1906)

and '80s, and regularly offered his recommendations in articles for *The Willamette Farmer*. The paper's editor described the Oregon Trail emigrant as "one of those enterprising and successful farmers who identify themselves with the State Agricultural Society," and noted yields of his various white wheats—White Velvet, White Chaff Mammoth, Sonora, and White Clawson, as well as White Russian rye. He also grew China Tea (Black Tea) wheat, a hard red spring variety named for kernels found in the 1840s inside a tea chest that had been shipped to New York from Asia.

Froments (Methodical and Synonymic Catalog of Durum Wheats) significantly expanded on the groundbreaking work of the same prosaic title compiled by his father, Louis, in 1850. The later catalogue presented an unprecedented taxonomy of fifty botanical categories distinguished by species, head characteristics, and other attributes of some two hundred featured landraces, improved selections, and early hybrid wheats. (Vilmorin had consolidated the number of wheat species from seven into five.) Most were from Europe and Asia, but Vilmorin included several varieties from the American Northwest with dates of his company's acquisition—Oregon Big Club (1878), Sonora (1879), and "Vala-vala" White (1887)—all likely supplied by Tacoma-Walla Walla entrepreneur William Reed. The Vilmorin family's agricultural legacy influenced a generation of grain breeders like Australia's William Farrar, Dominion cerealist William Saunders of Ottawa, as well as Missouri native William Spillman, whose experiences in Oregon and Washington from 1889 to 1902 would revolutionize Northwest agriculture.[16]

Northwest "farmer experimenters" also contributed significantly to the identification of varieties best suited to Northwest growing conditions. Englishman George Belshaw raised dozens of grains at his Irving area farm west of Eugene in the 1870s

In the 1880s, Vilmorin supplied Tacoma experimenter William Reed with fourteen wheat varieties for his farm near Walla Walla, including spring barley strains derived from Manchuria (Manchury), German Oderbrucher (from a landrace native to the Oder River Valley), and English Chevalier. The Tacoma grain trader and attorney was also among the first to actively promote the old semi-hard Australian Lammas descendant Pacific Bluestem east of the Cascades, where it came to dominate production in many areas by 1900. Reed sought to apply scientific methods to the trial-by-error approach of many Northwest farmers. In an 1893 article penned for the *Yakima Herald* titled "The Culture of Wheat," Reed advocated clinical trials of seeding rates and depths, soil type, climate zone, and exposure to vitrolization. After sending soil samples from his Walla Walla property to Vilmorin, the French firm recommended a group of wheats from Russia, Hungary, and France and supplied seed for Reed to continue his research.[17]

An unfortunate consequence of this global exchange was the introduction of weed seed that contaminated imported nineteenth-century foundation seed. The unwelcome cornucopia of alien invaders, like Jim Hill (tumble) mustard, Russian thistle, Scotch broom, Canada thistle, the

European foxtails, China (prickly) lettuce, and wild oats flourished in the Americas. Nevertheless, harvests in Washington and Oregon yielded a 300 percent increase between 1880 and 1900 with wheat production reaching as astounding twenty-five million bushels in 1900. Whitman County alone was contributing annual wheat yields of some ten million bushels and nearly an equal combined amount of barley and oats to become the nation's leading grain-producing county by the turn of the century. But grain

J. F. Seeber's Residence and Farm, Walla Walla
F. A. Shaver, *An Illustrated History of Southeastern Washington* (1906)

surpluses from 1880 to 1890 depressed Northwest wheat prices from about eighty-five cents to sixty-five cents per bushel during the same time, and in the Panic of 1893 prices plummeted to less than a quarter of a dollar. These factors contributed to the success of a network of entrepreneurs who provided storage facilities to area farmers, expanded milling operations, and sought stronger international markets for high quality Northwest flour.[18]

Marketing, Inspection, and Storage

Among the first to perceive opportunities afforded by the economic situation, including the completion of railroad networks, and the opening of foreign markets, was a group of Jewish businessmen who further contributed to regional development. Led by Colfax's Aaron Kuhn, a German immigrant of 1873, the tight-knit circle of Palouse Country grain traders also included Julius Lippitt and Simon Dreifus. All three operated general mercantile businesses in Colfax, became active in city politics, and regularly met with other prominent residents in the city's Masonic Lodge. In addition to shared marketing interests, Kuhn, Lippitt, and Dreifus also established local banks in order to extend operating

capital to Palouse area farmers of proven character and ability.

Kuhn arrived in America at the age of sixteen and operated stationery and cigar stores in Nevada, California, and Idaho before coming to Colfax in 1883. His mercantile business prospered with regional population growth and Kuhn invested a share of his profits in local real estate. Julius Lippitt settled in Colfax in 1878 and was soon shipping Palouse grain through his brother, Phillip, who lived in San Francisco at a time when the West Coast grain trade was headquartered in that city. However, by the 1890s, a shift in production northward moved West Coast market decision-making to Portland and Tacoma. By that time Kuhn and Lippitt had become important figures in the Northwest grain trade, with Kuhn shipping as much as one and a half million bushels annually through his network of sixteen warehouses in Whitman and Latah counties. In 1901 he also built the half-mile long Wawawai Tramway to transport grain off the Palouse plateau and down to the Snake River steamer fleet for export to Portland, while railroads moved much of the region's wheat to Puget Sound ports.

Port of Tacoma Grain Terminal and Ships, c. 1910
Robert Smith

Northern Pacific Railroad officials had decided in the 1870s to designate Tacoma as the line's western terminus to take advantage of Commencement Bay's deep water port. By 1900 Northern Pacific grain warehouses stretched for twenty-three hundred feet along Tacoma's boisterous mile-long eastern waterfront grain storage district. Touted as the "World's Longest Wheat Warehouse," the district was home to four of the region's largest mills—Puget Sound Flouring Mills, Albers Cereal Company, Cascade Cereal Mills, and the Tacoma Grain Company. The city also had the region's only dry dock large enough to repair the great vessels of the Pacific grain fleet. The cavernous enclosure measured three hundred twenty-five by eighty feet, and could displace eight thousand tons. Tacoma had become the state's leading grain exporter and the nation's fourth largest, exceeded only by shipments from Minneapolis, Kansas City, and Portland. Sixteen grain and flour warehouses spread

along eight miles of Portland waterfront with total storage capacity of seven and a half million bushels. Seattle's south waterfront near the present stadium district hosted sixteen warehouses for Hammond Milling, Centennial Mills, Albers, and other companies. Across the state large Spokane mills included Clarke & Curtis, Echo Mill, Spokane Flour Mill, and Centennial.[19]

As US grain production soared in the late nineteenth century, marketers and millers formulated an inspection system to assure commodity quality and fair compensation. Before 1860, transactions between farmers and grain buyers were largely determined locally on the basis of individual samples taken from wagonloads. The informalities of such arrangements were no longer efficient as the volume of trade and wider access to national and foreign markets burgeoned. The Chicago Board of Trade had organized the first grain inspection standards in 1856, followed by similar steps in

Minneapolis, St. Louis, Philadelphia, and Boston. Illinois again led with the first state-wide system in 1871. Wheat grading definitions underwent minor revisions in the late 1800s but generally conformed to the following criteria:

> Choice: Sound, dry, plump, of good color, free from smut, clean, not be mixed with more than 15 percent of any other variety, and weigh not less than 60 pounds to the bushel.
>
> No. 1: Sound, dry, reasonably plump, good color, reasonably free from smut, reasonably clean, and weighing not less than 58 pounds per bushel.
>
> No. 2: Sound, fairly good color, reasonably clean, and of good milling quality, weighing not less than 56 pounds per bushel.
>
> No. 3: So badly shriveled or from any other cause too poor to be graded as No. 2, but still not weighing less than 54 pounds per bushel, and suitable for milling purposes.

Although Washington, Oregon, and Idaho did not approve statewide inspection until after 1900, most Northwest warehouse owners entered into agreements to observe the standards and comply with inspection policies that determined pricing. Tacoma Grain Company manager John T. Bibb further ranked the most commonly grown Northwest varieties by their milling quality. Bluestem remained the region's "ideal miller" for its color, high grade gluten, and milling yield, followed closely by club wheat varieties. Red Russian, however, Bibb branded as a grain that "staggers the miller" due to its thick bran layer, which earned it the nickname "rhinoceros wheat." Further wheat and milling improvement, he opined in a 1906 Wheat Convention address, "will be under the hand of science."[20]

The Global Grain Exchange

In 1900, approximately seventy percent of West Coast wheat exports went to China and Japan as the result of an ambitious marketing campaign involving Northwest growers with some of the world's most influential leaders in the secretive global grain trade. As early as 1865, Inland Northwest wheat

had been shipped from Walla Walla on Dorsey Baker's famed "Rawhide Railroad" to Wallula for transfer to Columbia River steamers and on to Portland. In the 1870s Portland traders first shipped flour directly to the Liverpool trading exchange by sea. This period witnessed the transition of grain trading from the ancient continental traditions of bartering cartloads of produce to flour mills within a few miles of the harvest, to some of the earliest marketing schemes on a truly international scale. Spurred by the Industrial Revolution and concurrent population increases, European demand for foodstuffs during the early nineteenth century rose dramatically. The British Parliament's repeal of the protectionist Corn (Grain) Laws in 1846 represented a major opportunity for foreign traders to enter Great Britain's lucrative grain market. Among the first to seize upon the opportunity was a small group of European entrepreneurs whose separate efforts would lay the foundation for the great grain family trading empires of the modern era that reached to the Pacific Northwest. Two of the most prominent—Simon Fribourg of French Lorraine and Léopold Louis-Dreyfus of French Alsace—were traders who recognized and supplied the demands of Great Britain's markets with the abundant grain resources from Russia's Black Sea region.

Circumstances of the era also led the Bunges of Antwerp and Andrés of Switzerland to establish similar connections, since Russia at mid-century could not consume all the grain the Black Sea and Volga regions were capable of producing. By the mid-1800s, the Black Sea polyglot port of Odessa had become the center of Russian grain exports, as Greeks, French, English, Germans, and Italians mingled with native Slavic peoples to bargain for the region's ample produce. In doing so they also introduced both intentionally and by accident a number of the region's most popular wheat varieties as seed for farmers and breeders in Europe and the Western Hemisphere.

The 1870s "Communication Revolution," made possible by the completion of transoceanic cables greatly facilitated international trading, which also contributed to the rise of several American grain marketers. Brothers Will, Samuel, and

Barron Flour Mill; Oakesdale, Washington
Robert Smith

James Cargill began building and buying grain elevators from Minnesota to Chicago; "Elevator King" Frank Peavey launched his chain that would stretch from St. Paul to Portland by century's end; and Charles Alfred Pillsbury began construction of his first flour mills in Minneapolis. By 1875 the United States had replaced Russia as Great Britain's principal grain supplier, and six years later the US vessel *Dakota* inaugurated the first wheat shipment direct from Tacoma to England. Coming full circle, most of the grain exported to Europe had come from the seeds of varieties that had been raised for generations in South Russia and the United Kingdom.

The British-American firm Balfour, Guthrie & Company entered West Coast commerce in 1869 with the arrival of Scotsmen Robert Balfour and Alexander Guthrie in California. The pair's speculative commodity trading interests eventually turned to wheat and the company established warehouses in several strategic coastline locations. As grain production in Washington and Oregon soared in the 1870s, Balfour, Guthrie expanded operations accordingly to Portland (1878), Tacoma (1888), and Seattle in order to capitalize on markets in Europe and Asia. Alexander Baillie, also a native of Scotland, supervised the company's Northwest operations from Tacoma and entered into an agreement in 1900 with the Northern Pacific to lease one of three cavernous grain warehouses constructed that year along Tacoma's south waterfront. The broad roofs of the massive structures were supported by inverted railroad bridge trusses, and the adjacent Balfour, London, and Northwest docks each stretched for over a thousand feet where tall ships also plied toward nearby coal bunkers and lumber yards. Balfour, Guthrie advertised its grain as "Best in the West" and at the dawn of the new century the company could also boast being the nation's largest grain exporter.[21]

Attention to trans-Pacific Asia in the 1880s, however, led to economic relationships that would transform the marketing of Palouse and other Northwest soft white wheats preferred by consumers in China and Japan. During the same period that businessmen like Kuhn, Lippitt, and Dreifus were becoming established east of the Cascades, entrepreneur Theodore B. Wilcox had matured from a young Salem, Oregon, bank clerk to general manager of Portland Flouring Mills. The Massachusetts native quickly grasped the incredible economic potential represented by East Asia's half-billion inhabitants and began a series of acquisitions with backing from Oregon financiers to build additional flour mills throughout Washington in Tacoma, Spokane, Harrington, and Odessa.

Just when the first Northwest exporters began testing Asian markets, Wilcox formed Pacific Elevator Company to handle bulk storage and delivery to his mills. Two years later, in 1886, he established Puget Sound Warehouse Company to bring his network of grain handling facilities to three hundred fifty locations for shipping bulk wheat to England and flour to China. Wilcox established the Puget Sound Flouring Mill in 1889 adjacent to the Northern Pacific wharf in Tacoma where massive grindstones hummed rhythmically around the clock. Wilcox's foresight and methods—sometimes characterized by his competitors as ruthless—led to a pivotal move in 1890 when he arranged for Canadian diplomat Albert Rennie to represent his interests in Hong Kong. British brokers had previously established a monopoly on China's foreign trading arrangements, but Rennie represented a Commonwealth official who could facilitate the bargaining sought by Wilcox. Resulting sales accords with Chinese and Japanese grain brokers proved so successful that in 1895 Rennie began working full time for Wilcox as Northwest grain production continued to feed the capacity of his far-flung operations.

The period also witnessed the opening of Northern Pacific steamer shipping service from Tacoma to the Orient in 1890, Union Pacific Steamer Company operations from Portland in 1889, and Great Northern traffic on vessels from Seattle to Hong Kong in 1896. Elevator magnate Frank Peavey constructed a million-bushel capacity grain warehouse in Portland in 1895, and could ship grain to Liverpool via the Isthmus of Panama in a mere four weeks. Peavey's experience raised

WSC president urges cooperation in the wheat industry

Washington State College President Enoch A. Bryan sought to encourage a new spirit of cooperation among the often harshly competing and accusatory stakeholders of farmers, grain brokers, and shippers. In an address to the 1906 Wheat Convention in Pullman, he extolled wheat as the region's "greatest money making machine.... There have been times when the shipper was considered by the producer as little less than a pirate, while the transporter and miller were of so avaricious a character that they were beyond mentioning in the class of honest men.... By a gathering such as this wheat convention all these various interests will become better acquainted and get along infinitely better.... Throughout the world the production of bread, the staff of life, can by no means be considered unimportant, now or at any time. Of all the productions of humanity, this is the most fundamental, the most indispensable. The farmer...as he wisely sows and reaps and markets in the best possible way, the transporter and the miller as he does in the best and most economical way his part in the great work of production, each in his way and to his extent is a missionary, working for the betterment of humanity. There is no other industry in the world that is more important...."

his concerns regarding the challenges of storing and shipping sacked grain. He became interested in concrete bulk storage facilities like those he had seen in Romania and elsewhere, and decided in 1898 to sell his entire West Coast operation to Wilcox. In the famed "Million Dollar Deal," 256 of Peavey's warehouses were transferred to Wilcox's Western Warehouse control.[22]

While much of the rest of the world had lower harvests in 1900, Washington's farmers saw a twenty-five-million-bushel bumper crop, which represented a three-fold increase from the 1895 yield. In the 1890s, local farmer-owned cooperatives also emerged to warehouse and secure higher prices for commodities. (The region's first was the Ritzville Warehouse Company, established in 1893.) Burly Puget Sound longshoreman labored to ship a record 1,400,000 barrels of Northwest flour to Hong Kong in 1895 on exotically named vessels anchored along mammoth wooden docks. Ships regularly in port at Tacoma, Seattle, and Portland like the *Persian Empire, Pass of Melfort, Emin Pasha, Phra Nang, Victoria*, and *City of Delhi* were capable of holding five thousand tons of cargo and bore three and four masts spreading several acres of canvas. The Northwest grain fleet of American and foreign ships in 1900 consisted of 133 clippers, packets, schooners, and other vessels, and they carried about one-quarter (20,700,000 bushels) of all US wheat exports that year. Return trips from Hong Kong, Vladivostok, and other East Asian ports brought loads of Japanese tea and Chinese silks, rice, and burlap grain sacks to the region's chaotic docks where dockworkers in 1900 earned about thirty-five cents an hour for ten-hour shifts.

Reflecting the cycle of harvest, processing, and delivery, the export season was busiest from October to March with many vessels making several round-trip Pacific voyages annually. In 1905 President James J. Hill of the Great Northern

Steamship Company launched the largest vessel under American flag, the twenty-one-thousand-ton SS *Minnesota*, to transport American grain from Seattle's Smith Cove pier to Singapore and return with Asian commodities. The behemoth boasted the cargo capacity of twenty-five hundred Great Northern "Silk Train" boxcars, and a second ship for Hill's Pacific fleet followed later in the year—the SS *Dakota*.

In 1902, Wilcox and Balfour, Guthrie acquired Aaron Kuhn's Palouse grain operation, enabling Kuhn to purchase controlling interest in Traders National Bank of Spokane, forerunner of Spokane & Eastern Trust Company and Seattle First National Bank. By 1910 Wilcox was the Northwest's unrivaled "Flour Magnate" whose brands were known from the Malabar Coast and across China to Vladivostok. Following his death in 1918, Wilcox's warehouse and milling empire was acquired by Sperry and subsequently absorbed by the industry's largest, General Mills, in 1929.[23]

In a matter of just several decades, Northwest grain growers evolved from small, regional operations to being the nation's largest suppliers of wheat to the world.

Chili Club (Spain/Chile)
Soft Yellow Spring

Original Balfour, Guthrie Warehouse and Dock
Foss Waterway Seaport Maritime Museum; Tacoma, Washington

Yakima Valley Vines
Red Mountain near Benton City, Washington
John Clement

Beloturka (Russia/Ukraine)
Hard Yellow Spring

California Spring
Soft White Spring

Red May (England/France)
Soft Red Spring

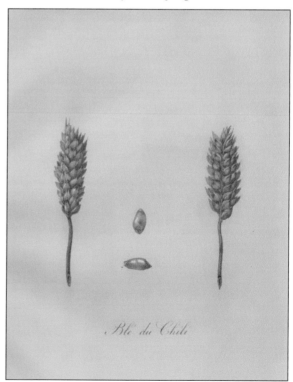

Chili Club (Spain/Chile)
Soft Yellow Spring

Eugene Graf Wheat Lithographs
Henri de Vilmorin, *Les Meilleurs Blés* (1880)

Beardless Odessa (Russia/Ukraine)
Hard Red Winter

Touzelle (France)
Soft White Winter

Red Chaff Danzig (Prussia/Poland)
Soft White Winter

Ghirka Red (Russia/Ukraine)
Hard Red Spring

Bartlett Pear
WSU-Mt. Vernon Research and Extension Center

Northern Spy Apples
WSU-Mt. Vernon Research and Extension Center

Wealthy Apples
WSU-Mt. Vernon Research and Extension Center

Red Astrachan Apples
Craigflower Manor National Historic Site, Victoria

Canola Skies
Near Potlatch, Idaho
John Clement

Dixie Hills Twilight
North of Walla Walla, Washington
John Clement

Boston Marrow Squash
Champoeg State Heritage Area, Oregon

Purple Hyacinth Beans
Champoeg State Heritage Area, Oregon

Evening Wheat
Seven Hills near Kennewick, Washington
John Clement

Spring Orchard Patterns
Near Selah, Washington
John Clement

CHAPTER V

Cradles to Combines

So freely drink to your lord's health,
Then to the plough, the commonwealth,
Next to your flails, your fans, your vats,
Then to the maids with wheaten hats;
To the rough sickle, and crook'd scythe,
Drink, frolic, boys, till all be blithe.

Before the late nineteenth-century revo-lution in agricultural mechanization, a hard-working farmer in 1850 could break out only about forty acres of land each year with an awkward, heavy-beamed, single-shear "foot-burner" plow. The next challenge was to pre-pare a proper seedbed, as the fibrous root sys-tem, especially thick on the Palouse, penetrated the ground for two to three feet.

An early farmer in the western Palouse, Fred Clemens, described the process: "[The] first plow to break the native sod was a single furrow one, pulled by two horses (sometimes three)…. As the team moved forward the share cut the sod and the moldboard turned it over. The plow-man walked behind in the newly made furrow, driving the team and steadying the plow with a pair of handles that extended backwards. With sod thus plowed…it lay in parallel strips…. The uprooted grass lay underneath; the root-bound soil on top."

Later, double-furrow "two-bottom" plows were used with six-horse teams, while "triple-bottomed" plows were usually pulled by eight horses. Belgians, Percherons, and Clydesdales were the most common work horses, but mules

Clipper Prairie Plow
Report of the Commissioner of Patents (1860)

Iron Cultivator
Report of the Commissioner of Patents (1860)

Plowing near Colfax, c. 1915
David Anderson Collection

were often preferred on Columbia Plateau farms because of their stolid temperament and ability to better withstand the summer heat. Pioneer Walla Walla County farmer Carl Penner recalled his approach to harnessing their attention: "You couldn't beat the meanness out of 'em. It just don't work. But if you'd treat 'em halfway right and pet 'em and curry 'em and give 'em plenty to eat, they soon learned who was the boss."[1]

To cultivate plowed ground, farmers first devised crude two- or three-row harrows by pounding long nails or wooden pegs into wide beams or logs, which they dragged across the field, often several times. Seeding was originally done using the ancient hand-broadcast method, considered an art form by pioneer farmers who moved at a measured pace with a sack slung over their shoulder to cover a swath about a dozen feet wide. Rancher William Snyder recalled hiring an experienced Russian-German immigrant to broadcast seed on his dryland Adams County acreage: "He went down there and seeded by hand and I paid him a dollar and a

half a day and he said that wasn't enough. 'Well,' I said, 'I could have gotten any of my neighbors to have done this for a dollar….' He raised up his hand toward the sky and said, 'You will find that whatever that hand soweth God Almighty will bless a thousand fold!' Incidentally, that was a twenty-bushel crop and my neighbors had five."[2]

Farmers usually harrowed again for a smoother surface, sometimes using only clumps of brush. They prayed for rain and an early sprout to firmly root the grain and create a ground cover before winter. The introduction of the shoe drill in the 1880s greatly improved plant emergence, as the seed was placed evenly at a calibrated depth. Threats from uncooperative weather as well as noxious weeds—especially cheatgrass and the tumbleweeds produced by Russian thistle and Jim Hill mustard—could still do considerable damage to a promising crop. After initial efforts to eradicate Russian thistle in the 1890s failed, a contributor to *The Ranch* opined that "the whole Russian army…if it were here engaged in destroying this thistle, could hardly exterminate it." Columbia Plateau farmers also faced legions of ground squirrels and periodic "coulee cricket," chinch bug, and grasshopper plagues. USDA range managers John Sandberg and John Leiberg warned Columbia Basin ranchers in an 1893 tour that overgrazing by livestock threatened to significantly degrade the region's complex mosaic of native grasses and forbs (non-grass herbaceous plants). They further noted the destructive impacts of poor rangeland oversight and fence-to-fence farming on the grassland habitats of animals— including deer, cougars, and black bears—that had lived in the fragile landscapes for millennia. Hawk, falcon, and sharp-tailed grouse were also in decline, as well as trout, steelhead, and other fish native to inland Northwest streams and rivers.[3]

Through trial-and-error, farmers in the late nineteenth century used tillage methods and specialized implements for summer-fallow field operations to conserve crop-sustaining moisture and nutrients in the semi-arid environs of the Columbia Plateau. Lands allowed to remain idle for a year and kept clear of weeds stored rainfall in humus that agricultural chemists like Pullman's R. W. Thatcher claimed could also "mineralize" valuable nitrogen for plant nutrition. But he also recognized the damaging effects of erosion by wind and water upon unprotected soils in a day when agronomists like his Washington State College (WSC) co-worker, Byron Hunter, and regional journalists recommended the "Campbell system" of intense cultivation widely used in the Midwest. "Dust mulch" advocates like Hunter encouraged area farmers to burn their stubble and till fallow ground from a half-dozen to ten times a year in order to create "the dustiest, smoothest, cleanest, least lumpy, and least trashy field surface." Most growers followed such advice in spite of Thatcher's warnings that in view of preeminent needs to conserve organic matter and prevent erosion, "conserving moisture is not enough."[4]

Boosters of regional development often proclaimed in newspaper editorials and farm demonstration lectures that the Columbia Plateau was blessed with "inexhaustible soil," and at the turn

of the century farmers generally followed a pattern of field operations consistent with such optimism. Grain fields were routinely burned soon after harvest to destroy weeds and dispose of troublesome stubble that otherwise might clog plows. Farmers who maintained stubble frequently commenced late summer field work by discing to break down the residue and then followed by plowing in the fall and sometimes again in spring. Harrowing one or more times with a common or heavier spring-tooth harrow usually followed plowing in order to smooth the ground and kill sprouting weeds and volunteer grain.

In drier districts, Hunter advocated the use of a corrugated roller or subsurface packer to conserve moisture. In the spring, farmers commonly hitched their teams to shank cultivators for at least two passes to break up the soil and open up small trenches for rainfall to better penetrate the ground. In order to prevent weeds from robbing soil moisture, gooseneck slicker blade or split knife weeders were used throughout the summer to root them up, although these primitive implements often clogged where fields were infested with Jim Hill mustard and vines like morning glory and bindweed. Seeding generally took place after harvest in late September or October with a hoe drill, or a disc drill in more trashy fallow, which was often trailed by a light spike-harrow. If weeds sprouted before the grain germinated, a farmer might lightly harrow the entire field again.

Such labor intensive patterns of field operations rendered the deep, heavier soils of the Palouse and Walla Walla regions highly vulnerable to water erosion; and the shallower, sandy soils of the Big Bend susceptible to destructive winds. A Country Life Commission appointed by President Theodore Roosevelt in 1908 characterized such approaches as soil "mining," and the annual tonnage loss of topsoil from periodic "gully washers" and gale force winds could be staggering. Although Washington State College agronomist William J. Spillman warned against the long-term consequences of "exploitive farming," his misconception that Palouse soils were composed of disintegrated basalt with "practically no bottom" may have contributed to widespread acceptance of intensive cultivation. In fact, the region's legendary black humus was a relatively thin layer built upon loessal soils composed of desiccated silts blown east by prevailing winds over eons in prehistoric times. A twentieth-century generational shift of consciousness would be needed to stabilize soils through modified tillage practices that would eventually vindicate Thatcher's theories.[5]

Northwest Harvests

The arduous task of summer harvest was first undertaken using a primitive cradle, or scythe connected to four to six long wooden ribs that could

Cradle Scythe and Sickle
R. Scheuerman Collection

hold several hand swathings. These were then dropped in the stubble and bundled into rows of shocks reminiscent of a van Gogh painting. (The basic design of the hand-sickle has remained essentially unchanged since the dawn of civilization, and use of this ancient implement endured throughout Europe well in the 1800s. Some ten swipes by an experienced fieldworker typically provided enough stalks to fashion a sheaf about one foot in diameter.) The calloused hands that knew this labor then either flailed the wheat, barley, and oat cuttings or led a team of horses around a hard-surfaced circular area to trample the stalks. The straw was then removed with pitchfork and the seed carefully shoveled with as little dirt and roughage as possible into burlap gunny sacks. The grain was eventually dumped and winnowed to separate the kernels from chaff and dirt. An entire family might harvest only two acres in a day from which might be gleaned fifty to seventy bushels of grain.

The US Patent Office registered more than two hundred and fifty hand- and horse-powered threshing machines between 1820 and 1845. One of the most popular was New England inventor Joseph Pope's hand-crank model operated on the "Scottish principle" and could thresh ten dozen sheaves per hour to yield about five bushels of grain, or double that amount if powered by horse. Pope's table-like platform held a cloth conveyor that carried the stalks under a revolving wooden beater at one end that knocked the grain from the brittle heads. But the golden remains still had to be winnowed in a separate operation to clean the grain. Few farmers could afford to order small mechanical fanning mills from the East, which were expensive and required considerable strength to turn the internal blades for sufficient wind to clean the grain before small steam engines were introduced. Oak Point, Oregon, farmer Joseph Hamilton is credited with bringing the first mechanical thresher to the Pacific Northwest. The Ohio native journeyed over the Oregon Trail in 1847 with a wagon containing the machine's components, which he reassembled and operated for several harvest seasons. That same year fabricator F. C. Cason was selling fanning mills built in his Oregon City shop.

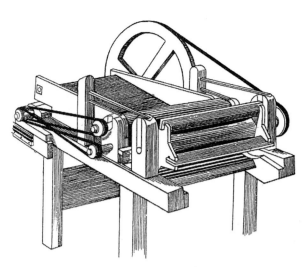

Pope's Hand Thresher
The American Agriculturist (1830)

In the summer of 1856, Hudson's Bay Company workers at Ft. Vancouver received a Buffalo-Pitt's threshing machine, which was shipped in pieces on bateaux to Cowlitz Farm. The nearly half-ton marvel combined both thresher and fanning mill and was powered by several teams of horses. The animals were led around a turntable of sweeps attached to a tumbler rod on the ground that connected to the thresher. The machine was operated by four farmhands and capable of threshing five hundred bushels in a twelve-hour shift—easily a ten-fold increase over the old flailing method and eight times more efficient than Pope's hand-machine. But the Buffalo-Pitts system experienced numerous breakdowns and the horses used in the operation were soon replaced with coal- or wood-fired steam engines. George Washington Bush introduced the first horse-powered reaper to south Puget Sound in 1856, and obtained a threshing separator the following year. In 1858 Ft. Walla Walla wagon master Charles Russell obtained the first threshing machine east of the Cascades for the small fields of oats and wheat he tended near the fort.[6]

In the 1870s small, horse drawn reaper-binders that could drop five or six grain bundles on the ground tied with wire and later with twine appeared in Northwest fields. Six to eight bundled sheaves were then arranged in shocks to further ripen or be hauled directly on open wagons to large stationary separators, or to threshing machines. A McCormick or Marsh reaper could harvest fourteen to fifteen acres a day and increased output tenfold over the hand scythe method. The machine's advent and economic significance were celebrated in Will Carleton's "Song of the Reaper."

> The grain-stalk bows his bristling head,
> As I clatter and clash along,
> The stubble it bends beneath my tread,
> The stacker's yellow tent is spread,
> And the hills throw back my song—my song—
> The hills throw back my song!
> Then hie! where the food of nations glows,
> And the yellow tide of the harvest flows,
> As we dash and crash and glide and run;
> And the world will eat when our work is done![7]

Grain collected by these early threshers still required further cleaning to remove chaff and weed seed in order to fetch full value in cash or trade. For this reason, pioneer Oregon inventor Daniel Best devised a hand-powered mechanical separator in the winter of 1869–70. An 1859 Oregon Trail immigrant from Iowa, Best relocated from Oregon to Sutter County, California, in 1869 where he

Pitts Horse-Powered Thresher and Cleaner
The Cultivator and Country Gentleman (1848)

built the first of many "Best Grain Cleaner" models. He returned to the Willamette Valley in 1874 and established his business in Albany. Best eventually acquired forty-three patents and his ingenuity would revolutionize agricultural mechanics worldwide. The "Best Combined Harvester" outfitted with header, thresher, and cleaner appeared in 1885, and the following year he sold the first and relocated his operation to San Leandro, California. In 1888, Best's company manufactured one hundred and fifty combines in an effort to keep up with strong demand. Under the skillful management of Best's son, Clarence Leo "C. L." Best, the firm eventually merged with California's Holt Manufacturing Company to form the Caterpillar Tractor Company. Washington's first manufacturer of threshing machines, Walla Walla's Gilbert Hunt, founded his company in 1888 and introduced growers to the popular "Pride of Washington" series.[8]

Best, Holt, and other manufacturers sold large headers in the 1880s with twelve- to twenty-foot sickle bars and reels. Some were three-wheeled contraptions pushed by horses or mules behind the header and driven by a "header puncher" who steered by means of a rudder wheel connected to a board between the knees. The operator's hands guided the lines to the horses and operated a lever

to adjust the height of the sickle that cut the grain, which fell onto a wide and rapidly moving canvas draper reinforced with hardwood slats. On the downhill side of the header was a sloped elevator where a flexible, wood-ribbed draper carried the cuttings upward and dropped them into a header box wagon, built with one side lower than the other to fit under the spout.

In addition to the wagon driver, a loader worked inside the wagon to equally distribute the grain with a pitchfork in a laborious routine considered one of the most strenuous of the entire operation. Another header box would move into place when the first was full, and the loader would jump into it to continue working while the other wagon was driven to the thresher, a beehive of harvest activity. At a centrally located area in the field, usually near a country road, a small army of workers moved continuously amidst the cacophony of roars and whistles from the steam engine, thresher, derrick table, and horse-drawn wagons. [9]

As many as two dozen experienced workers were needed for stationary thresher operations, and it was not uncommon to see women from the family driving teams. The overall harvest operation was supervised by the "straw boss," who was often the owner of the thresher and engine who rented them out to area farmers. He handled the hiring

Threshing outfit, Gus Anderson wheat harvest near Pullman, Washington, 1910
David Anderson collection

Binding wheat sheaves, 1910 Gus Anderson wheat harvest
David Anderson collection

of the core crew from reliable acquaintances and relatives, and other helpers from the several thousand "bindle stiffs" who converged on rural farming communities each summer looking for harvest employment. The going rate for such employment in 1900 was about three dollars a day. The boss also worked with the farmer to determine the sequence of fields to cut, and oversaw other aspects of the workers' myriad responsibilities. Teamsters were needed to drive the two or three headers that usually comprised an outfit's contingent, and for handling the two-horse teams that took the several header boxes back and forth to the threshing area from the headers relentlessly winding through the fields.

The wagon cuttings were unloaded onto large piles by the driver and "spike pitchers," and a "stacker" who properly arranged the grain into two or three tall piles. A "forker" then set to work on a large platform mounted on a wagon called a "derrick table," named for a high four-beam derrick that rose some fifteen feet above it. At the top of the poles a pulley was suspended, through which a rope ran, connecting a "derrick team" of six to eight horses to a six-pronged steel Jackson fork. The forker positioned the Jackson onto one of the piles and yelled to the derrick team driver to move the horses ahead so the fork's load could be hauled to the table and dropped with a trip rope. In later years the main pulley rope was connected to a net in the bottom of the header box wagon that could be lifted to deposit the load directly onto the der-

rick table, which eliminated the need for the Jackson fork.

Two workers called "hoe-downs" then used hoe-shaped forks to guide the grain at a measured pace onto a long canvas feeder that led to the thresher's gnashing mouth, out of which long metal fingers moved back and forth to pull in the grain. This grueling work usually went in shifts with pairs of hoe-downs trading off in half-hour intervals. These workers determined the maximum rate of intake by listening to the growl of the metal monster. Care was taken not to choke the creature with too much grain, which risked breaking a drive chain or shaft, or jamming the machine. The laborious task of extracting the partially digested stalks by hand from inside the tightly packed innards was usually tended to by several of the younger workers using every possible contortion of limb and colorful language. This chore was especially unpleasant if the straw was infested with countless miniscule spines of scabrous tarweed that stung like fire if touched.

Deep inside a rapidly rotating cylinder, rows of short steel tines were narrowly mounted above a set of stationary iron "concaves" with large teeth to shatter the kernels out of the heads. The particles then fell through a series of rocking sieves to an auger at the base of the machine and into a "bulk tank" storage bin. The sieve action combined with the effects of a wide-bladed fan created a virtual wind tunnel through which the straw and chaff were blown out the back of the thresher. These tailings were stacked by two "straw pitchers" until a long "wind stacker" pipe was introduced after the turn of the century that blasted the straw twenty feet away to form a pile. Other important needs of the thresher were tended to by an "oiler," who kept the moving parts well lubricated and assisted the mechanic, or "separator man," in maintenance work.

The inner workings of the thresher were turned by an enormous drive-belt, at least sixty feet long and crossed in the middle. It ran from the steam engine's power wheel to the thresher's main pulley. On the 1890s Case, Rumley, and other models it could deliver up to forty horsepower. The huge engines were ponderous steamers, some up to

Engine tender and fireman, 1910 Gus Anderson wheat harvest
David Anderson collection

twenty feet long, and tended by experienced engineers. The long distance of the engine from the thresher was a fire prevention measure.

The fireman's job was considered one of the most exhausting of all tasks in the sweaty crucible of harvest, and certainly the hottest. These workers earned the crew's highest wages. The fireman rose at 4 a.m. to clean out the ash pit and boiler flue soot, and light the firebox with straw. When sufficient pressure was reached, he blew the whistle to wake the rest of the crew who usually slept outside in their bedrolls. During the day he had to constantly fuel the flames, usually with straw. This was brought to the fireman by a "straw buck," who used a pitchfork to provide a steady supply from the main pile behind the thresher to the engine. A "water buck" was in charge of the cigar-shaped wooden water wagon, which carried up to five hundred gallons and a hand pump to keep the steam engine and horses satisfied.

Twirling sprockets run by flat chains turned the cylinder, fan, augers, and other components that howled throughout the day. A mechanic was needed to keep thresher properly operating, a "roustabout" to run errands, gather the enormous foodstuffs necessary for the crew's consumption, and facilitate communication among the workers. A "sack jig" filled gunny sacks with the grain while two nimble-fingered sack sewers sitting on two grain sacks raced to close the bags using long steel sack needles flared at the end. They formed a corner "ear" on the left side of the sack, rapidly tied it off with two half-hitch loops, and then moved across the top with nine lightning stitches before closing it off with an identical ear on the right side.

Weighing about one hundred forty pounds each, the sacks were then stacked nearby to await loading by a teamster onto flatbed wagons with short side-racks. The wagons were often hitched together in groups of two or three to be pulled by eight-horse teams to local warehouses and outside storage platforms. Here men carefully arranged the sacks into formations that could reach several stories high. During a good fourteen-hour day, eighteen workers, an experienced threshing crew running two headers, and a pair of sack sewers

Sack sewers and strawpile, 1910 Gus Anderson wheat harvest
David Anderson collection

Hauling grain with mule and horse teams, 1910 Gus Anderson wheat harvest
David Anderson collection

Moore Brothers sack pile, 1911
Manuscripts, Archives, and Special Collections; Washington State University Libraries (PC 70.631)

could harvest sixty acres and fill twelve hundred sacks with twenty-seven hundred bushels—about eighty tons of grain.[10]

Such intense labor and long work hours generated enormous appetites. One of the surest ways to keep a good crew was to ensure they were well fed with plenty of fresh meat and potatoes, vegetables, and applesauce. Sometimes workers were also treated to fresh fruit desserts. Women toiled in portable cookshacks from predawn hours to feed the workers up to five times each day—breakfast by 6 a.m., midmorning lunch break, dinner at noon, afternoon lunch break, and supper after 8 p.m. The men ate in shifts outside or on long narrow benches and tables in the cookshack behind screened windows. The abundance and quality of harvest food was legendary among most crewmembers, who considered the cook's job even more demanding

than their own. The provender was a source of considerable pride to farm wives and others who assumed this responsibility.

By the 1880s implement manufacturers like Holt, Deere, and McCormick were combining reapers and threshers to make "combines." On the steep slopes of the Inland Northwest, these machines could require as many as forty-four horses to pull and power by massive drive chains from large metal-cleated side wheels. Walla Walla farmer Robert Kennedy obtained one of the first combines in the region in 1884. Palouse Country "Wheat King" Lillis Smith drew crowds of gawkers to his farm near Endicott in the summer of 1893 to see what the *Palouse Republic* proclaimed Holt's "seventh wonder of the world." The reporter wrote that it required "all the horses in the neighborhood...to drag the great machine over the hills."

McGregor harvest crew and cook wagon at Wood Gulch Ranch near Hooper, Washington
Straw boss John Forrest (far left), separator man Joe Marmes (front row, fourth from right),
loader Dallas Hooper (seated far right), c. 1928
Dallas Hooper Collection

These complicated contraptions of chains, sprockets, and cogs still required sizeable crews. A driver, or "mule skinner" was needed to direct the horse or mule teams with long jerk lines from a seat perched precariously on a ladder far out in front of the machine. Drivers "spoke" to the enormous teams of draft animals with telegraphic movements on the lines and their own invented vocabulary beyond "gee" and "haw," and tried to minimize the trampling down of standing grain. (For this reason, some farmers sowed a swath along the fence-line of less valuable oats.) Just harnessing the herd could take several hands a full hour in the early morning and late evening. For drivers on the steep slopes of the Inland Northwest from Spokane to Walla Walla, the driver's role could be both exhilarating and nauseating. Historian Kirby Brumfield likened their role to riding ship's prow against violent waves: "There were times just before reaching the peak of a hill that the driver was far up and at a backward slant that he couldn't see the horses in

front of him. They were already over the hill and out of sight. Even the most experienced drivers had a sense of relief as the combine pulled over the hill and the horses came back into view." Pulling up hill, the lumbering machines often failed to gain sufficient speed to properly thresh.

Other members of the crew included a "header puncher," who stood behind on a wooden deck to raise and lower the cutting platform according to the slope and height of the grain, the "separator tender," and a machinist. A "leveler" standing on the main unit controlled the combine's rack and pinion leveling mechanism with a lever in front of the bulk tank where up to fifty bushels of clean grain could be stored. Vertigo was common after navigating slowly for hours along hillsides, but leveling was necessary to prevent the stalks from piling up on the downhill side of the machine to cause plugups or the "walking out" of unthreshed grain. One or two sack sewers sat on a bench beneath the bulk tank where the kernels fell through a downspout

Anderson-Jackson horse-drawn combine, near Moscow, Idaho, c. 1923
David Anderson Collection

into burlap sacks that were sewn shut and stacked nearby until six to eight could be dropped onto the ground. This process still required wagons for collecting the sacks and transportation to local storage flathouses.

Improved mechanization did not necessarily bring economic benefits to the region's farmers. At the 1906 Washington Wheat Conference in Pullman, A. J. Stone of Rosalia, Washington, decried the performance of itinerant threshing crews: "The farmer is now paying more for threshing bundles than the price of wheat in most seasons will justify…. The waste of the present bundle crews is simply outrageous. Eleven to twelve teams to the crew will not accomplish what eight wagons could do were the hands interested in the work. It is often remarked by Eastern farmers who observe our way of harvesting that we waste more here than they grow back there." In response to these problems, Northwest innovators teamed together to fabricate a new generation of affordable and labor-saving threshing equipment.[11]

Moscow, Idaho, inventors Andrew Anderson and Charles Quensnell had joined forces in 1904 to build a prototype thresher that could be operated by just two men. The "Little Idaho" header was only six feet wide, weighed only 2,200 pounds, and was designed to be pushed by just two horses from the rear of the machine. This resulted in sig-

nificantly less crop damage than that inflicted by the enormous teams needed to pull the eleven-ton models built by Holt and others. With funding from Idaho mining magnate Jerome Day, the Idaho National Harvester Company flourished, as did the Moscow manufacturer of a similar machine, the Rhodes Harvester, until the advent of gas-powered combines following World War I rendered the earlier equipment obsolete.

One harvest season incident in 1915 on the Washington-British Columbia border demonstrated the power of farmer friendships and ingenuity in foreign affairs. Molson, Washington, area thresher J. C. McDowell operated a steam engine-powered Rumley capable of threshing several thousand bushels of grain in a day. He had just finished the season on the Ernie Curtis place adjoining the international boundary near Bridesville, BC, when he was contacted by Curtis's Canadian neighbor, Robert Johnston, who had been unable to locate a machine to thresh his oat crop. Harvesting equipment could not operate north of the line without a special permit that might take weeks to obtain and Johnston was growing desperate for help. Following a bilateral field parley, McDowell placed the Rumley parallel to the border so the clean grain spout reached over the line while Johnson's crew pitched his grain bundles in the opposite direction. Not only was the grain bagged on the Canadian side, but McDowell swung the straw pipe around to also blow the oat straw northward. In this way, the American machine threshed the entire crop without ever touching Canadian soil.[12]

In his 1919 novel, *The Desert of Wheat*, popular Western author Zane Grey weaves detailed descriptions of Northwest farm life against a backdrop of regional labor conflicts and World War I. Protagonist Kurt Dorn confronts a series of challenges to his Big Bend wheat farm with threats from smutting bunt (a parasitic fungus) as well as Wobblies

Rhodes Harvester, c. 1915
Manuscripts, Archives, and Special Collections;
Washington State University (PC 70.5b.219)

seeking employment concessions from landowners. Grey traveled throughout the region in 1917 in preparation for the book and took copious notes on regional wheat varieties and diseases. Through Dorn and his German immigrant father, Grey introduced a nationwide audience to Pacific Bluestem, Turkey Red, and Fife wheats, and the crucial work of the Washington State Agricultural Experiment Station. Grey transports readers to Spokane, Walla Walla, and Yakima, though the expansive landscapes surrounding rural Big Bend hamlets like Odessa, Krupp, and Ruff evoke the popular author's most vivid prose:

> A thousand hills lay bare to the sky, and half of every hill was wheat and half was fallow ground; and all of them, with the shallow valleys between, seemed big and strange and isolated. The beauty of them was austere, as if the hand of man had been held back from making green his home site, as if the immensity of the task had left no time for youth and freshness. Years, long years, were there in the round-hilled, many-furrowed gray old earth. And the wheat looked a century old.... A singularly beautiful effect of harmony lay in the long, slowly rising slopes, in the rounded hills, in the endless curving lines on all sides.... Here was grown the most bounteous, the richest and finest wheat in all the world.[13]

Columbia Plateau harvest from Zane Grey's *The Desert of Wheat*

First Kurt began to load bags of wheat, as they fell from the whirring combines, into the wagons. For his powerful arms a full bag, containing two bushels, was like a toy for a child. With a lift and a heave he threw a bag into a wagon. They were everywhere, these brown bags, dotting the stubble field, appearing as if by magic in the wake of the machines. They rolled off the platforms.... He passed to pitching sheaves of wheat and then to driving in the wagons. From that he progressed to a seat on one of the immense combines, where he drove twenty-four horses.... [A]s a boy, he had begged to be allowed to try his hand; he liked the shifty cloud of fragrant chaff, now and then blinding and choking him; and he liked the steady, rhythmic tramps of hooves and the roaring whir of the great complicated machine. It fascinated him to see the wide swath of nodding wheat tremble and sway and fall, and go sliding up into the inside of that grinding maw, and come out, straw and dust and chaff, and a slender stream of gold filling the bags.

The late afternoon found him feeding sheaves of wheat to one of the steam-threshers. He stood high upon a platform and pitched sheaves from the wagons upon the sliding track of the ponderous, rattling threshing-machine. The engine stood off fifty yards or more, connected by an endless driving-belt to the thresher. Here indeed were whistle and roar and whir, and the shout of laborers, and the smell of smoke, sweat, dust, and wheat.... He toiled, and he watched the long spout of chaff and straw as it streamed from the thresher to lift, magically, a glistening, ever-growing stack. And he felt, as a last and cumulative change, his physical effort, and the physical adjuncts of the scene, pass into something spiritual, into his heart and his memory.

Northwest Patrons of Husbandry

The Patrons of Husbandry, or Grange, was an agricultural society organized in 1867 as a result of President Andrew Johnson's and journalist-farmer Oliver Hudson Kelly's efforts to develop means for reconciling animosities that persisted between the North and South after the Civil War. The term "Grange" was derived from a word used in the Middle Ages for a country manor with barns, stables, granaries, and other structures necessary for husbandry, or agriculture. Grangers were familiar with the ancient Greek Eleusinian (Elysian) tradition and used the order as a pattern for the new organization's structure and ritual. The role of each local Grange officer was associated with an occupation on a typical English estate including a master, overseer, steward, gatekeeper, and chaplain, which were generally associated with the four highest officials of the Elysian republic—hierophant (master of sacred relics), daduchos (torchbearer), keryx (herald), and epibomios (priest).

The Grange movement was envisioned to be progressive and women were equally represented in the leadership with designated titles drawn from classical mythology—Ceres, the goddess of grains; Pomona, goddess of fruits; and Flora, goddess of flowers. The organization was organized at the local, county, state, and national levels with seven farm implements used as symbols in the formalities of each degree. The plow, for example, "should teach us how to drive the plowshare of thought diligently through the heavy soil of ignorance;" the hoe "is emblematic of that cultivation of the mind…, thus promoting the growth of knowledge and wisdom;" while the "ancient and honorable" sickle "speaks of peace and prosperity, and is the harbinger of joy…." The Horn of Plenty and Bible were all-encompassing symbols representing the values of harvest blessing and divine wisdom.

A panoply of problems faced Northwest farmers when the first Granges were formed in Oregon (1873), Washington (1873), and Idaho (1874). Membership swelled as over three hundred Northwest Granges were organized by 1875 and their leaders decried excessive profits made by several farm implement manufacturers as well as artificially high railroad freight rates. Putting into practice their preachings about citizenship activism, the organization sought every legal means to improve their economic plight by lobbying state legislatures and Congressional regulatory commissions. Their first efforts brought concessions from manufacturers and the Northern Pacific Railroad in the 1890s, which enhanced the role of Granges throughout the country.

In 1918 the Washington State affiliate formed the Grange Wholesale Warehouse Company, later known as Grange Co-op Wholesale, which combined the purchasing power of smaller Grange cooperatives to more economically market equipment and petroleum products to farmers. The prime-mover behind this effort was Pullman-area Granger William Smith. A dozen years later the cooperative merged with the Midwest's Farmers Union Central Exchange (CENEX) to create one of the nation's largest agricultural supply enterprises that integrated ownership of oil wells and refineries with bulk handling and services at the regional and local levels.

Grangers were also known across the Northwest for campaigns at educating youth and the general public about the importance of agriculture to all segments of society. No visit to the county fair was complete without viewing Grange displays fashioned in intricate designs of rural scenes and messages using multicolored mosaics of grains and legumes. Annual exhibition themes focused public attention on the importance of agriculture in daily life and evidenced members' spirit of fellowship and hard work. The *Pacific Grange Bulletin* (later the *Agricultural Grange News*) began publication in 1908 to better coordinate activities within the organization and to feature prose and poetry by rural authors who merited publication. Sara Archer penned lines to commemorate the Spokane interstate agriculture fair:

> Another year of garnered hopes, of bending
>   boughs on orchard slopes;
> Of stubble-fields where Ceres reigns, of
>   bursting barns and stagg'ring wains;
> The tardy sun seeks southern skies; and
>   Hesperus is quick to rise.

Northwest Granges also used their growing influence in the 1920s to fight for rural electrification and conservation practices. Efforts to bring electrical power to the farm were greeted with widespread support and contributed during the following decade to the organization of public utility districts and Columbia River hydroelectric dams. The Grange campaign to promote an ethic of land stewardship was rooted in the moral principle and enunciated by Grange enthusiast Theodore Roosevelt. The former president visited Moscow, Idaho, in April 1911 and addressed an enormous audience from a platform made of Palouse wheat sacks. His words echoed a theme from earlier speeches: "The conservation of our natural resources and their proper use constitutes the fundamental problem which underlies almost every other problem of our national life. Unless we maintain an adequate material basis for our civilization, we cannot maintain the institutions in which we take so great and so just a pride; and to waste and destroy our natural resources means to undermine this material basis...."

Roosevelt went on to define stewardship of the land in terms that balanced principle with practicality: "Conservation means development as much as it does protection. I recognize the right and duty of this generation to develop and use the natural resources of our land; but I do not recognize the right to waste them, or to rob, by wasteful use, the generations that come after us."[14]

Roosevelt's reasoned ethic of land stewardship was promulgated by national Grange leadership that sought innovative farming practices. The steeply rolling Palouse had acquired the unenviable reputation as an area where an average of twenty-five tons of topsoil per acre eroded away annually resulting in a loss of twenty million tons of topsoil each year. The epochal forces of nature that required more than a century to form one inch of fertile humus could be washed away in a single day of heavy rainfall on an unprotected sidehill. In just two generations such neglect had begun to transform the dark chestnut soils of one of the most fertile regions on earth into the exposed pale clods of clay nubbins.

The magnitude of the problem not only decreased Palouse fertility, but degraded fish and wildlife habitat and formed massive silt deposits in the Palouse, Snake, and Columbia rivers. Grangers worked with USDA soil scientists in Pullman and Moscow to identify and advocate measures to moderate the crisis. Grange publications and farmer workshops recommended various practices like divided slope farming and stream greenbelts to reduce Palouse erosion rates by over half without significantly reducing income.

As a reader of Plato, the Grange's erudite founder O. H. Kelly would have been aware that the ancient Greeks were among the first civilizations to note with grave concern the effects of unbridled farming on once abundant landscapes. Plato regarded the environmental changes of Hellenic Greece with alarm, as reflected in his dialogue with Critas: "What now remains of the formerly rich land is like the skeleton of a sick man, with all the fat and soft earth having wasted away and only the bare framework remaining.... The soil was deep, it absorbed and kept the water in the loam, and the water that soaked into the hills fed springs and running streams everywhere. Now the abandoned shrines at spots where formerly there were springs attest that our description of the land is true." In Greece, soil erosion continued at an alarming pace and fouled the waters of the northeast Mediterranean, weakening the region's economy, and forcing the Greeks to plant their grains and vines on the increasingly marginal soils of Attica's highest slopes.

It was one thing for researchers and observers to warn of impending calamity. Quite another was to implement changes on a farm during the grinding financial calamity of a postwar agricultural market collapse, widespread crop failure in 1924, drought, dust storms, and the Great Depression several years later. Grain growers had earlier urged scientists to get out of the laboratory and provide practical help in the field—the beginnings of a shared commitment of growers, researchers, and local agricultural businesses working together that would, over time, pay significant dividends in productivity and conservation. This collaboration soon began to show promise. In a daybook entry when wheat sold for 32 cents a bushel or used for livestock feed, Maurice McGregor wrote "a good farmer is one who farms his land with full regard for duty to the soil."

Landmark Congressional action advocated by Franklin Roosevelt created the USDA Agricultural Adjustment Administration (AAA) in 1933 and the Soil Conservation Service (SCS) in 1935. Not since the Lincoln administration had agricultural policy been so high on the federal agenda. The AAA introduced subsidy payments to farmers who voluntarily reduced production acreage by 15 to 20 percent. Maurice McGregor accurately predicted in 1936 "that it will probably fail of its purpose to greatly reduce the surpluses of wheat.... The payment for good farm practices will however be valuable and farmers can do some of the soil building they have wanted to do on each farm but which the pressure for money and cash crops have prevented them from trying." In September 1930, Pullman was designated one of the USDA's first ten Soil Erosion Experiment Stations under the leadership of William Rockie and Paul McGrew and in cooperation with the two nearby land-grant colleges. Following organization of the SCS, soil conservation enabling acts were passed in Washington, Idaho, and Oregon to fund state committees that would work with the new federal agency.[15]

Whidbey Island Pastoral
Ebey's Prairie near Coupeville, Washington
John Clement

Heirloom Plums
Tlithlow Farm, Joint Base Lewis-McChord, Tacoma

Glen Ian Apple Label
Alexander McGregor

Touchet Valley Fields
Near Waitsburg, Washington
John Clement

Long Anglais Cucumber
Ft. Vancouver National Historic Site

Parma Onion
Ft. Vancouver National Historic Site

Montreal Muskmelon
Ft. Vancouver National Historic Site

White Emergo Beans
Ft. Vancouver National Historic Site

Black Emmer
WSU-Mt. Vernon Research and Extension Center

Buckwheat
Ft. Vancouver National Historic Site

Scots Bere Barley
McGregor Research Station, Colfax, Washington

Sonora Wheat
WSU-Mt. Vernon Research and Extension Center

Yesteryear's Grain Samples
Tom Simpson Ranch near Rock Lake, Washington

Cradle Scythe and Red Fife Wheat Bundles
Ft. Nisqually Living History Museum, Tacoma, Washington

Furrows and Rainbow
Near Lowden, Washington
John Clement

Freeze Church Summer
North of Potlatch, Idaho
John Clement

CHAPTER VI

Hybridization at Home and Abroad

Be mindful that the lab'ring neat,
As you, may have their fill of meat.
And know, besides, ye must revoke
The patient ox unto the yoke,
And all go back unto the plough
And harrow, though they're hanged up now.

When the Washington Agricultural College, Experiment Station, and School of Science was established in Pullman in 1891, it was among the first colleges in the western United States to function as both an educational and research institution. With the 1890 reauthorization of the Morrill Act, land-grant schools were also established at Corvallis College (subsequently Oregon State University) and the University of Idaho in Moscow. Federal legislation enacted through the 1887 Hatch Act established agricultural experiment stations in cooperation with these affiliated Northwest schools.

The Washington Agricultural Research and Extension Office initially met with some skepticism from area farmers and ranchers, who were wary of outside experts. The Panic of 1893, coincidental with an unseasonably wet year, sent grain prices and production plunging to eighteen cents per bushel and much of the harvest was left to rot in the field. In spite of these circumstances, however, a group of progressive Palouse farmers joined together to purchase a 200-acre Pullman farm for test plots near the new school. Within several years the research teams had won over considerable numbers of their constituents by showing respect for their experience and demonstrating the practical results of scientific methods for crop and livestock improvement.

Missouri native William Spillman arrived in Pullman in 1894 to teach agriculture and direct related research at the behest of his longtime mentor and newly appointed school president, Enoch Bryan. Spillman's appointment marked the beginning of his career as one of the nation's foremost agricultural scientists and USDA administrators.

As Spillman began his research at the century's turn, farmers had learned that varieties suited to areas west of the Cascades did not thrive as well as others on the Columbia Plateau. Puget Sound weather reports from before 1900 indicate the driest years on record were wetter than the average years in eastern Oregon, while the coldest years in the Willamette Valley were still warmer than the average year on the Columbia Plateau. As they considered weather patterns along with distinct soil conditions and tillage practices, scientists like Spillman came to understand the need for selective crop breeding based on regional conditions. The advent of winter varieties suited to the more extreme climate of the inland Pacific Northwest held promise for enhanced yields since grains sown in the

William Spillman, 1900
Manuscripts, Archives, and Special Collections, Washington State University Libraries (MC 250.1.7)

fall commonly outperformed spring crops that matured in fewer days, and earlier ripening winter grains were generally less vulnerable to destructive diseases like stem and leaf rust.

When Spillman arrived in Washington, the most widely grown Northwest wheats were primarily spring varieties introduced from either Europe or Australia. These included the Palouse's soft yellow-white spring Little Club; Red Chaff, which was widely raised in transition areas and eastern Oregon; and the drought-resistant White (Lammas) Australian descendant Pacific Bluestem, which prevailed in the arid Big Bend country near Wenatchee. Many farmers in the Waterville Plateau area of Douglas County favored soft white Spanish Sonora. Substantial stands of Old White "Hudson Bay" Winter wheat still grew west of the Cascades. Popular Inland Northwest barleys at the

time included Coast, a Mediterranean descendant from Spanish California; early maturing Manshury, an Oriental six-row; and the two-row English Chevalier. Farmers used all for feed, but the latter two were also widely grown for brewing. Spillman found that most farmers were planting these and other tall, low-protein wheats in the spring instead of risking winterkill, since earlier plantings of these popular grains were susceptible to such damage.

Spillman's pioneering research would lead to the independent rediscovery of the groundbreaking Laws of Inheritance formulated by Mendel in the 1860s through his work with peas, a single genome species. Mendel's results had been buried in an obscure German scientific journal in 1866, and remained unknown to most of the world's scientific community, including Austria's own preeminent cereal hybridist of the time, Erich Tschermak von Seysenegg, who independently discovered Mendel's laws in 1900, as did Karl Correns in Germany and Dutch scientist Hugo de Vries. Adding to Spillman's challenge was his work with wheat's complex triple genome.

During Spillman's formative Pullman years, he also deliberated on other important issues related to grain production. Through research and observation, he came to understand that agricultural and social wellbeing depended on crop diversity, sustainable farming practices, and vibrant local markets. The region's grain monocultures, soil erosion rates, and dependency on Liverpool and Chicago grain sales threatened ruination. Spillman was challenged by the demands of a complex

global industry in flux. He would apply his scientific knowledge to grain hybridization in order to improve production, as well as his good sense as an outspoken early advocate for sustainability through holistic systems of farm management.

The historic decade of Spillman's tenure in Pullman witnessed the introduction of many new wheat varieties by the USDA, private Eastern seed firms, and Northwest land development groups seeking to promote sales of their properties. The Northern Pacific Railroad's Oregon Improvement Company, for example, tested over a hundred varieties in 1900 at its experimental farm near Walla Walla. Virtually all crops grown in the region at that time, however, experienced problems. Red

James "Cashup" Davis's Steptoe Butte Hotel Foyer Grain Display, c. 1885
Washington State Library Archives (WCL WSU033)

Chaff was often damaged by Northwest winters; Baart, a South African spring variety introduced via Australia, did not yield well; and semi-hard Red Russian (not to be confused with soft winter Russian Red), was of inferior milling quality, so brought lower prices. The earliest true winter habit introductions took place in the 1890s with varieties from the Midwest and East including Diehl Mediterranean (Michigan Bronze), and Martin (Michigan) Amber—a Red May selection. These tended to shatter easily, however, so were soon discontinued. Others that endured, like the Goldcoin (Fortyfold) and soft red winter Jones Fife, were still susceptible to similar loss.[1]

The most promising grains for the soil and climatic conditions of the Columbia Plateau appeared to be the starchy soft white spring wheats, which found ready markets for domestic and foreign consumption in noodles, pastry, and breakfast cereals. Spillman reasoned that crossing the dependable Columbia spring wheats Little Club and Red Chaff with winter wheats of desirable traits offered the best hope for a breakthrough new variety ideally suited to the region. Spillman also sought to hybridize for higher gluten and less bran to satisfy millers. With these ambitious intentions in mind, Spillman embarked on a five-year quest "to combine [traits] into a single variety of winter wheat that will not fall down, be subject to smut or rust, will sell as well as Bluestem, and yield as well as Red Chaff or Little Club." He studied profiles from a global array of samples including semi-hard red Lancaster (resistant to Hessian fly), Tasmanian Red (high yielding), soft white Theiss (an early maturing "Turkey Red" variety from Hungary), and familiar Oregon Club (strong straw). In the end he decided to cross the four dominant Northwest varieties with six other winter *vulgare* types from the Midwest—rust-resistant Valley (German Amber), high yielding Jones Fife, soft red Farquhar, semi-hard Lehigh, white chaff Emporium, and red-grained McPherson and White Track.

Armed with years of practical experience and newfound regional insights, Spillman initiated an ambitious breeding program in 1899 using Little Club, Bluestem, and Red Chaff for foundation stock with which he crossed eleven winter wheats, including Turkey Red and Jones Fife, which he felt offered the best prospects for hybridization. Assisting in Spillman's initial crosses were Professor E. E. Elliot and a research assistant, H. F. Blanchard. Of the one thousand plants they pollinated, only 303 became fertile, and a late winter wash-out on the plots near the school's barn further reduced the number of survivors to just 149. Second-generation plants were seeded in the fall of 1900 and these headed out the following spring as mixtures of "all sorts of types," which Spillman organized by head shape (club/common), awn (bald/bearded), glume (pubescent/glabrous husk), and glume color (brown/light). Meticulous inspection and record keeping produced mathematical tables that led to the momentous formulation of the Law of Recombination: "The first rows that headed out revealed nineteen distinct types of wheat [later found to be twenty-two].... Instantly the thought occurred that we did not simply have great variability, but that in each row we simply had new combinations of the characteristics of the original parents." The modern science of crop genetics had been born.[2]

Recognizing the significance of Spillman's work for Northwest farmers and the world of science, President Bryan encouraged the young researcher to personally present his research to a national audience. Equipped with a three-by-three-foot display case of hybrid exemplars, Spillman journeyed to Washington, DC, in November 1901 to address the convention of American Agricultural Experiment Stations Association. In a paper soon published by the USDA and London's Royal Horticultural Society, Spillman reported, "...[I]t seems entirely possible to predict, in the main, what types will be result from crossing any two established varieties and approximately the proportion of each type that will appear in the next generation." The pragmatic possibilities of predictive selection through hybridization stunned many in the audience, who unacquainted with Mendel's work, still relied on crop improvement through the exhausting and essentially random process of landrace selections.[3]

Varieties Spillman used in his original crosses, as presented in his 1901 Washington, D.C., convention paper

COMPACTUM-VULGARE CROSSES

-Little Club♀ x Emporium♂
-Little Club♀ x Jones' Winter Fife♂
-White Track♀ x Little Club♂
-Little Club♀ x Valley♂
-Emporium♀ x Little Club♂
-Farquhar♀ x Little Club♂
-Valley♀ x Little Club♂
-Little Club♀ x Turkey♂

INTER-VULGARE CROSSES

-Red Chaff♀ x White Track♂
-Red Chaff♀ x McPherson♂
-Red Chaff♀ x Jones' Winter Fife♂
-Red Chaff♀ x Farquhar♂
-Red Chaff♀ x Lehigh♂

Spillman summarized resulting hybrid "types" in a series of trait tables indicating ratios of occurrence. The Little Club♀ x Turkey♂ cross, for example, provided the following results:

	Awnless	Awned	Ratio
Types I and II (heads long)	130.5	44.0	21.9 : 1
Types II and IV (heads intermediate)	222.0	125.9	1.7 : 1
Types V and VI (heads short)	120.6	46.0	2.6 : 1

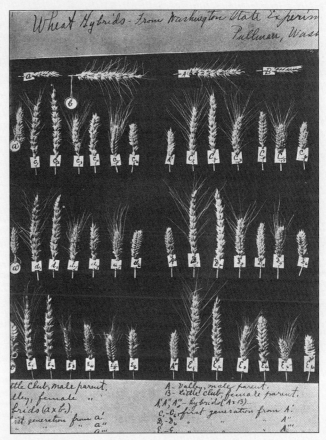

William Spillman's Hybrid Wheat Display, 1901
USDA, *After a Hundred Years: The 1962 Yearbook of Agriculture*

THE GILDED AGE OF GRAINS

Northwest grains competed well against varieties from throughout the nation and around the globe at the 1893 World Columbian Exposition in Chicago. The themes of agriculture and nature were especially prominent at the fair and would significantly influence twentieth-century American culture. Songwriter Katharine Lee Bates drew inspiration for the "amber waves of grain" in her *America the Beautiful* after viewing the hundreds of bountiful sheaves on display. Visitors were awed by Kirtland Cutter and Karl Malmgren's spacious Idaho Building, a two-story log structure with distinctive structural and furnishing motifs of cereal grains and Native American art. Salem author Olive S. England represented Oregon writers with

Lewis & Clark Centennial Exposition
Palace of Agriculture, Portland, 1905
Special Collections, University of Washington Libraries (UW 35770)

the publication of her anthology, *Ceres, A Harvest Home Festival*. The book featured twenty-eight poems and namesake four-act pageant featuring the kind of melodramatic interplay between the Greek goddess of agriculture and rural Americans that delighted nineteenth-century audiences.

Analysis of the Columbian Exhibition's wheat entries by USDA Chief Chemist Harvey Wiley revealed that three Northwest landrace improved selections exceeded commercial "best quality" standards—soft white spring Sonora, hard winter Turkey Red, and semi-hard white spring (Pacific) Bluestem. A specimen of the latter was entered with sheaves of White Wonder oats, Northumberland barley, and Pride of Butte (California) club wheat by Tumwater's William Owen Bush, who had traveled the Oregon Trail with his father George Washington Bush and established prosperous farms near Olympia. Other highly rated regional wheats exhibited at the 1893 Exhibition included the Old Oregon Country's enduring White Winter from the Willamette Valley, and the spring varieties Red Fife and a new high yielding Canadian introduction, Campell's White Chaff from Spallumcheen in the upper Okanogan Valley. Other British Columbia

wheat entries included Seneca Chief, a semi-hard red winter, the white bearded winter Blue Democrat, and Ladoga. Vernon-Spallumcheen farmers also displayed a recent two-row barley selection from England, Carter's Prize Prolific.

Owen Bush's prominence at the World's Fair led to his appointment that fall to the Advisory Council of the World Congress Auxiliary on Farm Culture and Cereal Industry. He had long promoted Northwest grain research and marketing and had been a prime mover in organizing the Western Washington Industrial Association for this purpose. His Washington grain display at the 1876 Centennial International Exhibition in Philadelphia—the first World's Fair to be held in the United States, had received the gold medal for "World's Best Wheat." Smithsonian officials offered to make the resplendent display a special exhibit at the nation's preeminent museum where it was viewed by tens of thousands of visitors in the 1870s and '80s.[4]

With the theme, "Westward the Course of Empire," Oregon residents were also keen to showcase the region's economic accomplishments to a world audience. The 1905 Lewis & Clark Centennial Exposition in Portland provided an opportu-

---

Milestones of Early Modern Crop Improvement

(After M. Carleton, 1920, et al., with representative wheat varieties)

1690-1720: Rudolf Camerarius (Tübingen, Germany), *De Sexu Plantarum Epistola* (1694) first describes plant fertilization

1750s: Carl Linnaeus (Uppsala, Sweden), *Species Plantarum* (1753) introduces modern classification of wheat species

1760s-90s: Joseph Kölreuter (Karlsruhe, Germany) and "Parental Transformation" in first controlled hybrid crosses (tobacco)

1810s-20s: Patrick Shirreff (Haddingtonshire, Scotland) and "Variety Isolation" (Shirreff's Squarehead)

1830s: John Le Couteur (Bellevue, Isle of Jersey) and "Individual Form Separation" (Bellevue Talavera)

1840s-50s: Louis de Vilmorin (Verriers, France) and "Individual Variation 'Force' Factor Theory"

1850s: Frederick Hallett (Brighton, England) and "Generational Pedigree Selection" (Hallett's Golden Drop)

1860s: Gregor Mendel (Brünn, Austria) and Mendel's Laws of Inheritance

1870s-80s: Henri de Vilmorin (Verriers, France) and "Pure-Line Selection" (Dattel)

1870s: Cyrus Pringle (Charlotte, Vermont) and Eastern Wheat Hybridization (Defiance)

1870s: A. N. Jones (Leroy, New York) and "Composite Crossing" (Jones Fife)

1880s: Ainsworth Blount (Ft. Collins, Colorado) and Rust-resistant Prairie Hybridization (Ruby)

1890s: Hjalmar Nilsson (Svalöf, Sweden) and "Single Plant Pedigree Culture" (Sol)

1890s: John Garton (Newton-le-Willows, England) and "Multiple Cross Fertilization" (Regenerated Fife)

1890s: Willett M. Hays (St. Paul, Minnesota) and "Centgener Pure Line Selection" (Minnesota 163)

1890s: William Saunders (Ottawa, Canada) and Northern Great Plains Hybridization (Marquis)

1890s: William Farrer (Lambrigg, Australia) and "Selective Crossing" (Federation)

1890s: William Spillman (Pullman, Washington) and Rediscovery of Mendel's Laws for Hybridization (Hybrid 128)

1899: (First) International Conference on Hybridization and Plant Breeding, Royal Horticultural Society, London

1906: Aaron Aaronsohn (Haifa, Palestine) identifies wild emmer at Rosh Pinna as the progenitor of modern wheats and proposes ancestral grains as valuable sources for crop breeding programs

---

nity to do so, and twenty-one nations participated in the event commemorating the American explorers. There, visitors could also stroll through rows of cereal grain and other international crop exhibits in the domed Spanish Renaissance-inspired Palace of Agriculture.

In addition to displays of grains like Hudson Bay White Winter wheat, Pacific Bluestem, and Scotch barleys, other award-winning Oregon and Washington varieties indicate the wide reach of progressive farmers who displayed new and obscure grains found through attempts to identify those best suited to Northwest microclimates. Among other cultivars that scarcely appear in any USDA reports of the era were the wheats Carter's Queen, Dooley, Fishpole, Tracy, Sweetbread, Salt Lake Club, and German Red; while barleys included Wharton, Benyon, and Highland Chief (likely

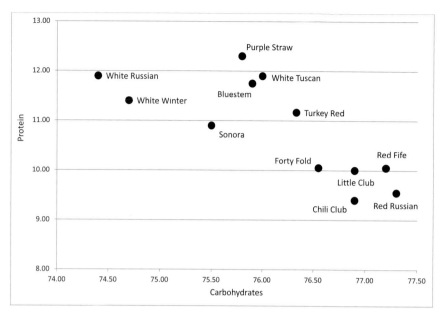

Nutritive Values of Northwest Wheats (1905/1910)

Sources: R. Thatcher (Washington), 1907:20-21; J. Jones, et. al. (Idaho), 1911:27-34; D. Stephens and C. E. Hill (Oregon), 1917:34.

Processing for flour tends to reduce overall protein and increase carbohydrate levels due to removal of bran and other parts. Remaining percentages of kernel composition include moisture, ash, and other trace minerals. The relative range of nutritive values remains consistent among varieties, but varies in samples due to climate, soil conditions, seeding date, and farming practices.

named for Highland, Oregon, rather than a Scottish homeland). Perhaps more surprising are the number of new oat varieties that had been introduced to the region by the early years of the new century—Harper's, White Holland, Danish Island, Haggett's, and two with names suggesting Spanish/Moorish landrace origins, Texas Red and Ambler's Rustproof.[5]

In June 1901, the *Colfax Gazette* proclaimed a breakthrough in crop improvement at Pullman with the capitalized headline, "NEW SPILLMAN WHEAT," and reported on his speech that month to growers in Portland where the Pullman scientist explained his methodology and challenges. The new varieties—all of which were club-headed—included hard white winter Hybrid 60 (released in 1905), followed in 1907 by Hybrid 63 (Little Club x Turkey Red = White Hybrid), and the soft red springs H108 (Jones Fife x Red Russian = Red Hybrid) and H123 (Jones Fife/Little Club x Red Russian = Red Walla Walla). Soft white winter H128 (Jones Fife x Little Club) and H143

(White Track x Little Club = Shot Club) were also released in 1907. Of this historic collection, Spillman's Hybrid 128 seemed to represent the best combination of preferred traits—winter hardy, rust-resistant, and productive. Within just three years of their release, broad stands of Spillman's new varieties pulsed magnificently on a half-million acres across the Columbia Plateau. They remained in production for decades and typically yielded ten to twenty bushels per acre higher than the parent varieties.

The Pullman plant breeder drew world acclaim for his accomplishments, but he lamented farming practices throughout the region and especially in the Palouse that resulted in severe water erosion and depletion of soil fertility. Many growers who sought increased production with Spillman's new hybrids ignored his recommendations on soil conservation and improvements. "Farmers make no effort to keep up the stock of humus in the soil," he wrote in the 1903 USDA *Yearbook* with renewed suggestions for green manure cropping and commercial mineral amendments. The opening lines of his article on farm management included a holistic definition of farm management expressed in more than empirical terms: "The most successful system of farming is that which gives the largest profit, leaves the soil in condition to yield more crops, and brings to the farmer and those dependent on him the largest measure of happiness."[6]

During Spillman's eight-year tenure in Pullman, William Farrar's experiments in Australia produced the drought-hardy "great wheat" Federation that would be widely grown across the Columbia Basin in the early twentieth century. His experiments had begun in 1894 after he selected an early maturing purple straw wheat, possibly a

Hybridization

Mark Carleton described the tedious process of artificial hybridization used by breeders like Spillman and Lawrence in a manual for farmers and agronomists: "The lemma and palea of the flower to be cross-pollinated are spread apart, and with the forceps, the three stamens [of the female parent plant] are taken out bodily.... At the same time, or soon after, pollen is taken from the fully ripened flowers [anthers] of the plant selected for the male parent, and scattered within the opened flower that is emasculated, after which it is smoothed back into its former condition as nearly as possible....[If pollination] is at all delayed, the spike or panicle should be covered with a paper bag, as a precaution against the accidental introduction of foreign pollen."

The seedling progeny, designated an "F1 hybrid" (for Latin *filium*, child) was adroitly collected and tended in pots and trays under supervision of a farm foreman and workers to provide increase for promising stands in rows and small plots. First and second generation (F1 and F2) specimens were usually raised at the main state research units near Pullman and others established at nearby Moscow's University of Idaho (1892) and at Oregon State College in Corvallis (1888). Successful new strains were then distributed to regional stations for third and fourth generation field trials to "breed true" to the desired traits on the distinct soils of each district. Capable oversight of the process required the patience and indulgence of a caring parent since desired heritable traits often do not appear until after several years of generational development.

At each stage extensive testing and documentation was done on yield, weight, disease resistance, milling quality, and other agronomic traits. The few crosses that emerged as commercially viable were then distributed to growers.

Developing hard red wheats better adapted to the Columbia Basin proved challenging since crosses with popular white wheats created low-protein, high-starch qualities yielding overly viscous bread flour. While strong markets continued overseas for Northwest soft white wheat pastry and noodle flours, Idaho agronomists increasingly turned attention in the early 1900s to improving hard red varieties like Turkey Red that thrived with others like Fultz and Silver Chaff (Red Clawson) on the state's southeastern Snake River plateau.[7,8]

pure Purple Straw variety of Italian landrace origin, from a field of Improved Fife. He crossed the plant with Yandilla, an earlier cross of Improved Fife with Indian Etawah, to produce soft white Federation, released in 1901, which became Australia's dominant variety by 1910. Early-maturing Federation also yielded well in the Columbia Plateau and was used for crosses by Claude Lawrence and E. E. Elliot for production in low rainfall areas. Two Australian selections of the grain, White and Hard Federation, were found to be excellent hard white spring bread wheats and were widely raised on the Columbia Plateau in the 1920s.

Only about half of the increase in American grain production between 1870 and 1940 can be attributed to labor-mechanical improvements. The other half resulted from biological innovations of professional grain breeders and farmer culturists whose persistent work with selections and hybrids made significant strides in developing disease-resistant varieties adapted to regional environments. Agricultural historian J. F. Shepherd observes that grain breeders have long characterized their work as having to "run fast to stand still." Their work enabled farmers nationwide to maintain pre-war average yields of about twenty bushels per acre, although Northwest harvests were commonly twice that amount.[9]

American brewers likewise turned their attention at this time to research for improved barley selections to improve product consistency. In a 1906 address to the American Brewing Institute, senior USDA barley researcher David Fairchild lamented the fact that "no such thing as a pure race of barley is yet grown [in the United States] on an extensive scale," and pledged the department's resources to developing "consistency from mixed stands." The Pacific Slope hosted some of

Morrill Hall
Robert Smith

the nation's most extensive acreage of brewing barleys at the turn of the century with Chevalier, Manshury, Scotch, and Bay Brewing (California Coast) still representing the most widespread. However, Fairchild recognized that as descendants of European landraces these grains exhibited a wide range of physical attributes and kernel characteristics within each group. Willamette Valley and Columbia Plateau farmers also experimented during these years with winter, shatter-resistant White and Purple Hulless barleys.

Using a metaphor that likely appealed to his audience, Fairchild asked, "Why should a brewer expect to manufacture a uniform quality of beer from barleys of varying character any more than a wine-maker should expect a uniform wine from a mixture of different kinds of grapes?" Fairchild then cited Moravian Hanna and a Swedish variety from Svalöf as recent examples of "pure races" could also be developed for North American growers through careful "inspection and selection." Robert Wahl of Chicago's prestigious Wahl-Henius Institute of Fermentology responded by suggesting that traditional European two-row malting barleys might prove wholly unsuited to the distinct agronomic conditions in the United States and Canada. He wrote that six-row "pure races" might prove superior to "Old Country" varieties. The give-and-

take played out in issues of the *American Brewers Review* for some months resulting in USDA initiatives to test a range of both two- and six-row malting barleys for improved Midwest and West Coast production.[10]

CARLETON AND EXPERIMENT STATION GRAIN BREEDING

Following Spillman's departure from Pullman in 1902 to serve as founding director of the USDA Bureau of Farm Economics, the wheat breeding program was capably continued by Claude Lawrence and E. E. Elliot. In his new capacity, Spillman collaborated with USDA Head Cerealist, Mark A. Carleton, the legendary "Plant Explorer" (an official department title) who had extensively studied Midwestern grains like the high protein Turkey Red brought to Kansas in the 1870s and White Spring (Vernal) Emmer to the Dakotas soon afterward by German immigrant farmers from southwestern Russia. Carleton's research at the department's Botany Division benefited from the work of his predecessor, Niels Hansen, a native of Denmark and Iowa Agricultural College graduate who traveled extensively throughout Russia, Turkestan, and China from June 1897 to March 1898. Hansen's primary interest was in forage crops but among the several boxcar loads of seeds he collected were grain samples including high quality Volga and Black Sea region hard red bread wheats. Such work helped inaugurate a new era of grain globalization.

Agronomists like Hansen and Carleton became convinced that U.S. crop improvement would best benefit from crosses with Eurasian landraces like the winter hardy and rust-resistant Crimean Turkeys. These were a group of hard wheats with Slavic geonyms like Ghirka, Kharkov, and Stavropol of the Ukraine-Russian Kursk region—Canadian Red Fife's likely ancestral homeland; and the spring durums Arnautka (from Taurida), Kubanka, Pererodka), and Beloturka, the Volga "White Turkey" highly prized by millers for pasta. Long considered Europe's bread basket for exporting substantial quantities of wheat to the continent's major urban centers, Ukraine's remarkable variety of geoclimatic conditions had spawned a wide range of winter and spring grain varieties which Carleton sought to correlate to similar conditions in the United States. His other breeding considerations for use of Turkeys in the America—where strains were sometimes known as Red Russian—included early maturation and resistance to lodging and shattering.

Carleton taught himself conversational Russian, studied Eurasian geography, and corresponded with A. F. Batalin, founding director of Russia's Ministry of Land Cultivation's Bureau of Applied Botany and director of the Imperial Gardens in St. Petersburg. Batalin facilitated Carleton's ambitious travel arrangements. The burly American traveled widely across Russia in the summer of 1898, from the bountiful golden harvests of the lower Volga and Crimean Taurida to the dun-colored desolations of the Khirgiz Steppe. Carleton obtained seed for experimental use and met other prominent Russian grain researchers like M. C. Flaksberger, who had extensively studied Crimean and Volga wheats. Carleton's itinerary also included a side trip to Sweden, where research by N. Hjalmar Nilsson on the famed Svalöf Institute's 2,500 acres had begun to show the limits of landrace improved selections. Nilsson had meticulously noted botanical changes in many generations of pedigreed cereal grain "elementary species" and concluded that traits influencing production offered a finite range

"Carleton's Fantastic Hunt for Wheat in Russia"
The Country Gentleman (1926)

of possibilities. But the newly emerging methods of hybridization provided plant breeders with a seemingly endless universe of combinations for crop improvement. Varieties could be refined for desired product qualities and specific geographic settings to develop "the right kind of cereal for each place."

When Carleton arrived home several months later, rural newspapers in the Northwest carried numerous articles on his travels and grain improvement work. He returned from this first trip abroad laden with 130 vegetable, grass, and grain accessions. These included thirty-seven bread and durum wheat varieties, as well as millets, oats, ryes, and barleys. Based on comparative studies of Russian and American soils and imbued with the zeal of a missionary, Carleton recommended a group of flavorful grains with breeding potential for the Pacific Northwest including Ghirka, Volga Sandomir (native to Poland's Radom district), and Kharkov (Ukraine) bread wheats, Khirgiz Kubanka and Sari-Bugda (from Baku) durums, Shugan (from Turkestan) rye, and emmer. In 1904 Carleton procured hardy winter Black Emmer (Russian polba, Italian farro), through de Vilmorin in France.[11]

Carleton's prolific range of USDA publications on grain production included an unusual 1904 work through which he sought to acquaint American consumers with the wider culinary array of wheat-based foods popular throughout Europe.

Although Carleton's peculiar single-mindedness did not endear him to USDA colleagues, the labors of this Johnny Appleseed of global grains revolutionized American grain production and consumption. He noted that most Americans had long used flour almost exclusively for breads and simple noodle dishes, but his advocacy for wider use of durum for "graham" whole grain flour was unpopular with many millers who operated equipment unsuited for its production.

Carleton's two European tours had introduced the inquisitive traveler to the savory universe of continental tables and whole grain dishes through acquaintances with prominent chefs and the newly thriving cookbook industry. Scouring through such works as *French Cookery for English Homes*, *Harland's Complete Cookbook*, and *European and American Cuisine*, Carleton assembled a delicious feast of recipes little known to the mainstream American palate except in ethnic enclaves. His *USDA Plant Industry Bulletin 70* included a substantial section of recipes for raviolis, timbales, croquettes, and puddings, as well as vermicelli, macaroni, and semolina soups. He also listed leading US producers of quality pasta products including A. F. Ghiglione of Seattle, Tacoma's J. C. Martinolich, and Portland's Columbo Paste Company.[12]

On Carleton's 1898 visit to Russia, he sampled festive Russian white *kalách* bread (from Old Slavonic *kolo*,"round, circle") in Moscow and judged it to be the most flavorful he had ever tasted. His hosts said the flour came from wheat raised on the Kirghiz Steppe of southwestern Russia, which also influenced Carleton's decision to procure samples from that region. By 1930, Russian landraces and hybridized variants represented approximately forty percent of all wheat raised in the United States.

Selections by Carleton, Hansen, and Spillman significantly contributed to Northwest wheat development in the early 1900s by replacing many spring varieties with hardier and higher yielding winter wheats from Ukraine and Russia. Hard red Karmont, a Kharkov selection made in 1911 at the Montana's AES Judith Basin Branch in Moccasin, was grown throughout northwestern Montana after its commercial release in 1921. Black Emmer

was also grown on a limited basis in the Skagit Valley, an area with mild climate and black loam that had long been synonymous with oat production. Among oat varieties Carleton collected during his European travels were several he recommended for Northwest growers including Tobolsk (Early Siberian) and Svalöf's Swedish Select (Silvermine), a white spring oat derived from the French landrace, Ligowa. Swedish Select soon became popular in the area along with an 1892 Svalöf Probsteier white oat selection, Victory. But closure of many upper Skagit Valley logging camps by 1900 depressed the price of oats, and Skagit farmers sought alternative grain and vegetable crops. Immigrants continued to come to the scenic region, however, including a substantial colony of Dutch farmers who began settling around Oak Harbor in 1895 to establish dairies and orchards that contributed to the area's economic recovery.[13]

Results of Northwest college and experiment station grain research were more fully disseminated among area farmers following the enactment of the Smith-Lever Act of 1914, which established an agricultural extension service cooperative among federal, state, and county levels. The work of county extension agents facilitated rural education in farm management practices, 4-H programs, and home economics demonstrations. Dozens of Northwest extension service bulletins covered practical topics for farmers and homemakers ranging from grain disease prevention and potato storage to home canning and chicken coop design. State legislatures funded a series of Farmer Institutes and demonstration trains in cooperation with the Northern Pacific Railroad. Seventy-one institutes were held in Washington from 1907-08, and four special trains toured dozens of rural communities during those years throughout the Inland Pacific Northwest.

Millers worldwide came to prize Northwest wheats for their high quality flour and named both improved strains and hybrids among the best—Goldcoin (also known as Fortyfold and in Canada as American Banner), Federation, Baart, and Bluestem for pastries; and Turkey Red, Baart, and Marquis (usually pronounced mar´kwiss) for breads.

Lawrence and others patiently worked for years with experimental varieties in Pullman and Moscow and in 1918 released Triplet, the two stations' first lax, or head-type selection. The soft red winter variety was a four-way cross of Jones Fife/Little Club with Jones Fife/Turkey Red. From about 1910-1920, Turkey Red and Jones Fife prevailed in the Big Bend; Red Russian (Turkey Red) and Goldcoin (Fortyfold) competed with Little Club in the Palouse. Triplet substantially replaced Red Chaff in transition areas despite severe irritation to horses and field hands during harvest from its pubescent chaff. However, like other varieties of the time, Triplet's kernels became infested with the black fungus dwarf bunt, or "stinking smut" (*Tilletia caries* or *T. foetida*) that drastically reduced yields in the 1920s and resulted in crops that failed the meet the quality standards demanded by shippers and millers.

The soft red spring wheat Mayview, named for the Snake River railway siding southwest of Pullman opposite Wawawai, was found growing in a field there by Washington State College plant breeder Edwin Gaines in 1917 and had come from a Goldcoin (Fortyfold) admixture stand that had been raised for several years in the vicinity. Another club variety unique to the area, the soft red winter wheat Coppei, grew from a 1907 selection found in a field along Coppei Creek near Waitsburg and was believed to be a natural cross between Jones Fife and Little Club. Mayview spread to some parts of Idaho and Oregon, but its popularity declined due to the large awn size. Mayview's namesake grain tramway from the top of the bluff to the Snake River siding became a regional architectural wonder that could transport nearly one hundred thousand sacks of grain each year from Garfield County growers. Area farmers in the 1880s had first fashioned a simple chute down which bulk seed flowed, but the distance created enough friction to injure the grain. They next replaced the pipes with a mile-long tram resembling a ski lift with buckets that snaked back and forth down the canyon, but mechanical problems recurrently interfered with its operation. Finally in 1890, a straight flatcar tramway, eighteen hundred feet long and supported by beamed trestles was built to transport as many as twenty-seven hundred sacks a day down to the river siding. The Mayview Tram remained in operation until 1942, providing a critical link in the region's grain transportation network.[14]

INTERNATIONAL COOPERATION: GAINES AND VAVILOV

Plant geneticist Edwin F. Gaines began breeding for resistance to smutting bunt fungus in 1915 at Washington's Main Experiment Station in Pullman using resistant Crimean varieties collected by Carleton in Russia. Gaines's research led nine years later to the release of the hard red variety Ridit, followed by the soft white club wheat Albit in 1926, a popular variety originally developed in 1920 by crossing Hybrid 128 with a bunt-resistant Black Sea winter wheat, White Odessa. The scientists also took into account farmer concerns about marketability since the hard classes were used domestically for breads and breakfast cereals while most whites were still exported to China and other Asian markets for making noodles.

Gaines selflessly shared the results of his research with scientists worldwide while also devoting attention to his considerable teaching load in Pullman and doctoral studies at Harvard. In 1921 he completed his dissertation on the genetics of bunt resistance in wheat. He felt a special sense of gratitude to his Soviet contemporary, the renowned biologist and geographer Nikolai Vavilov, whom he visited during a European research tour in 1930. Vavilov, originator of the "centers of origin" theory for world grains (a phrase first used by Darwin), had been a protégé of Robert Regel, Russia's preeminent pre-war era botanist. Regel appointed the brilliant young Saratov University scientist head of all Russia's agricultural experiment stations on the very day the Bolshevik Revolution broke out in 1917. Vavilov was a prime-mover in the organization of the first All-Russian Conference of Plant Breeders in Saratov in 1920. The group's June 4 opening session marked a milestone for world science as Vavilov delivered his famous paper, "The Law of Homologous Series in Hereditary Variation," in which he put forth the first hypothesis on mutation. For subsequent related research that led to the formulation of a law on the periodicity of heritable characteristics, Vavilov was proclaimed the Mendeleyev of biology. Although Vavilov's enthusiastic grasp of problem definition in crop breeding proved easier than problem solving, upon Regel's death later in 1920 he was named director of the Agricultural Ministry's Department of Applied Botany and Plant Breeding, and went on to organize the Soviet Academy of Agricultural Sciences.

Vavilov derived many of his insights from extensive travels "across the whole of Scripture" in Transjordan (Israel) and Palestine where he pored over religious texts in order "to reconstruct a picture of agriculture in biblical times." His ideas were significantly influenced by the field studies of German botanist Frederich Körnicke (1828-1908), curator of the Imperial Botanical Gardens in St. Petersburg in the 1850s, and Aaron Aaronsohn, Director of the Agricultural Experiment Station at Haifa, Palestine. In an article published in 1889 on the history of world grains, Körnicke identified a specimen of wild emmer found in the collection of the National Museum of Vienna as the progenitor of all modern wheats. He urged botanists to conduct expeditions in the foothills of Mt. Hermon where it had been found in order to better document its origin and range.

Aaronsohn subsequently recorded his historic 1906 discovery of the grain: "When I began to extend my search to the cultivated lands [near Rosh Pinna], along the edges of roads and in the crevices of rocks, I found a few stools of the wild Triticum. Later I came across it in great abundance, and the most astonishing thing about it was the large number of forms it displayed." Vavilov followed Aaronsohn's itinerary to locate this relict stand of the famed "Mother of Grains" and found it growing nearly forty inches tall with stiff, six-inch long beards. His further research demonstrated that emmer's ancestral range extended throughout northern Trans-Jordan and into Turkey.[15]

Vavilov met Edwin Gaines and his botanist wife, Xerpha, at the celebrated 1932 Sixth International Genetics Congress at Cornell University in Ithaca, New York, which was attended by some five hundred fifty of the world's leading geneticists. The conclave's highlight was the much-anticipated delivery of Vavilov's presentation on geographic distribution of wild cultivar relatives. His paper focused on the importance of preserving threatened landraces and their progenitors for future breeding stock and pure research. He further postulated the origin of modern hard red wheats in the Fertile Crescent ("southwestern Asia") and soft whites in northwestern Africa. Vavilov also described ancient selection methods by which early agriculturalists unconsciously conducted spontaneous variety selections.

In spite of myriad challenges in hosting such a prestigious event in the midst of the Great Depression, the Gaineses invited Vavilov to Pullman while on his extended trip to several western states. Vavilov accepted the offer and spent several weeks in the late summer and fall of 1932 touring grain research stations in eastern Washington and Oregon, clad in an ever-present tie and fedora. A decade later, Vavilov died in prison, a victim of Stalin's purges.[16]

OREGON RESEARCH

Corvallis's Eastern Oregon Branch Experiment Station for cereal grain research opened at Moro in 1910. Outlying nurseries affiliated with the extensive Moro operation were developed in the 1920s at Pendleton, Dufur, Lexington, Burns, and Kent. The problem of treating wheat, barley, and oat seed for bunt was the focus of intense research begun in 1912 headed by David E. Stephens at Moro and Jessie Rose at Corvallis. Chemical compounds with formaldehyde, copper, mercury, and calcium were tested on a range of grains. Stephens and Rose eventually recommended that seed grain be soaked in a one pound to five- to ten-gallon solution of copper sulfate (blue vitrol or "bluestone") for up to four hours, which substantially reduced the problem. Moro station superintendent H. J. C. Umberger and E. F. Gaines at WSC focused attention on trials of a smut-resistant oat selection made by Mark Carleton from grain exhibited by Louis Dreyfus at the 1904 Louisiana Purchase

Exposition in St. Louis. The resistant oat, which was named Markton, a contraction of Carleton's name (and renamed Carleton in 1922), resulted from a selection made by Umberger in 1911. Subsequent crosses in the 1920s at Aberdeen, Idaho, with Carleton and the Baltic oat landrace Victory, led to a half-dozen smut-resistant varieties that virtually eliminated effects of the disease in the Pacific Northwest for over a decade.

Northwest barley production also benefited from USDA research at Moro and Aberdeen. White Smyrna was introduced from a 1901 selection of the two-row Turkish spring barley and yielded well in the drier districts of eastern Oregon and southern Idaho. Six-row spring Trebi, released at Aberdeen in 1918, came from a 1909 selection made by H. V. Harlan from a sample of barley from the Black Sea coastal city of Trebizond, Turkey. The variety proved to be resistant to Northwest rusts and became a highly sought Northwest brewing grain. Enduring California Coast (Bay Brewing), a six-rowed eighteenth-century remnant from Spanish America, grew along the Pacific Slope to Washington. A spring variety used for brewing and feed, Coast was also notable for its distinctive blue-tinged kernels. A 1920s selection by botanist Luther Burbank of a hulless sport in a field of California Coast led to his release of Burbank Hulless in 1927.

Eastern Oregon experiment station staff developed important soft white club wheats like Alicel (Goldcoin x Hybrid 128) in 1919, Rex (White Odessa x Hard Federation) in 1926, and Elgin (1932) that were raised on hundreds of thousands of acres in the 1930s. This research proved the value of shorter stalk, smut-resistant grains and would lead Northwest grain breeders a generation later to the forefront of the Green Revolution. The Puget Sound (Ross) Station had opened near Puyallup in 1895 to conduct research for the needs of west side farmers, and other Washington agricultural units followed near Lind (Dryland Research Station) in 1915, followed by Vancouver, Prosser (irrigation), Wenatchee (tree fruit), Mt. Vernon, Winthrop, and Waterville.[17]

Oregon agronomists had made great effort since the establishment of the Oregon State College (OSC) Main Experiment Station to determine which wheats from other parts of the country and world might yield better than the Pacific Bluestem, White Winter (also called Oregon Winter), and other varieties that farmers had been growing since the frontier era. Early field reports list myriad wheats seldom found anywhere else in the literature of the time and indicate the remarkable reach of pioneering Oregon agronomists like Hiram T. French and George Coote. Some one hundred different wheats were grown on OSC test plots by 1900 using samples collected from experiment stations and commercial vendors in the US and worldwide. Some colorful names suggest continental and overseas origins—Tuscan Island, Hindustan, German Emperor, French Imperial, Tasmanian Red, Assiniboia Fife, Ontario Wonder, Mayflower, New York Spring; while others reflect Colorado breeder Ainsworth Blount's interest in mineralogy—Granite, Jasper, Chalcedony, Gypsum, Amethyst, Beryl, Emerald, Sapphire, most of which were Red Fife (Halychanka/Ghirka) crosses.

Unknown sources contributed to some of the most poetic sounding—Lost Nation, Northcotis, Black Prolific. The patient labors of scientists and workers who tended these plots year after year found only a few to recommend as equal to or superior to varieties already growing in the region: Golden Cross, Centennial, Ruby, Sardonyx, and Missoyen (Altanti).

Northwest Farmer Experimenters

Across the Northwest farmers had resorted to their own creative methods to obtain new varieties from relatives and friends in the East. Substantial stands of Genesee Giant, a mixed selection from a New York field of Clawson, grew on San Juan Island in the late 1890s, as did Arcadia in the northern Palouse and soft white Landreth (Martin Amber) in the Willamette Valley. But problems with lodging, milling quality, and threshability led to their short-lived existence in these diverse environments. Other wheat selections made by Northwest farmer-experimenters were more enduring. The popular soft white spring Jenkin (Jenkin's Club), first reported in the vicinity of Wilbur, Washington, in

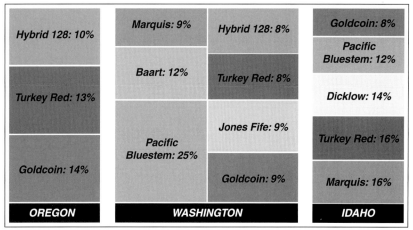

Predominant Northwest Wheat Varieties, 1920
Washington: 2,494,000 acres; Idaho: 1,141,000 acres; Oregon: 1,080,000 acres
Source: J. Clark, et. al., 1922:210-16.
Totals are less than 100% due to varieties grown on smaller acreages
and surveys unreported to the USDA.

1895, was raised widely across the Columbia Plateau in 1920. By that time, soft white Bluechaff (Calvert Club), plucked in 1897 from a field in Junction City, Oregon, and named for the distinctive color of its bloom, was found in fields throughout the northern Willamette Valley.[18]

Northwest farmers also experimented with several varieties of European Poulard wheats (*T. turgidum*) which may be among those represented by generic references to "durum" in late nineteenth-century newspaper and government reports. Grown in Great Britain as English Rivet or Irish Cone for its distinctively shaped head, one of the earliest references to a specific Poulard strain in the Northwest is from a Juliaetta, Idaho, farmer who reported a good stand of beardless spring Alaska in 1908. In a peculiar case of provenance that offers insight into various seed peregrinations to the region, Lopez Island farmer Harry Towell returned to his native England in 1912 and returned on the maiden voyage of the ill-fated Titanic. While on his visit, Towell had obtained a dozen kernels of a British Poulard and was among the fortunate ones rescued from the freezing waters of the North Atlantic along with the precious grains he had safely pocketed away. Towell dubbed the variety "Titanic," and grew it for several years on his farm near Port Stanley. Other Northwest varieties grown at the time were Clackamas Wonder and Alaska Winter, but

millers judged the quality of Poulard flour generally inferior to Northwest common wheats.[19]

CANADIAN GRAINS

Canada's principal western agricultural experiment station was at Agassiz, British Columbia, where work focused on the introduction of improved hard red spring grains after the calamitous Red Fife crop failure from an early frost on the Canadian prairies in 1888. Canadian Minister of Agriculture John Carling contacted a grain trader in Riga, Latvia, to obtain samples of the Russian hard red spring wheat Ladoga that grew well in the cold northern climes of the St. Petersburg area. The following spring one hundred pounds of the grain were planted for field trials across the country. Work led by Canadian cerealists William Saunders, Dominion Experimental Farm Director in Ottawa, and Seager Wheeler focused on US red wheat varieties from Ukraine as well as India because of their resistance to cold, rapid fruiting, and the high quality of their flour—routinely determined by Saunders' habit of chewing kernel samples to see if sufficient quantities of gluten would make gum. But Saunders and Wheeler found that Ladoga neither matured earlier than Fife nor produced better flour. However, the promising hybrid Preston (Red Fife x Ladoga) emerged from their work in 1895.

William Saunders's son, Charles, went on to serve in the same capacity after the turn of the century and brought his father's work to a climax in 1904 with the release of Marquis, an 1890s spring Red Fife/Red Calcutta cross that would revolutionize the Canadian grain industry. (Red Calcutta is a hard amber landrace probably indigenous to India's Punjab district.) The variety matured some two weeks earlier than Red Fife and regularly yielded over forty bushels per acre. General distribution took place in 1909 to farmers from British Columbia to Ontario and soon US dealers were placing substantial orders. By 1918 Marquis represented approximately 90 percent of the Canadian crop for a market value of five hundred million dollars. The cultivar would remain Canada's dominant wheat variety for several decades, and was the leading US hard red spring wheat in the 1920s.

Work undertaken by the Saunders father-and-son team, with Wheeler and others, also produced improved spring barley and oat varieties and the complex spring red wheat crosses Garnet (Preston x Riga) and Reward (Marquis x Prelude). Along with Marquis and Red Bobs, these became the most widely grown spring wheats in British Columbia in the 1920s. Production of malting barley declined significantly on both sides of the international border during the 1920–1933 Prohibition Era. Northwest Germans, Italians, and other immigrant groups with distinct brewing and wine-making traditions felt improperly targeted by crusaders who caused unintended changes in consumer habits. Touted as a measure to improve health, Prohibition zealots effectively replaced the ancient European "beer as bread" culture since brewing companies shifted production to soda and other high sugar beverages that became a staple of the American diet.

Because of more severe climatic conditions to the north, approximately 85 percent of British Columbia's grain was planted in the spring, and the total crop was only about 5 percent of Washington's. Other spring wheats that Canadian growers tried with limited success were Bishop Ottawa, Charlottetown, Mindum, Onac, Pelliser, and Vermillion. These varieties were little known in the states. In addition to popular American winter varieties like Jones Fife and Genesee Giant, British Columbia farmers also experimented with Harvest King, Harvest Queen, Kanred, Mealy, Pansar, Red Velvet Chaff, Rocky Mountain, Washington Sun, and more than a dozen others. The Minnesota Agricultural Experiment Station's 1934 release of rust-resistant Thatcher in St. Paul was shared with Canadian crop breeders and led to a series of important descendants that represented approximately 70 percent of Canadian acreage by mid-century. This high quality hard red spring wheat emerged from a 1921 double-cross hybrid of Marquillo (Marquis x Iumillo durum) with Marquis x

Kanred, and was a progenitor of the popular Canadian varieties Saunders, Chinook, Canhatch, and Manitou.

Canadian farmers also grew the old White Winter that Hudson's Bay Company Governor George Simpson had likely first brought down the Okanogan Valley a century earlier. This original Pacific Northwest English landrace, also grown as Wold's White Wonder, remained popular well into the twentieth century.[20]

KARL SAX AND THE DAWN OF CYTOGENETICS

One of Edwin Gaines's most acclaimed students at Washington State College was Karl Sax, son of a Spokane area farm family and an agriculture major at the Pullman school from 1912 to 1916. Dr. Hally Jolivette served as one of Sax's instructors in botany and the two were married by the time he graduated, forming a remarkable research and writing partnership that endured for over a half-century. She was offered a teaching position at Wellesley College in 1916, so the couple relocated to Massachusetts where, upon Gaines's recommendation, Karl enrolled in graduate studies at the Bussey Institute for Applied Biology, where he studied under the eminent geneticist E. M. East. While subsequently serving as Director of Plant Breeding at Riverbank Laboratories in Geneva, Illinois, Sax completed his doctoral dissertation in 1922 on the emerging field of cytotaxonomy which sought to identify the mechanisms of inheritance that had been observed by Gaines, Spillman, and their predecessors. Sax's training in Pullman, combined with a farmer's penchant for practical advancements and a prodigious intellect, would contribute to a lifetime of significant contributions to biological research.

Prior to publication of Sax's influential 1918 paper, "The Behavior of the Chromosomes in Fertilization," genetic research had been devoted almost entirely to animal species beginning with German biologist Walter Flemming's first description of chromosomes in 1879 in his study of cell division (mitosis) in salamander eggs. Subsequent breakthroughs soon after the turn of the century included American biologist Calvin Bridges's "Theory of Chromosome Inheritance" using fruit flies, followed by E. Eleanor Carothers' studies of chromosomal assortment factors in grasshoppers. Sax was the first researcher to relate these discoveries to hybridized flowers and grains and propose the linear arrangement of heritable factors—anticipating the discovery of the genetic code half-century later.

Sax's classic two-part study "Sterility in Wheat Hybrids" published in 1921 and 1922 in the journal *Genetics*—to which he would contribute thirteen articles by 1938—was substantially based on studies of five wheat varieties obtained from Gaines at the Washington Agricultural Experiment Station, including Pacific Bluestem, Australian Amby, Marquis, Kubanka, and Hybrid 143. This work also led to his acquaintance with Vavilov's related investigations in Russia. Sax's research with these grains and four others, including einkorn obtained from the Maine Experiment Station in Orono, revealed the distinct polyploidy (having a chromosome number that is a multiple greater than two of the monoploid number) of wheat species and related genetic influences in hybrid crosses (i.e., 14 chromosomes in diploid einkorn, 28 in tetraploid emmer, and 42 in hexaploid common vulgare wheats). Guided by these insights, Sax could then propose the prehistoric origins and sequence of wheat evolution as well as locate and identify genetic traits on individual chromosomes.[21]

In 1935 Sax initiated the pioneering radiation studies that would garner his widest scientific acclaim and earn him distinction as "Father of Cytogenetics"—forerunner of modern molecular biology. Ever mindful of practical steps that might improve hybridization, and intrigued by recent radiological studies in Germany and the United States, Sax embarked in 1935 on research using x-rays to induce chromosome translocations, or mutations, in plants. German biologist Herman J. Muller had discovered x-ray mutagenesis in 1927, and this work was applied to plants and other organisms in the United States by Sax and a small circle of scientists including Lewis Stadler and Croatian émigré Milislav Demerec. Sax joined both men at the historic Sixth International Genetics Congress at Ithaca, New York, which was also attended by his mentors Edwin Gaines, E. M. East, and USDA bar-

ley researcher Harry Harlan. Together they met with other towering figures in the field at what came to be considered the capstone of the golden era of pre-war classical genetics. Among prominent foreign participants were Muller, Roger de Vilmorin, one of the heirs to the prominent French seed company, and the ill-fated Russian scientists Vavilov and Nicholai Timofeeff-Ressowsky. Collaboration among these scientists would lay the foundation for significant post-war research on mutagenesis and hybridization at the Northwest's land-grant universities.[22]

Enduring Heirlooms, Emerging Hybrids

In 1920, three wheat varieties that had been grown in the Pacific Northwest for several decades still dominated regional production, although hybrids introduced since 1890 were gaining popularity. Farmers' reliance on Pacific Bluestem, Turkey Red, and Goldcoin (Fortyfold) testified to the enduring productivity of these heirlooms, which accounted for 40 percent of cropland that year. Yet the dedicated efforts of grain breeders like Spillman and Saunders had introduced a host of new crosses that would soon replace the earlier varieties by boosting yields with hybrid strains better adapted to area conditions like Hybrid 128 for eastern Oregon, Baart in eastern Washington, and Dicklow in southern Idaho (see Appendix III). Crop breeders also turned their attention to improved rye varieties in the early years of the twentieth century. Prior to that time most rye in the Northwest as elsewhere in the US and Canada was grown as mixed landrace Common Winter for fodder and bread flour, and to a limited extent for distilling. The improved winter variety Rosen was introduced to the US from Russia in 1909 and was soon found to yield well in sub-humid districts of southern Idaho and eastern Oregon, as did the Italian spring landrace Abruzzi.[23]

Estonian scientist-nobleman Fredrich Magnus von Berg used the German landrace rye Probsteier for experiments in natural cross-pollination with winter ryes that had grown for centuries in areas surrounding his Sangeste estate. This work led to von Berg's selection of heads exhibiting good winter hardiness that had large brown kernels. This "Sangeste rye" received high honors at the 1911 All-Russian Tsarskoye Selo Exhibition in St. Petersburg commemorating the 150th anniversary of Catherine the Great's ascension to the Romanov throne. Encouraged by this and other successes, von Berg's grandson, Rene R. A. Berg, continued to improve the variety after he immigrated to Edmonton, Alberta in the 1940s. Within two decades Sangeste became one of the most widely grown winter ryes in Alberta and Saskatchewan.[24]

The discovery of the Haber-Bosch process, for which German scientist Fritz Haber won the Nobel Prize in 1918, allowed atmospheric nitrogen to be converted to a stabilized form that could be used to replenish depleted soil nutrients. Previous sources—guano from remote Pacific islands and nitrates from the deserts of Chile—were in increasingly short supply. After the war, munitions companies like DuPont—whose operations threatened the few remaining buildings at old Fort Nisqually—found peaceful markets producing commercial fertilizers, though demand grew slowly at first. In spite of their previous differences over grain land tillage methods, prevailing opinion by that time among agronomists like WSC's

Hunter and Thatcher had settled on the need for nitrogen-based fertilizers to boost production and conservation measures to protect farmland. Grain production soared both east and west of the Cascades with these innovations just as the availability and affordability of internal combustion engines greatly reduced manual labor and enabled growers to manage larger acreages.

Farmers and rural townspeople had reason to be optimistic about the future, but concerns persisted about soil conservation. Oregon pioneer farmer-politician Leslie Scott in 1917 contrasted the general attitudes of nineteenth-century settlers with their twentieth-century rural counterparts. He described the admirable traits of the former: "a stirring race of men and women—hardy, untiring, and thrifty," but "unready to change methods of tillage." Traditional summer-fallowing threatened fragile topsoil in highly erodible areas, and the removal of streamside grass buffers sacrificed water quality. Scott warned farmers of the hazards of antiquated tillage practices and the temptation to over-expand farm size, admonishing that indifference to agricultural stewardship could sacrifice the vitality of future generations.

The farmer and every one of us: every citizen should be put right toward the earth, should be quickened to a relationship with the natural background. The whole body of public sentiment should be sympathetic with the one who works and administers the land for us; and this requires understanding.

—Liberty Hyde Bailey, *The Holy Earth* (1916)

CHAPTER VII

Grass, Grains, and the Green Revolution

And, you must know, your lord's word's true,
Feed him ye must, whose food fills you;
And that this pleasure is like rain,
Not sent ye for to drown your pain,
But for to make it spring again.

From the inception of agricultural instruction at the Northwest's state colleges in the 1890s, plant scientists sought to understand the complex botanical ecosystems and soil composition of the region's legendary grasslands. Pioneering agronomists at the state colleges in Pullman and Moscow also expressed concern about erosive farming practices and overgrazing in the steeply rolling Palouse region and adjacent Washington-Idaho mountain rangelands. William Tolmie's Hudson's Bay Company experiments with European red and white clovers, cocksfoot (orchardgrass), foxtail, and timothy had shown that forage crops could flourish on both sides of the Cascades. Soon after the founding of Washington State College (WSC), Charles Piper, the school's first agrostologist-botanist (a specialist in grasses), established an extensive plant nursery on property covered by the present university's football practice field, as well as the school's acclaimed herbarium. Piper and William Spillman shared many interests and became close personal friends.

The herbarium benefited from dedicated cadre of Northwest volunteer field botanists who collected for the college. Wilhelm Suksdorf lived at Bingen, Washington, and thoroughly explored the greater Mt. Adams region as well as the Spokane and Palouse areas. William C. Cusick studied primarily in northeastern Oregon's Blue and Wallowa mountains, while Thomas J. Howell collected for Piper in the Willamette Valley. Piper planted dozens of plots with introduced grass species in order to determine which varieties were best adapted to the region, and in partnership with R. Kent Beattie, undertook a comprehensive botanical survey of the greater Palouse at a time when isolated areas of the region still hosted native habitat. The pair explored widely in northern Idaho and eastern Washington, and identified blue bunch wheatgrass, blue bunchgrass, ryegrass, and other mixed prairie perennials as the Palouse's predominant climax vegetation.[1]

PRAIRIE FLORA AND THE BLUEGRASS INDUSTRY

For centuries these grasses had provided luxurious forage for deer, bison, and antelope, and later for the horses that reached the Northwest in the 1800s. The region's native Sahaptin peoples referred to the wild graminae species simply as *wasku*, or forage grass. In early summer these grasslands became a tufted universe of slender stalks, emerging petioles,

119

and curling leaves inhabited by herbivorous nations of crickets, beetles, and grasshoppers. Equipped with tiny serrated sickle jaws, these species were integral to the grassland's ecological renewal by their ingestion of vegetative growth and its deposition into forms essential to plant nutrition. Biblical numbers of wraithlike mayflies, midges, and damselflies appeared with the first warm days of spring to feed creatures of larger wing that nested during seasonal migrations. Underground earthworms worked diligently in the fibrous darkness to transform soil minerals into organics also usable by prairie flora. Their infinite twisting tunnels, together with the penetrations of decaying roots, kept the ground open to aeration and percolation.

Seven large tribes of the grass family (*Poaceae*) representing at least eighty-five native species once blanketed the Washington-Idaho borderlands in a rippling expanse of fecundity. Piper and Beattie described these varieties in detail and assembled a comprehensive taxonomy of grasses forming the woof and weft of the inland Northwest's pulsing patina. The groupings are distinguished by the number and arrangement of the miniscule spikelet flowers during inflorescence.

Panicae: Spikelets with one perfect flower or neutral and perfect flowers which fall with the seed-previously widespread on the sandy banks of the lower Snake River (e.g., *Panicum barbipulvinatum*).

Phalarideae: Spikelets with one perfect flower which does not fall with the seed, typically occurring in wet places, and often in shallow water as with reed canary grass.

Agrostideae: Spikelets with a staminate or neutral flower in addition to the perfect one, found in both dry and moist places including *Calamagrostis rubescens*, the most abundant grass in the northern Idaho pine forests.

Aveneae: Spikelets with a perfect and an imperfect flower which do not fall with the seed, including the once abundant annual *Deschampsia calycina* and introduced members of the oats family.

Festuceae: Spikelets with two or more perfect flowers on a longer modified leaf (bract), the widespread bromus (which later included foreign cheatgrass), *poa*, and *fescue* genera.

Chlorideae: Spikelets which do not fall with the seed and are crowded in two rows, coarse perennial grasses.

Hordeae: Spikelets with two or more perfect flowers which do not fall with the seed and are arranged in opposite rows-including the Palouse's famed six native wheatgrass (*Agropyron*) and five ryegrass (*Elymus*) species.[2]

Efforts by university scientists and extension personnel to persuade area farmers to preserve areas of native vegetation, establish streamside buffers, and reduce overgrazing brought mixed results. But the 1933-34 Dust Bowl years prompted national leaders to consider the ideas of America's prophet of conservation, Hugh Hammond Bennett, who had long advocated a campaign to save the nation's soil. In response, the Department of Interior's "Erosion Service"—forerunner of the Soil Conservation Service (SCS)—was formed in 1934, leading to regional efforts across the country to better manage vegetation in order to improve and conserve soils. SCS nurseries were established the following year in Pullman, Moscow, and Bellingham, where collections of native and introduced grass species were expanded in order to evaluate their performance for erosion control as well as for forage production. This research led to recommendations and seed releases for slender wheatgrass and clovers in grass mixtures, beardless wheatgrass and Sherman bluegrass for dryland ranges, intermediate wheatgrass for pasture mixes, and Manchar (Manchurian) bromegrass for high mountain rangelands.[3]

The first Department of Agronomy at a Northwest land-grant college had been established at WSC in 1929 under the leadership of S. C. Vandecaveye. During his quarter-century tenure at the institution, he recruited a cadre of notable agronomists, including Louis Kardos, Ralph Weihing, and B. Rodney Bertramson. Under their guidance the Pullman school, in cooperation with the Soil Conservation Service, established the largest grass nursery of its kind in the world. Thousands of species of grasses, legumes, shrubs, and trees were tested at the facility for erosion control properties which led to the release by the 1940s of twenty-five new certified strains of grasses using many selections of plants native to the Pacific Northwest as progenitors.

These scientists influenced a generation of agronomy graduates who became leaders in regional grass, legume, and grain production, including brothers Manuel and Elmer Schneidmiller of Post Falls, Idaho; Robert Dye of Pomeroy; and Doyle, Don, and Duane Jacklin of Dishman, Washington. The Jacklin family's Spokane Valley enterprise, Jacklin Seed, began in 1936 when the brothers' grandfather and sons established a legume seed business. In 1942 the family began raising blue wildrye and chewings fescue on farmland south of Mt. Spokane, and in the late 1940s the Jacklins' father, Arden, obtained Kentucky bluegrass seed from a Klamath Falls, Oregon, grower. He planted a field near Post Falls, which led to the production of high quality Merion Kentucky bluegrass

followed by the first bluegrass proprietary variety, Fylking.

The nation was experiencing a post-World War II boom in demand for grass seed for lawns, golf courses, parks, and public spaces. In response to these opportunities and associated research needs, WSC agronomists organized the first Pacific Northwest Turf Conference in 1948, and enterprising seed grower participants like the Jacklins began seeking area growers to help meet demand. Manuel and Elmer Schneidmiller, sons of Volga German immigrant parents who had settled in the St. John-Endicott area, acquired a dairy and farmland on the fertile Rathdrum Prairie east of Spokane in 1949 after obtaining agronomy degrees at WSC and distinguished military service in the Pacific during World War II. Soon after relocating to the Post Falls area, the Schneidmillers were

Schneidmiller Farms Rathdrum Prairie Harvest, c. 1955
Gary Schneidmiller Collection

contacted by Arden Jacklin about raising Kentucky bluegrass for his family's burgeoning business.

The crop flourished on the Schneidmillers' acreage, irrigated from a dozen hand-dug wells. With strong prices contracted through the Jacklins, the brothers began expanding their holdings on both sides of the state line from Coeur d'Alene to Liberty Lake. By the mid-1950s, the Schneidmillers had become the largest supplier of grass seed to the Jacklins and partnered together with WSU agronomists Alvin Law and Robert Warner to develop rigorous seed inspection measures to ensure varietal purity as well as innovative seed curing systems. The progressive research, production, and marketing alliance provided 60 percent of the nation's grass seed supply by 1960, and contributed to the development of new varieties for turf and conservation management, and for irrigated forage crops made possible by the expansive Columbia Basin Project.[4]

COLUMBIA BASIN IRRIGATION

Echoing Hudson Bay Company Governor George Simpson's optimism for regional development, Chief Columbia District Surveyor Thomas W. Symons of the Army Corps of Engineers had predicted in 1881 that the vast rangelands of the Pacific Northwest would one day become "waving fields of grain." The 1902 National Reclamation Act funded significant irrigation development projects through the newly created Federal Reclamation Bureau for arid districts across southern Idaho, central Washington, and eastern Oregon where populations surged between 1900 and 1920. With settlement on most of the region's last remaining unclaimed lands during that decade, and impending revolutions in agricultural mechanization and production, Pacific Northwest farmers would soon feel far less isolated.

Many state and federal officials had long been convinced that irrigation of the arid Columbia Basin was possible and could be done cost effectively. The basic resources were available: an abundant water supply from the Columbia River and the region's lakes and connecting scabland channels; a vast expanse of fertile drylands in central Washing-

ton and Oregon; and legions of farmers who had been lobbying for years in vain attempts to secure government assistance for an undertaking of such magnitude. Farmers in the Yakima Valley formed the Washington Irrigation Company in 1892 in the region's first substantial cooperative effort to bring water from Cascade mountain lakes to fields and orchards. Wenatchee Valley fruit growers followed with similar herculean projects in the 1890s which contributed to the state's national prominence in volume and quality of Delicious, Jonathan, Macintosh, Winesap, and other apple varieties and pears. Cashmere's Oscar Redfield drew international acclaim when a forty-two-and-a-half-ounce Wolf River specimen from his orchard garnered the 1898 World's Fair prize for the largest apple ever recorded. The popular variety began in 1875 as a Grand Alexander seedling in Wolf River, Wisconsin. The winter hardy Alexander, named for Tsar Alexander I, came to England from Russia in 1817. An excellent drying apple, it was widely grown in New England by the 1840s and in Northwest family orchards by the end of the century.

In 1900 western basin farmers formed the Quincy Irrigation District, the first such jurisdiction east of the Columbia River. But geography did not favor gravity flow systems from high lakes for Columbia Basin farmers. Many pioneer families dug their own wells for domestic needs, but supply was insufficient to irrigate large acreages, and without electrification all pumps had to be operated by wind or hand. The 1902 federal legislation championed by President Theodore Roosevelt authorized significant funding for irrigation plans that had fallen victim to the nation's economic woes of the previous decade. Roosevelt loved the American West and his experiences here as a young man shaped his national agenda. During a 1906 Northwest campaign swing he remarked that development of the Columbia Basin would present an appropriate challenge to the recently created bureau. Since many other Western lands could benefit from irrigation, Roosevelt formed the Inland Waterways Commission in 1907 to prioritize and plan these projects with interested state officials. The most widely discussed Columbia Basin plan at the time was to divert water from Lake Pend Oreille in northern Idaho to the Spokane River and then into an enormous gravity flow canal that would run across the arid basin.

The 1909 National Irrigation Congress held in Spokane convened development partisans from across the country and members of the Quincy District organized a strong presence to draw attention to their plight and prospects. Dozens of delegates paraded through the streets of the city singing a theme song to the tune of the spiritual "Beulah Land":

> We've got the soil and attitude
>   We've got the sun to grow the food.
> We've got the space for everything
>   But water we ask Congress to bring.
> Oh, Quincy land, my Quincy land
>   On this burning soil we stand;
> Then look away across the plain
>   And wonder why it never rains,
> Till Gabriel blows the trumpet sound
>   And says, "The rain has gone around."

Although the Spokane gathering could not authorize project funding, Northwest delegates did come together to establish the Washington Irrigation Institute to draft a master development plan among regional competing interests and in cooperation with federal efforts. The region endured years of drought from 1908 to 1913 and area fundraising challenges were then compounded by the nation's involvement in World War I. Furthermore, problems had been encountered with Idaho legislators reluctant to provide Washington farmers with lake water from their state, and plans to extend the Cascade high lake canals from the Yakima and Wenatchee valleys were fraught with supply and engineering problems.[5]

In July 1918 Ephrata attorney William "Billy" Clapp suggested a novel basin irrigation plan to *Wenatchee World* owner-editor Rufus Woods. He proposed construction of a mammoth high dam across the Columbia River near the mouth of the Grand Coulee, a vast and deep Ice Age remnant violently carved out in the cataclysmic Lake Missoula floods. The Grand Coulee ran southward into the

heart of the Columbia Basin, and water impounded behind the proposed dam could be directed down its course to the drylands. The bold scheme would require a dam nearly a mile across, and that would form a reservoir along the upper Columbia channel nearly to the Canadian border. Captivated by the plan, Woods ran editorials endorsing the project to give area farmers and government officials a grand but realistic plan to consider.

Impressed with the prospect, state legislators formed the Columbia Basin Survey Commission in 1919 to select the most feasible comprehensive irrigation plan. Although the commission's work was forestalled by America's plunge into the Great Depression, basin irrigation advocates found formidable allies in two victors in the 1932 national elections, eastern Washington Democrat Governor Clarence Martin, and President Franklin Roosevelt. That year the commission formally recommended the Grand Coulee Dam proposal and contracted with the Federal Bureau of Reclamation for its construction, which took eight years. The complex irrigation plan named the Columbia Basin Project was organized in 1939 with three districts formed to cover the entire one-million-acre area. Grand Coulee Dam began generating electricity in 1941 and water diverted for irrigation finally began to flow to the basin three years later.[6]

GAINES AND THE GREEN REVOLUTION

The proliferation of new hybrids that required grading, along with appearance of the fungal diseases rust and smut, led to the organization of the eleven-state Cooperative Western Regional Wheat Improvement Program in 1930. Funded by Congress through the Department of Agriculture, the organization's Pacific Northwest affiliate was formed in 1943 and administered at WSC by Gaines, Orville A. Vogel, and O. E. Barbee; and V. H. Florell and C. A. Michels at the University of Idaho in Moscow. The two teams worked closely together to develop more and larger nurseries by acquiring additional lands adjacent to the experiment stations and in areas of various microclimates and soil classes across the region. Vogel, who grew up on a small farm in Nebraska, arrived in Pullman in 1931—the year William Spillman died—to begin a distinguished forty-two-year career with the school and USDA Agricultural Research Service. Wheat breeding projects he directed led to the development of more specialized stiff-strawed and disease-resistant soft white wheat hybrids like the Hymar (a Hybrid 128 x Martin cross released in 1935), Orfed (1943), Marfed (1947), Brevor (1949), and the superior miller Omar (1955) for areas of high rainfall. Washington and Oregon agronomists primarily used various combinations of Turkey Red, Federation, Florence, Fortyfold, and Oro for these varieties. Other semi-hard varieties were released during these years for intermediate lands, and several hard reds for low rainfall areas.[7]

Vogel's work with Brevor and Omar coincided with post-war introduction of the remarkable Japanese semi-dwarf wheat Norin-10 (Nōrinshō) to the

Orville Vogel, c. 1965
Manuscripts, Archives, and Special Collections, Washington State University Libraries (MC 524.10.278)

United States in 1946 by S. Cecil Salmon, a senior Agricultural Research Administration (ARA) consultant serving with the Natural Resources Section of General Douglas McArthur's US occupation forces in Japan. Salmon had inspected the nine Imperial Agricultural Experiment Stations located throughout Japan and seen vigorous stands of short wheats growing on Honshu. At one of the stations, Marioka Experimental Farm at Iwate in northeastern Japan, he collected sixteen seed samples, including Norin-10, and sent these to the USDA Small Grain Collection in Beltsville, Maryland, where they were processed in August. Subsequent studies indicated that Norin probably descended from the bearded landrace Daruma, which had likely been introduced to Japan from Korea as early as the sixteenth century. Norin was a true dwarf with yellow kernels that grew only about twenty inches high and was used for soft noodle flour (udon).

Japanese agronomists at the Central Agricultural Experiment Station in Nishigahara, Tokyo, had originally crossed Daruma from Kanto Prefecture in 1917 with the American hybrid Glassy Fultz (Fultz [Red Mediterranean] x Mealy, an 1880 Fultz field selection in New York) to yield a cultivar subsequently crossed in 1925 with an American Turkey Red selection. A promising semi-dwarf, rust-resistant seventh generation selection made by Gonjiro Inazuka in 1932 at Morioka and named Norin-10 (an official designation as a sequenced hybrid). The cultivar's physiology directed energy from the normally higher stalks into a prodigious head and kernels.

The USDA Norin samples were grown during the 1946–47 season in Sacaton, Arizona. Vogel, whose work in Pullman was also associated with the ARA (after 1953 a part of USDA's Agricultural Research Service), obtained enough breeding seed for a couple dozen starts among some 225 lines gathered from twenty-one countries. Planted in March 1948, the initial nursery trials of Norin-10 grew only about sixteen inches tall in row number 1215. The uncharacteristic shaky handwriting in Vogel's field notebook that summer may indicate comprehension of the variety's peculiar significance: "Very short straw about 6" shorter than Idaed, fairly (surprisingly) good kernel for such a short plant." Vogel assigned a graduate assistant, Masami "Dick" Nagamitsu, the delicate task of crossing the first progeny as female stock with Brevor pollen in the late winter of 1948–49 as part of about a hundred experiments. On the day of the historic cross that would spark the Green Revolution, the fertilized Norin/Brevor head (Selection 14) became just one among many shrouded inside protective parchment envelopes that fluttered inconspicuously on Roundtop's windswept slopes just east of the main campus. Nagamitsu collected fourteen seeds from the plant in the spring which were planted as second generation in the fall of 1949 and allowed to self-pollinate.[8]

Vogel reasoned that late-maturing, higher-yielding winter wheats like Brevor would serve as good candidates for parent stock, while the Asian variety could contribute winter-hardiness and the dwarfing genes for resistance to lodging. Soft white Brevor's complex pedigree also included a hard Turkey Red cross with William Farrar's Australian white winter Florence (Fife/Eden x White Naples—an Italian bald Lammas descendant also known as Carosella), combined with a soft white Goldcoin (Fortyfold) cross with Farrar's famed Federation. A subsequent cross was made in 1952 between Brevor-Norin 10 and the widely adapted American hard white winter hybrid Burt (see Appendix V). A final 1956 selection produced the world's first semi-dwarf variety that Vogel named Gaines in honor of his mentor and predecessor at the Pullman school, Edwin F. Gaines. The two semi-dwarfing genes (Rht1 and Rht2) were subsequently identified by agronomists Robert Allan and Clarence Peterson, Jr., who Vogel hired in the late 1950s to conduct collaborative research on the genetics of wheat improvement and disease resistance.

In spite of able assistance from USDA agronomist colleagues at WSC like Prosser native Harley Jacquot, Vogel's extensive series of crosses brought initial disappointment due to considerable male sterility. But promising results with some fertile specimens by 1952 led to field tests of Gaines at the Pullman, Pendleton, Lind, and Prosser experiment stations in 1953. Vogel's successful progeny—a short, bearded soft white wheat of high milling quality—still had problems with emergence due to reduced coleoptile length characteristic of dwarf wheats. Further work showed the matter to be one of seeding depth, which led to John Deere's development of the innovative deep-furrow, split-packer HZ drill based on a prototype designed and built by Almira farmer Robert Zimmerman. When the new cultivar was sown in deep furrows sixteen inches apart in late summer with Zimmerman's equipment, the seedlings flourished in early fall even in low rainfall areas. Moreover, Gaines flourished beyond expectation in maturity with fertilizer, as application of nitrogen increased yields by over 20 percent compared to non-semi-dwarfs. Research published abroad in 1953 also unlocked the secret of the genetic code. British scientists' Francis Crick and James Watson famous article in *Nature* in 1953 explained the helical structure of DNA, and this discovery would have significant implications for grain breeders seeking to identify the biological mechanisms of inheritance.

Enhancing grain yields with supplementary nitrogen fertilizers had become a special interest of Jacquot's since his early years at the Lind Experiment Station. His research there led to the conclusion that availability of nitrogen to grain was a more critical and potentially controllable factor for yield than rainfall. Although prevailing professional opinion was skeptical of the notion, Jacquot found valued encouragement for his ideas from Hooper's Maurice McGregor, who managed McGregor Land and Livestock Company's vast land holdings in the southwestern Palouse, where the economics of dryland production was marginal. When funds for Jacquot's USDA research were diverted to other projects, McGregor offered him a position with the company in 1950 to continue his work.

Recalling McGregor's influence in this pivotal era of Northwest cereal grain development, Jacquot wrote, "He's the one that really put this fertilizer program on the map." The veteran agronomist relocated his operation to the McGregor Ranch near Hooper with instructions from his new employers that the research must return profits as well as satisfy scientific curiosity. Within two years dozens of

Sherman McGregor, c. 1970
Alexander McGregor Collection

test plots appeared on McGregor land around the tiny hamlet along the Palouse River. Jacquot and the McGregors tested a range of nitrogen-based fertilizers in dry, aqueous ("aqua"), and from 1952, anhydrous ammonia (an 82 percent gaseous nitrogen) forms. By the mid-1950s the evidence was startlingly clear that the value of higher yields significantly outweighed the fertilizer's cost: Untreated plots yielded thirty-three bushels per acre, those with thirty pounds of nitrogen produced forty-six bushels, sixty pounds yielded fifty-nine bushels. Seventy bushel yields could be raised with ninety pounds on land where twenty-five bushels per acre had long been considered average.

The McGregors and Jacquot also advocated stubble mulch ("trashy") summer-fallowing, streamside grass buffers, and other soil conservation measures that hearkened back to the advice of agronomists a generation earlier like Thatcher and Leiberg. Jacquot participated in dozens of farmer and scientific meetings and published numerous journal articles about his research that earned him distinction as the "father of nitrogen-moisture testing." McGregor field days became popular annual events each June as farmers from throughout the

country and overseas found their way to Hooper, and in 1951 Maurice's cousin, Sherman McGregor, founded The McGregor Company to distribute fertilizers, soil amendments, and agrichemicals from the Hooper General Store.

McGregor envisioned building a wholly-owned regional distributorship, and with the help of employees Cliff Rollins and Chester Field, and area farmer–improvisers like Donald Morasch and Ed Kramlich, the new enterprise also began fabricating specialized field application equipment which was marketed widely in the Northwest and Canada. In 1952 the company's first branches opened in LaCrosse and Endicott, followed by one in Colfax a year later, where the company headquarters was eventually established at nearby Mockenema. Several dozen outlets followed in rural communities across eastern Washington, Oregon, and northern Idaho. Due in large measure to the innovations of the decade, the Columbia Plateau counties of Whitman, Lincoln, and Adams led the nation in wheat output in 1955, with Whitman alone producing twelve million bushels.

Vogel's "shorty wheat" trials on fertilized ground frequently exceeded one hundred bushels per acre by 1960, and word soon spread among area growers and other researchers about the spectacular potential of Gaines. Pullman's 382-acre Spillman Farm southwest of campus came to resemble a military camp as summer field hands were provided small arms and worked extended hours to deter threats of pilfering. Theft of Gaines seed from a Lincoln City, Oregon, test plot led to intervention by the FBI which prevented illicit use of the grain. Vogel released limited quantities of Gaines to farmers in 1961—the same year virulent stripe rust struck the region's Omar crop, sending clouds of orange dust exploding into Northwest summer skies. In 1962 five hundred thousand bushels of the Western Hemisphere's first commercially successful semi-dwarf wheat were made available to North-west farmers. Approximately one million acres in the Pacific Northwest were seeded with stunning results, although millers continued to prefer Omar until its production had greatly diminished by the middle of the decade. Seventy bushels per acre dryland yields of Gaines were commonplace, and a world record was set in 1962 on eleven irrigated acres near Quincy in central Washington that yielded one hundred fifty-five and a half bushels per acre. That year Vogel received USDA's Distinguished Service Award, the first of many state, national, and international accolades for his scientific achievements.[9]

The soft-spoken Vogel, who joked about learning to improvise and solder moonshine equipment during his hardscrabble Midwest Depression-era boyhood, also made notable contributions to agricultural mechanics during his four-decade career in the Palouse. With grant and research support facilitated by WSU Agronomy Department Chair B. Rodney Bertramson and others, Vogel invented complex miniature equipment including a field tractor rototiller (with support from the Ford Foundation), eight-row seeder (supported by the Rockefeller Foundation), and a self-cleaning plot thresher (supported by the Washington Wheat Commission) to facilitate planting and harvesting test plots worldwide. Due to the interests and alliances of Northwest agronomists like Vogel, Gaines, and Spillman, the enduring efforts of the college experiment station staffs, cooperative extension service agents, and local farmers, the Pacific Northwest became the twentieth century's highest yielding dryland grain region in the world.

Gaines wheat along with a parent (Selection 101) and its superior milling sister-line kin, Nugaines (1965), sired over one hundred fifty commercially successful descendants worldwide by 2000 and accounted for some 75 percent of the planet's entire one-hundred-sixty-million-acre wheat production area. The homelands of their genetic progenitors represent an international heritage—Russia, the United States, Canada, Mexico, Europe, Australia, India, Japan, and Korea—and distinct attributes of yield and disease resistance

remain a continuing legacy of untold commercial value. New varieties continued to be developed to contend with threats from new kinds of smut, mold, foot rot, and other diseases driven by global winds and trade. Gaines significantly contributed to the Green Revolution following the transfer of samples in 1953 by Vogel to Norman Borlaug, the zealous Director of the Rockefeller Foundation's International Maize and Wheat Improvement Center in Mexico City, known by the Spanish acronym CIMMYT (sím-mit). Vogel's research enabled Borlaug, a tireless advocate of famine relief and solutions, to cross Vogel's high-yielding, semi-dwarf accessions with old Mexican varieties like Sonora. Subsequent hybrids like Pitic and Penjamo vastly improved wheat production in Central America in the 1960s, as did the cultivar Sonalika for India, Bangladesh, and Pakistan, as still others did for Africa, and, appropriately, for Turkey. In tribute to this work, Borlaug received the 1970 Nobel Prize, and President Gerald Ford awarded the National Medal of Science to Vogel in 1975.[10]

Smith, Nilan, and Radiobiology

Concurrent with post-war advances in conventional hybridization of grains involving collaborations between the USDA-ARS and Northwest land-grant universities were related initiatives in radiobiology. In the late 1940s, WSC agronomist Luther Smith built upon the work of Sax, Demerec, and Timofeeff-Ressowsky to undertake pioneering biotech studies on mutations in grains induced by ionizing radiation and a range of mutagenic chemicals. Pullman's proximity to the Hanford Atomic Works facilitated such studies that were supported by the Atomic Energy Commission, and Smith helped lead research in 1946 on radiation effects with exposed grain seeds from atomic bomb atmospheric testing. Since the nucleus of diploid barley cells contain far fewer genes than hexaploid wheat (~30,000 vs. 90,000 genes), barley seed became the focus of these studies as mutagenic effects could be more accurately determined. Smith then focused in 1947 at his Pullman laboratory on six-row barley and durum wheat seeds using x- and gamma-rays and such chemicals as diethyl sulfate and ethyl methane sulfonate. The project's objectives were to induce a range of genetic effects and then determine the process that created specific mutations. With colleagues Richard Caldecott, Mary Hafercamp, and others, Smith embarked on an ambitious agenda to study the related influences of heat treatments and the ages of experimental seeds using samples that had been stored at Lind's Dryland Research Station for several decades.

Between 1948 and 1952, Smith and his associates contributed a series of landmark articles on their work to the journal *Genetics* and as Washington Agricultural Experiment Station scientific papers. In 1951 he helped recruit agronomist and geneticist Robert Nilan who extended Smith's work at WSC and teamed with Harvard graduate Cal Konzak, who joined the faculty in 1958, to apply the principles of mutagenesis for induced grain breeding. The scientists found that a single mutation event tripled the recombinational genetic variance of genotypes within in the first generation. This discovery greatly accelerated the time needed to produce desired breeding traits and fostered a more bewildering array of possible combinations. In this way, the twelve- to fifteen-year generational cycle required for conventional hybridized breeding approaches could be reduced by two-thirds to four to five years.[11]

Ithaca, New York, again provided an international forum for Northwest scientists to share the results of their work when the National Academy of Sciences' 1960 Symposium on Mutation and Plant Genetics was held at Cornell. Nilan and Konzak delivered an address on "Increasing the Efficiency of Mutation Induction" in which they elaborated on effective approaches in the manipulation of conditions and screen techniques to maximize genetic variation. Mutagenesis was understood to essentially advance the natural system which led one reviewer to characterize it as "nothing more than controlled evolution" involving the same fundamental processes of variability and selection. Participants at the 1960 Ithaca gathering voiced concern that the considerable headway made by scientists like Nilan and Konzak had not been widely applied by crop breeders. Reviewer S. C. Stephens observed

that advocates of induced mutations and conventional hybridization should "judiciously" borrow from both approaches and not be "set in opposition" as prevailing attitudes suggested, and which did exist to some extent at Washington State and Oregon State Universities.

Nilan and Konzak eventually formed the innovative Program in Genetics and Cell Biology in 1965 to facilitate interdepartmental and intercollegiate relations. This collaboration procured millions of dollars of research funding from state, federal, and private sources. These efforts, largely conducted in Johnson Hall on the Pullman campus, led to the development of some of the world's first commercially released mutagenic barley varieties including the short-strawed winter feed variety Luther (1966), named by Nilan in memory of Luther Smith. Luther seed was released in a record four years from the time the Alpine mutant had been isolated and outyielded its parent cultivar by a quarter-ton per acre in intermediate to high rainfall areas. By the early 1970s, Luther was the Northwest's highest yielding barley and was grown on over 100,000 acres. Northwest malting barleys were also introduced in the 1970s using chemical mutagens, especially sodium azide, which induces a wide spectrum of mutations with few chromosome aberrations. This work accommodated brewer preference for beers without chill-haze. Barleys developed at WSU using these techniques include the malting barleys Vanguard (1970), Blazer, Advance, and Andre; and the six-rowed feed barleys Kamiak (1970), Steptoe, Boyer, and Showin. Mutagenic oats included Cayuse (1966) and Appaloosa.[12]

Direct Seed Farming and the Green Bridge

Although the stunning success of conventionally hybridized wheats like Gaines and the mutagenic barley Luther significantly increased grain production across the Northwest, agronomists like Vogel and Jacquot surmised the new hybrids were still not living up to their potential. "I knew it," Vogel once quipped, "there was something wrong with my wheats." WSU plant pathologist and Vogel protégé R. James Cook at WSU was tasked with studying the implications of soil biology in the 1970s and his research led to the conclusion that root diseases caused by host of ubiquitous micro-organisms infected Northwest cereal grains enough to impair the absorption of vital plant nutrients. Cook estimated that the damage done to US crops annually represented the entire annual grain output of Kansas, or about ten million tons. The primary culprits whose pathology had come to be accepted as normal were the root rot fungi *Gueumanomyces*, *Rhizoctonia*, *Pythium*, and *Fusarium*.

Concurrent with Cook's research was an innovative tillage approach pioneered in 1974 on the Morton Swanson farm near the rural community of Palouse, Washington. Swanson had used a conventional drill that fall to attempt seeding wheat directly into the stubble of his previous crop because the weather and other circumstances had delayed normal fall plowing. In spite of the heavy residue, Swanson's trial resulted in a good stand of spring wheat and successful harvest. He speculated that the crop would have significantly benefited from deeper seed drill penetration with the application of fertilizer and herbicides in the same operation.

Swanson went to work in his spacious farm shop designing and fabricating an enormous implement twenty feet wide that weighed fifteen tons when empty and twenty-five when fully loaded. Equipped with a row of paired steel discs to open the ground, followed by coulters to deposit seed and fertilizer, and trailed by narrow sealing packer wheels, Swanson's "Old Yellow" lumbered over his rolling slopes in time for fall seeding. Results the following year exceeded expectations with a harvest yield nearly as high as previous years using traditional approaches, but virtually without soil erosion. Swanson's break-through idea had eliminated the need for additional costly tillage operations. In 1978 Swanson began commercial production of his aptly named Pioneer and Yielder no-till drills, and by 1990 over two dozen models were in production by regional equipment manufacterers.[13]

During these same years, Cook and his team at WSU not only identified the parasitic cereal grain root rot offenders, but came to understand the biological process of their damage. He discovered that the presence of host material represented a "green bridge" by which diseases spread to seedlings. This work led to important recommendations for crop improvement with special relevance for emerging no-till methods, since the diseases were hosted in subsoil crop residue. Following summer harvest and seasonal rains, these microbial populations exploded in the weeks that preceded fall seeding. The problem was exacerbated by the increased organic matter from the higher yielding hybrids coupled with conservation-minded minimum tillage methods like those championed by Swanson and others.

Extensive field testing in the 1990s with a range of innovative cultivation practices, seed fungicides, and other measures led Cook to recommend a series of effective interventions. These included (1) removal of residue from seed rows, (2) use of "paired-row" drills to better warm dry soil for seed germination, (3) fresh seed treated with protectants to improve seedling vigor, and (4) placing plant nutrients including phosphorus in close proximity to the seed. The implications of this research for tillage practice and equipment design led to the next generation of heavy minimum- and no-till applicators and drills. These continued to be combined with substantial fertilizer and soil amendment applicators to form slow-moving field trains over fifty feet long with names like the Strawboss,

McGregor Company MD 1610 Deep Furrow Drill
Landrace Grain Trials
Alex McGregor (left) with Lead Designer Paul Buchholtz
McGregor Research Station near Colfax, Washington (2012)

Triple Shooter, Till-n-Plant, and Eagle. These behemoths, in turn, require ever-larger tractors to pull them, enabling a farmer to seed three hundred acres in a single day.

In the foreword to Cook and fellow agronomist Roger Veseth's authoritative 1991 book, *Wheat Health Management*, Orville Vogel credited them for bringing "together in one place the essentials of the scientific literature and practical experiences of farmers and scientists in North America and the world," noting that the work pioneered in the Northwest represented "the first truly integrated approach" to grain production. The advent of modern direct-seed cropping practices has led to record yields in the Pacific Northwest while significantly reducing soil erosion by water and wind. Conventional winter wheat-summer fallow tillage systems continue in low-precipitation areas, while farmers in the intermediate and high regions generally follow three-year rotations (e.g., WW-SW-SW [or spring barley] or WW-SW-legume). An Agricultural Research Service farm northeast of Pullman and named in Cook's honor was established in 1998 and he subsequently received the prestigious Wolf Prize for outstanding contributions to humanity through science.[14]

Turkey Red Wheat
McGregor Research Station near Colfax, Washington (2013)

Swords into Plowshares

When Hudson's Bay Company Governor George Simpson met his Russian counterpart at Sitka in the fall of 1841 to facilitate delivery of Columbia grain to Russian America, Governor Etholén surprised his British guest with an invitation to also provision settlements in the Russian Far East. Exactly one hundred and fifty years later, and a half century after the United States and USSR joined forces as World War II allies, requests to send Northwest agricultural commodities to the same region came from the Soviet Union under very different circumstances.

America's longtime Cold War rival now teetered on the brink of political and economic collapse in the wake of democratic reforms sweeping across Eastern Europe. Severe disruptions to the regular delivery of food and other necessities to eastern Russia raised the specter of famine for the region's most vulnerable—the elderly and orphans. Mike Lowry, then Washington governor, had been aware of the situation because of a lifelong personal interest in Russia and his rural Northwest upbringing. Lowry's father had managed the grain cooperative in the small Palouse community of Endicott, an area heavily populated by first- and second-generation Volga Germans who had long been accustomed to raising the Russian wheat varieties and hybrids that Lowry spent much of his youth harvesting and hauling.

In the late 1980s, Washington's Secretary of State Ralph Munro had worked with Lowry to promote a series of state trade delegations to Sakhalin Island. Munro had extensive experience in the USSR since leading a "People to People" group of Northwest business and community leaders to Russia and Ukraine in 1984. Bruce Kennedy of Alaska Air Group had personally directed Alaska's 1988 inauguration of the first regular flights by an American carrier to the Russian Far Eastern cities of Magadan, Providenya, and Khabarovsk. He later privately confessed these had been "more of a humanitarian than business endeavor" in order to foster better relations between both nations.

To facilitate humanitarian work in the Russian Far East in 1991, the international mission Deyneka Russian Ministries joined forces with Washington-based WestWind Ministries, an aid organization headed by eastern Washington's Stan Jacobson, a Lutheran pastor. Deyneka Ministries co-founder Dr. Anita Deyneka also had Washington roots, having been raised on a small farm in the Plain Valley near Leavenworth. Deyneka Ministries and WestWind representatives participated in late-1991 meetings in Vancouver, British Columbia, with democratic reform leader General Nikolai Stolyarov, who sought assistance for families of recently decommissioned Russian soldiers returning from Warsaw Pact countries previously occupied by Soviet forces. The Vancouver meetings led to an appeal to Northwest commodity producers for assistance. Following a meeting at the Russian White House with Ruslan Khasbulatov, at which the Duma president requested similar help, the Deynekas contacted co-workers and donors in the Northwest about marshaling a strategic response to the growing crisis.[1]

Since the US State Department had not designated funds for trans-Pacific delivery to eastern Russia, transportation expense represented a significant stumbling block. Bruce Kennedy advised contacting Governor Lowry and Secretary of State Munro because of their special experience in Russia. Munro's response was clear: "Anything you can get to a West Coast port I'll get over there if I have to take it over on my back!" The pledge would be often invoked in the coming weeks.[2]

Formation of the non-profit "Operation KareLift" relief campaign followed in January 1992 as a partnership among Deyneka Russian Ministries, the offices of the Washington Governor and Secretary of State, and WestWind Ministries. Northwest wheat, barley, pea, lentil, and other farmer commodity groups quickly pledged more than seventy-five tons of dry measure and dehydrated food products packaged in bulk Spokane and Pullman as nutritional soup mixes, and flour. Washington and Alaskan Rotarians assembled an additional twelve tons as food parcels for families in greatest need. Other private donors contributed forty tons of clothing and substantial amounts of medical supplies for total deliveries exceeding several hundred tons. To transport the cargo, McGregor Company fleet drivers carried commodities from eastern Washington and Oregon to West Coast ports, while Munro and his indefatigable deputy, Michelle Burkheimer, arranged delivery through the Russian-American joint venture Far East Shipping Company. The firm operated trans-Pacific vessels departing Washington ports, and Vancouver, BC, to port cities of the Russian Far East.

The generous outpouring of assistance coupled with reports of dire needs in Russian Far East orphanages prompted Munro and Senator Slade Gorton to request White House intervention for military airlift flights from Washington State to Khabarovsk. These were personally authorized by President George H. W. Bush in late February 1992 and the cargo planes were the first American military aircraft to land on Russian territory since World War II.

Russian and American reporters covered the campaign in articles featured in *Izvestia*, the *Seat-tle Times*, and *Spokesman-Review*. Although the total volume of relief was less than what the US government had pledged, the project was of special symbolic value to a Russian government beleaguered by mounting civil unrest. As noted by Russian Ambassador Vladimir Lukin, almost all other Western aid at the time was being directed to European Russia, while KareLift focused on the hardest hit areas in the Russian Far East. Moreover, the work was almost entirely undertaken by a partnership of private donors and volunteers among Northwest growers, private donors, and civic and mission leaders in the United States and Russia.[3]

Russian President Boris Yeltsin in Seattle, 1994.
Foundation for Russian-American Economic Cooperation

When President Boris Yeltsin journeyed to the United States in September 1994 to address the United Nations and meet with President Clinton, he surprised White House officials just days prior to arriving with a request to visit the Pacific Northwest, this in spite of invitations from prominent Eastern cities. On the morning of September 29, Yeltsin's Ilyushin jetliner emblazoned with Russia's new double-headed eagle insignia landed in Everett and he was taken to Seattle to attend a luncheon hosted by US Commerce Secretary Ron Brown, Lowry, and Munro. "He threw away his prepared speech," Lowry observed, and spoke extemporaneously to the enthusiastic crowd of eight hundred invited guests.

In addition to encouraging investment in Russia by American and Russian entrepreneurs to enhance political stability, the Russian president thanked his listeners for their special role in contributing to progressive civic change. "We have a real opportunity to foster friendship and democracy, a real chance to help make the world a better place," Yeltsin observed, and then referenced the uncommon mission recently undertaken by the region's citizenry: "Your willingness to help in our hour of need was a major factor in my decision to normalize relations between our two countries." Yeltsin and Russian Ambassador Vladimir Lukin then met with Operation KareLift representatives to offer thanks for the food and medical aid, and related partnerships to improve relations between both countries.[4]

The encounter provided opportunity for a Karelift worker to retell an incident that had taken place when the first shipment of KareLift supplies was unloaded at the port of Vladivostok. A group of burly stevedores clad in wool coats and black stocking hats had labored throughout the morning to hoist foodstuffs out of the hold of the Russian ship *Pestova*. American supervisors kept an uneasy distance. No words passed between the two parties until one of the Americans found himself sitting

near the stoic leader of the dockworkers, who had taken a break on a mountain of burlap sacks filled with Northwest grain and lentils. After an awkward silence the Russian pointed skyward to a large bird circling high above the ship and said with a slight smile, "In Russian folklore this bird's appearance is a good omen." He then paused and wistfully added, "You know, we should have been friends all these years."[5]

ENVIRONMENTAL STEWARDSHIP AND FOOD SECURITY IN THE TWENTY-FIRST CENTURY

Pulitzer Prize-winning naturalist E. O. Wilson optimistically finds a solution to the twenty-first-century East-West challenge of sustainable food security in a world with unprecedented population levels in "an exuberantly plentiful and ingenious humanity." The prescient conservationist offers hope through advocacy for the affirming forces of an indigenous land ethic rooted in traditions of sacred responsibility, and scientific advances to enhance crop production. Such an "Evergreen Revolution," Wilson observes, offers the best way forward for

Ft. Vancouver Heirloom Vegetable & Herb Garden
R. Scheuerman Collection

the wellbeing of regional living environments and for humanity writ large. Advocates of food security point out that over-emphasis on production alone can be counterproductive. Fully one-third of the world's annual grain harvest is lost to spoilage from moisture damage and consumption by pests. Since food production presently exceeds the global population's caloric need by over 35 percent, scientific and policy-making attention directed to matters of proper storage and economic distribution could significantly allay world food shortages.

The historical and scientific dimensions of an Evergreen Revolution would be mutually reinforcing as agricultural economists like CIMMYT's Melinda Smale note the essential value of farmers' personal accounts to understand cultivar sources, pedigrees, and trait selection. Related considerations of growing social significance in the United States, Europe, and the developing world include burgeoning interest in both heritage and modern grains for household and commercial uses ranging from artisanal breads and pastas to craft brewing malts. This work both affirms the value of biodiversity and sustainability while preserving cultural knowledge that attaches meaningful protection to landscapes.

Growing numbers of small-scale Northwest millers, artisan bakers, and craft brewers identify distinct flavors in grain varieties and enhancing product taste and marketability. Such desirable traits with recently introduced landrace grains like "Simpson White" Lammas wheat and "Tolmie Bere" barley—names associated with nineteenth-century Hudson's Bay Company agriculture—are akin to the idea of variety and *terroir* with fine wines. The Red Fife breads of Victoria baker-restaurateur Clifford Leir have been characterized as "yellow crumb with an intense scent of herbs and vegetables rich with a slightly herby and spicy flavor," while George De Pasquale of

Seattle's Essential Baking Company tells of specialty bread wheats imparting "chocolaty overtones and a hint of spice." A loaf made from Skagit Valley Red Russian wheat won the professional baker flavor test at the 2012 Kneading Conference in Mt. Vernon. Maltster-entrepreneurs Wayne Carpenter and Mike Doehnel founded Skagit Valley Malting in nearby Burlington that year to process reintroduced heirloom and modern grains for the region's burgeoning beverage and specialty food market. Eel River Brewery owner Ted Viratson alludes to the intangible value of heritage: "There's a reason we do what we do. This is what our grandparents drank.… It was wholesome, fresh, and flavorful, with a lot of heart and soul."[5]

Larger conventional, transitional, and organic commodity producers also seek innovative approaches to promote grain identity preservation. Reardan, Washington, area farmers Karl Kupers and Fred Fleming established Shepherd's Grain in 1999 in order to improve marketing by fostering closer associations between growers and consumers. The company soon grew to include Palouse growers Read Smith and John Aeschliman, and now includes forty Columbia Plateau partners who produce over six hundred thousand bushels of grain annually, using sustainable farming. Wheat varieties are selected on the basis of nutrient profiles related to flour qualities preferred by artisan and commercial bakers. Smaller, certified organic grain operations like Washington's Bluebird Farms in the Methow Valley and Azure Farms of Dufur, Oregon, market their produce to local bakers as well as to urban outlets east of the Cascades. Marlin, Washington's Lentz Speltz Farms advertises "yesterday's Elysium wholesomeness" in its Resurgent Grains line of einkorn, emmer, and spelt products. Pacific Natural Foods founder Chuck Eggert of Tualatin, Oregon, notes the

Pacific Natural Foods
Heirloom Vegetable Test Plots
R. Scheuerman Collection

marked interest and numbers of health-conscious twenty-first-century consumers who take time to read about product ingredients, origins, and packaging. "Folks today are caring more about taste as well as convenience," he observes, "and how food can be produced in socially and environmentally responsible ways." To this end, the company's livestock are all pastured, and development of soups, beverages, and other products draws from extensive company experience with heirloom vegetable and grain test plots.

Along with twenty-first-century entrepreneurial skills practiced by Northwest growers, educators also find relevance for today's youth in lessons on abiding agrarian values from America's past. Organizations like 4-H, FFA, Northwest Granges, and grower associations promote educational programs, hands-on activities, and career education to promote the virtues of personal responsibility, hard work, problem-solving, and teamwork familiar to scholars of Jeffersonian democracy. In the 1960s, rural Edwall, Washington, native Meryl Green Pruitt and Seattle Pacific University's Margaret S. Woods formulated a place-based pedagogical philosophy of "experiential homestead education" for urban youth. In 1975, Pruitt's Pioneer Place Museum in downtown Seattle developed into the Ohop Valley's 1880s-era Pioneer Farm near Eatonville and the Pioneer Trails History Education Program for area schools. Students, teachers, and others are taught today not only about nineteenth-century crops, harvesting techniques, and food preparation, but also about cultural values of earlier generations and indigenous populations relevant to environmental stewardship and sustainable lifestyles. Cultural historians at Ft. Vancouver National Historic Site, Tacoma's Ft. Nisqually Living History Museum, and Ft. Langley near Vancouver, British Columbia, have established heirloom vegetable gardens and stands of wheat, barley, buckwheat, and other crops that flourished at these places in the frontier era.[6]

The Greenbank Farm Agricultural Training Center on Whidbey Island opened in 2008 to offer a seven-month program for aspiring small farmers on sustainable crop production and business planning. Practical experience and coursework is offered on the historic 150-acre farm through a collaborative between the WSU-Mt. Vernon Research Center, Island County Extension Service, and the Port of Coupeville. Puget Sound developer Calvin Philips established Greenbank Farm in 1904 which today features renovated original barns, farmhouse, and community supported agricultural plots. The center also hosts educational programs open to the public throughout the year as well as the ATC Seed Project through which students conduct variety trials, marketing studies, and field days.[7]

New agronomic approaches being pioneered through the state land-grant universities in Washington, Oregon, and Idaho also hold promise for Northwest farmers and in the developing world, where farmers are increasingly compelled to cultivate marginal lands at high risk of degradation using conventional annual cropping methods. Crop breeders Stephen Jones and Steve Lyon at WSU's Mt. Vernon Research Center have teamed with Oregon's Patrick Hayes, Robert Metzger, and others to develop the evolutionary participatory breeding (EPB) method through which traditional mass selections of wheat and barley are combined with varieties developed worldwide that have been adapted to needs of smaller-scale farmers.

Crop breeders have long tended to overlook the circumstances of these low-input growers. Research they have conducted in cooperation with Wes Jackson at the Land Institute in Manhattan, Kansas, is also exploring the development of perennial grains to further increase global food security and regional sovereignty. Jones observes that, "Although we use new tools in our work, most of our new ideas turn out to be old if we look carefully enough at previous studies. It is a continuum that we work in, and the foundation was laid by Spillman, Gaines, and Vogel. We must embrace this past, not ignore it...." Vogel's WSU colleague Robert Allan further notes how the Pacific Northwest's remarkable growing conditions facilitate crop diversity: "We're not just 'one-trick dogs.' We grow all classes [of wheat] except soft red, probably because it's not as valuable a crop as soft white in the export market. But we have the ability to grow all classes."[8]

Northwest farm families and scientists will be called upon to meet the challenge of feeding a burgeoning world population, estimated to reach 9.5 billion during the lives of young people just getting their start in the field. Though it took more than 10,000 years to reach twenty-first-century production levels, scientists and farmers now beginning their careers must increase an additional 70-100 percent. Doubling food production to feed a hungry world on fewer acres, as urban growth continues and while using resources ever more efficiently and astutely, represents one of the most rewarding and challenging careers imaginable.

In remarks on "Food, Agriculture, and National Security in a Globalized World" at the 2009 Des Moines Borlaug Dialogue, Bill Gates warned of "an ideological wedge" offering the dangerous "false choice" of productivity or sustainability. "The fact is, we need both…and there is no reason we can't have both." To this end, he reaffirmed the Gates Foundation's commitment to comprehensive programs that use advanced wheat breeding techniques adapted to the conditions in the developing world so poor farmers will reap long term prosperity. With most Americans now two or more generations removed from their rural roots, restoration of publically funded research and administrative oversight is essential to show that technology is being used with sound science so nutritious and safe food is the paramount priority.[9]

Progress in Northwest agricultural development amidst these challenges and opportunities remains rooted in the early nineteenth-century experiences of pathfinders like George Simpson, William and Jane Tolmie, George and Isabella Bush, and thousands of other farm families who followed in their wake. Industrious teams of British and French Canadian settlers and Native Americans like the Kamiakin and Moses families tilled fields and tended livestock to improve their livelihoods. These were then followed by waves of pioneering Americans and recurrent pulses of immigrants to the region from Great Britain, Russia, Russia, Scandinavia, Mexico, and elsewhere. These groups contributed distinct cultural traditions and an ancestral cornucopia of heirloom grains for productive crops that ripened on both sides of the Cascades and eventually spurred the global Green Revolution. Improvement in tillage practices is erasing the memory of chin-high ditches caused by erosion, as a new generation of Northwest farmers values greater stewardship of the land while the region's crop breeders devote more attention to the plight of farmers elsewhere in the world where hunger is chronic.

Historian Oscar O. Winther observed that the frontier era "contributed immeasurably to the development of farming, ranching, and dairying…. [They] put crop raising beyond the experimental stage and made planting and sowing easy for the Americans who followed. They gave assurance to… settlers that the region was agriculturally rich."[10] The far ranging enterprises spawned at trading posts and frontier immigrant communities across the region led to conflict and accommodation with Native peoples in the 1850s. But the cultures also learned from each other in ways that continue to shape contemporary understandings of environmental stewardship and agricultural production, enriched with living history.

Appendices

Copy of Map of Cowelitz Farm

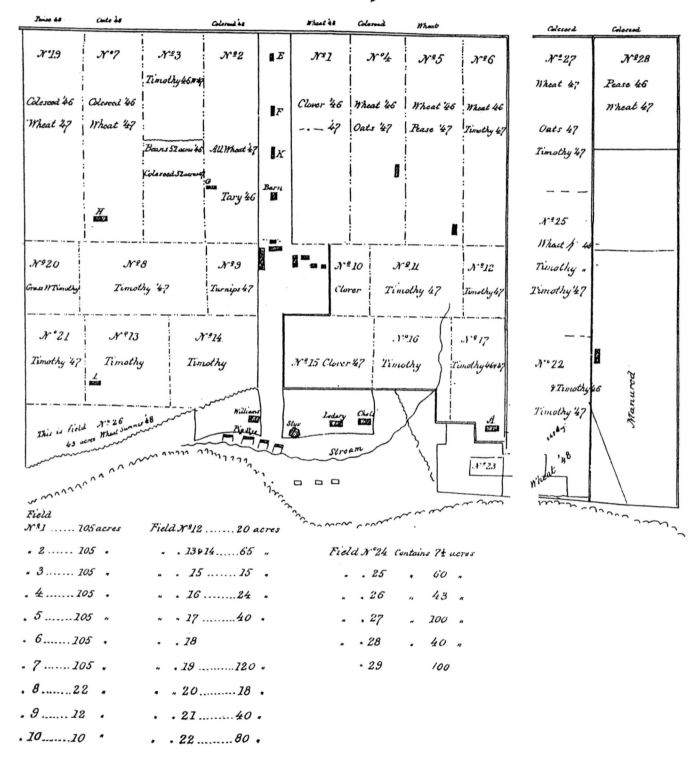

Map of Cowlitz Farm, 1843
Hudson's Bay Company Archives, Provincial Archives of Manitoba
(HBCA, F25/1.fo.10; F26/1,fo.66d-67)

Appendix I:
The Puget Sound Agricultural Company
Nisqually and Cowlitz Farms Year and Map (c. 1845–1860)

The following schedule of farm work is based journal entries by workers affiliated with the PSAC. Abbreviations: **C: Cowlitz Farm**, 1847–51 (near present Toledo); **H: Joseph Heath Farm** (at present Steilacoom, Washington); **M: Muck Station,** 1858–59 (north of present Roy along Muck Creek); **N: Ft. Nisqually** (1851–53); **T: Tlithlow Farm**, 1851, 1856–57 (along Murray Creek on present Joint Base Lewis-McChord).

Sources: George Roberts, "The Cowlitz Farm Journal, 1847–1851"; *Oregon Historical Quarterly* 63:2 & 3 (June–September 1962); George Dickey, *Journal of Occurrences at Fort Nisqually, 1833–1859*; *Tlithlow Journal, 1851* and *1856–57;* and *Journal of Occurrences at Muck Station, 1858–1859*, Tacoma, Washington: Fort Nisqually Historic Site, n.d. Map: "Cowlitz Farm with Field Rotations, 1845–46," Record Group 76, Boundary and Claims Commissions and Arbitrations, Cartographic Division, National Archives.

	Jan	Feb	Mar	Apr	May	June	July	Aug	Sep	Oct	Nov	Dec
Dipping sheep (in tobacco water)	T,H		H			H			M	C	M	
Winnowing & sorting wheat and peas[1]	T,H	T,H			C				M			M
Wild horse round-ups	T											
Moving grain to Dwelling House	T											
Gathering prele[2] for fodder		H	H									
Cutting pine boughs for sheep feed	T											
Pruning apple trees		N										
Cutting drains (ditches)			T									
Piling dung, gathering manure		T										
Repairing stables	T									T		
Repairing equipment[3]	H	T	H		M							
Corning beef[4]		T										
Spreading manure	C	T,H,C	C	M		T,H		C	C		C	C
Plowing	H	T,H	T,H				M		C	H	M,C	
Breeding sheep			M									
Sowing vegetables (onions, carrots, turnips)		C,M	C									
Sowing & harrowing oats and rye seed[5]		T,T	T,T	M,C						C		C
Sowing & harrowing wheat seed	C	C,T,M	C,M						C	C	C,H	H
Sowing & harrowing peas & coleseed[6]		T	C,T,H	C,T,M	C							
Sowing & harrowing buckwheat[7]				H								
Planting potatoes[8]		C,T	T	T,M,H	C,T,H							
Branding livestock			T,M	M	M							
Digging potatoes							M	C,M	C			
Weeding fields (hoeing vegetable & grain crops)					C,H	T,M	M	H	H			
Cutting roads			T									
Cutting green hay[9]			T	T								
Cows calving				H	C							
Ewes lambing[10]	M	C	C	C,H	T,H	T,M						
Grubbing brush, clearing trees		H	H	T			H					
Setting fence				T								
Breaking clods (with hoes)					T							
Field rolling				M	M							
Castrating horses			T,M	T								
Planting turnips[11]		C		T	H	H						

	Jan	Feb	Mar	Apr	May	June	July	Aug	Sep	Oct	Nov	Dec
Transplanting cabbage starts				C	M	M,H						
Castrating/docking lambs			M	M,H								
Shearing sheep, sorting wool, sharpening shears					T	H						
Separating ram lambs (to put with ram band)			M									
Moulding potatoes[12]					H	H						
Propping apple trees						N						
Breeding horses					M							
Washing and shearing sheep						M,H						
Cutting hides for cabresses[13]						M						
Garden weeding and thinning (carrots, turnips, onions)					M							
Castrating calves									T	M		
Harvesting grain (cutting, binding, shocking oats, barley, wheat, rye & flax)[14]		T,H	C,H,M									
Collecting, thrashing, and cleaning clover seed							C					
Thinning & weeding turnip fields							M					
Pulling peas (harvesting)			C		T	H	H,M					
Harvesting cabbage							H					
Picking potato blossoms							H					
Weaning lambs								H				
Opening & reshocking grain (to dry and ripen)							M					
Harvesting apples								N				
Digging potatoes								C,H	C			
Harvesting buckwheat									H			
Slaughtering hogs			C									C
Melting fat (for tallow)									M			
Bailing wool (to ship)											M	
Flailing/threshing grain, tacking straw[15]	C,T		M	C				C	C	M	C,T,M	
Thrashing peas				M							C,M	
Repairing grain sacks											M	
Hauling wheat to mill					M							
Claying houses, whitewashing chimneys										H		
Breeding ewes											C	
Breeding horses											M	
Salting & pickling beef tongue											H	
Smoking meats (tongue, venison, geese, cod)											H	H
Cutting, hauling & splitting firewood	T,H	T			M						H	T,H
Repairing harness & tack	T		M								T	
Digging parsnips											M	
Preserving & ironing cranberries										H	H	
Cutting, charring & pointing pickets												H
Sewing clover												C

Year-round PSAC chores included cutting, hauling and splitting rails, moving and building sheepfolds, breaking horses, cleaning stables, carting potatoes, hauling and feeding rye and oats to livestock, and butchering livestock.

[1]The "tedious work" of cleaning and sorting seed grain and peas by hand—chores usually done by Indian women—was to remove ragwort and wild vetch seed and to obtain "true kinds" (e.g., red, white, and yellow wheats) that could be sown "by sort" (J. Heath, 1845).
[2]Prele is native horsetail rush and marsh grass gathered for livestock feed.
[3]Equipment repair routinely included fixing oxen yokes, harrows, plows, and the building of tumbrel carts. The latter were tipcarts used to carry and dump dung, stones, and other bulk materials.

[4]Corning is the dry curing of beef with coarse salt ("corns"), sugar, and spice rubs.

[5]The general crop rotation sequence on company fields was wheat > peas & oats > potatoes. In Scotland oats and rye were often grown together. In England and Scotland a four-year rotation was common in varying sequences of potatoes or turnips, barley or oats, clover, and wheat.

[6]Coleseed is a headless cabbage raised for fodder.

[7]Although neither a grain nor grass, buckwheat produces a nutritious seed commonly used for human consumption.

[8]Potato varieties included Spanish, Lady Finger, Early Blue, Early Ashleaf Kidney, and reds.

[9]Tolmie experimented with a number of pasture grasses in the 1850s including red and white clovers, rye grass, cocksfoot (orchardgrass), foxtail, and timothy.

[10]To improve wool quality the company imported Merino and Sussexdown rams, Southdown ewes, and Leicester ewes and rams.

[11]Common globe turnips and rutabagas ("Swedish turnips") were often raised in England and Scotland in the nineteenth century for both human consumption and as fodder to supplement the winter diet of sheltered livestock or in the field. Much of the mature root is above ground so could be eaten *in situ* by sheep.

[12]A hoe or other tool is used to "mould," or draw up soil around a potato plant to protect shallow tubers and prevent disease.

[13]Hair rope for packing furs and hides.

[14]Grain was typically cradled with a scythe leaving stubble about a foot high. The stalks were then tied into sheaf bundles and shocked in piles to prevent lodging, or being knocked down by rain or wind. The 1859 crop at Muck and possibly on other company fields was cut with a reaper.

[15]Grain was flailed by striking low piles of stalks with wooden cylinders attached to poles by leather straps, or "treaded out" by horses led in circles around a hard threshing floor on the ground or inside a barn.

Appendix II:
Pacific Northwest Heritage Grain Development Chronology[1]
Italicized names indicate approximate time of the variety's introduction to the region

A. Wheat

1500–1600s	1700s	1800	1825	1850	1875	1900

Northern Europe (primarily soft white & red winter bread and hard amber Poulard wheats):

White Lammas>————————————→"Scottish Winter (HBC)?" ———→ *"White Winter"* ———→*"Hudson Bay"*[2]———————— *Oregon Winter*———→
(Winter) \————————————————————*White Australian*[7] ————→*Pacific Bluestem*[3] ————————————→
            ?————————Genesee Red Chaff>————————————————————————————*Red Chaff*————→*Goldcoin (Fortyfold)*—→

Red Lammas (Red English)[1]>———————————————————————→————————Old Squarehead————————————*Brown Squarehead*————→
(Winter)   (1868)   (Lewis County, WA)

Velvet Cone (Irish Poulard)————————————→Jerusalem ——————————————————————————————————————*Alaska*———→
(Spring)   (1808)

Southern Europe (primarily hard red and soft yellow-white winter wheats):

                    /Sonora (MX) ————→Sonora (CA)————————————————————*Sonora Spring, Oregon Spring*[7] ————————————→
                  /   /————————————————*White Clawson* ———→
Mediterranean>←————————————→Lancaster Red————→Fultz———→*Fultz*————————————
                 \   /————————————————*Hybrid 128*[4]—→
                  \Little Club (MX)——→Little Club (CA)————————————————→*Little Club*   >
                  \
                   Chili (Chile) Club>————————————————————→*White Chile Club,*[7] *Oregon Club?*→*Big Club*—→
                                                         \——————x/w Michigan Club=*Surprise* ———————*Dicklow*—→

                                                                                          /*Federation*[6] ————————→
Black Sea/Ukraine>———————————————————————————→Halychakna/Ghirka>*Red (Scotch) Fife*[5] ———→*Red Fife* ———→
                                                                                          Marquis————————————→
                                                                                           (x/w Red Calcutta)

Crimean/Ukraine> —————————————————————————————————→Turkey Red—*Turkey Red/Red Russian* ———————→
                                                               (to Kansas 1870s; 1890s to the Palouse)

---

[1]Documentation of varieties grown in the Northwest and indicated here in italics is based on period journal and newspaper articles, government research reports, and oral histories. Although evidence indicates those shown here were widely grown in the region at the times indicated, the list is by no means complete. Early nineteenth-century landraces and "improved varieties" provided by European firms like Gordon, Forsyth and Vilmorin were often identified generically as "yellow wheat" and "six-row barley," although some 100 different named wheats alone were grown in England and Scotland. (The most common were Red "Celtic" Lammas, the Spanish landrace selection Talavera, Browick, Childham, Golden Drop [Canada Club], and Spalding; see J. Percival, 1921:89.) Moreover, later "farmer experimenters" and nurserymen like Tacoma's William Reed and Phillip Ritz of Walla Walla likely distributed varieties not mentioned in available records. The emergence of plant genetics and selective crossing in the late nineteenth century further led to the development of many cultivars that were grown at government research stations at Pullman, Washington; Corvallis, Oregon; Agassiz, British Columbia; and elsewhere, although relatively few achieved widespread commercial use. By 1920 just ten varieties grown on at least 100,000 acres in the Pacific Northwest accounted for approximately 80 percent of production (see Appendix III). At that time leading USDA cerealist Carleton Ball sought to standardize varietal nomenclature to enable farmers and scientists to more accurately identify strains in accordance with American Society for Agronomy guidelines (J. Clark, 1922:2) and the following names were recommended for some Northwest wheats: Jones Fife for Jones Winter Fife, Red Chaff for Red Chaff Club, Baart for Early Baart, Jenkin for Jenkin's Club, Surprise for Pringle's Surprise, Red Clawson for Early Red Clawson, and Clackamas for Clackamas Wonder.

[2]Raised at Ft. Nisqually in 1845, and likely the Willamette Valley "Hudson Bay wheat" reported there in the 1880s.

[3]According to J. Klippart (1850), Bluestem, a white winter introduced to Ohio in 1804, "no doubt descended from Flint." Purple Straw is variously noted as descended from English Red Straw and Purple Straw, though the Bluestems and Purple Straws of the American Southeast may not be closely related genetically (L. Newman et al., 1946).

B. Barley

c. 1850	c. 1875	c. 1900	c. 1925

SIX-ROW

North African Coast ⟶ ——— California Coast ⟶ ——— *"Coast barley"*
Mediterranean landrace to Mexico, a fall barley dominant on West Coast, c. 1890

Scots Bere ⟶ *"Scotch Six-Rowed"*?
A Viking-Norman era landrace, the only one still raised commercially in Great Britain (Orkney and Shetland islands)

Oderbrucher ⟶ ——— *Oderbrucher* c. 1880s to Canada and PNW
A German landrace from the Oder Valley, widely grown in Midwest, c. 1900

Manshury ⟶ 1872 to Madison, WI ⟶ *Golden Queen, Silver King*
(Manchuria, Amur River)   (1881 "New Manchuria" from Russia to Ottawa)
A tall, late maturing spring malting barley, dominated Upper Midwest, c. 1890

A Balkan/Caucaus landrace ⟶ to Canada ⟶ Tennessee Winter
Primarily a high protein feed barley, dominant in the Southeast, c. 1900

A Turkish landrace ⟶ 1905: *Trebi* from Trebizond, Turkey via USDA
(1912 grown in Idaho, widespread c. 1920 PNW[8])

TWO-ROW

Chevalier[9] ⟶ Hallett's Chevalier, Old Island Two-Row ⟶ *California Chevalier*
(1885: possibly the "Canadian Malting Barley" of the Walla Walla Valley)[10]
A low protein variety and excellent malter, widely planted on the West Coast

Moravian ⟶ Hanna ⟶ Bethge/*Viktoria*
"[O]f very old Moravian origin."—E. Ritter Proskowetz

Stavropol ⟶ to Kansas with Russian-Germans[11] ⟶ Kansas Common

Scotch ⟶ *Scotch Two-Row* (1870s: Willamette Valley)

---

[4]From an 1890s W. Spillman cross of Little Club with Jones Fife, the latter was a hybrid descendant of Mediterranean Longberry, Fultz, and Russian Velvet released in 1889 by A. N. Jones of Newark, New York. Jones Fife was widely grown in the Pacific Northwest and known as Crail Fife in Montana and British Columbia.

[5]M. Carleton (1900) observes that Fife is "similar to the Ghirkas of the Volga region"; A. Buller (1919) identified it as Halychanka from Galicia, then a province of Western Ukraine, a designation confirmed by modern agronomists.

[6]The spring hybrid Federation was developed in the 1890s by William Farrar in Australia who crossed Improved Fife with Australian Purple Straw and Indian Yandilla.

[7]Reported in "Oregon Exhibit," *The Willamette Farmer*, August 22, 1879, where "Scotch Two-Rowed, Six-Rowed" barley are also listed.

[8]John C. Weaver, American Barley Production, 1950:40.

[9]*Spokane Falls Weekly Review*, March 28, 1885.

[10]Chevalier and Beaver were among the best two-row Canadian malting varieties; Manshury, Odessa, and Common were among the best six-row in the Midwest (Early Vernon and Clarence Smith, Farmer's *Cyclopedia of Agriculture*, New York, 1904.) For an overview of nineteenth-century British varieties, see John R. Walton, "Varietal Innovations and Competitiveness of the British Cereals Sector, 1760–1930," *British Agricultural History Society Paper*, 1997.

[11]Ellis or Common (spring) barley is six-row and likely brought to the Hays, Kansas, area by immigrants from southern Russia in the 1890s. The prominent Midwest spring barley Stavropol came from Russia about 1910. See Arthur Swanson, "Cereal Experiments at the Fort Hayes Branch Station, Hays, Kansas, 1912–1923," *USDA Technical Bulletin No. 14* (November 1927).

C. Oats

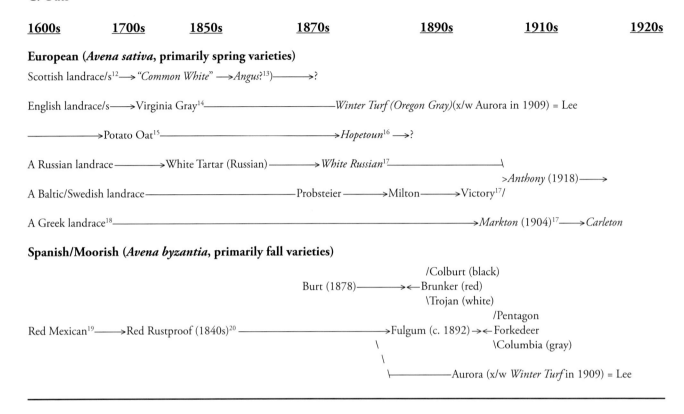

1600s	1700s	1850s	1870s	1890s	1910s	1920s

European (*Avena sativa*, primarily spring varieties)

Scottish landrace/s[12]⟶*"Common White"* ⟶*Angus?*[13])⟶⟶?

English landrace/s⟶Virginia Gray[14]⟶*Winter Turf (Oregon Gray)*(x/w Aurora in 1909) = Lee

⟶Potato Oat[15]⟶*Hopetoun*[16] ⟶?

A Russian landrace⟶White Tartar (Russian)⟶*White Russian*[17]⟶\

>*Anthony* (1918)⟶

A Baltic/Swedish landrace⟶Probsteier⟶Milton⟶Victory[17]/

A Greek landrace[18]⟶*Markton* (1904)[17]⟶*Carleton*

Spanish/Moorish (*Avena byzantia*, primarily fall varieties)

/Colburt (black)
Burt (1878)⟶←Brunker (red)
\Trojan (white)
/Pentagon
Red Mexican[19]⟶Red Rustproof (1840s)[20]⟶Fulgum (c. 1892)⟶←Forkedeer
\   \Columbia (gray)
\
\⟶Aurora (x/w *Winter Turf* in 1909) = Lee

---

[12]Nineteenth-century British agriculturalist John M. Wilson (1851) observed that "Common White" was an expression used by Scottish farmers "to designate simply the variety with which a person is best acquainted," and that these included Blainslie, Kildrummie, Bothrie, and Halkerton oats. Others grown in England at the time included Lancashire, Essex, Irish (Strathallen), White Tartarian (Russian), and Danish.

[13]Identified by cultural historians at Ft. Vancouver as an oat variety likely cultivated on area Hudson's Bay Company farms. Prominent Scottish horticulturalist Patrick Shirreff identified the "esteemed species" Angus to be an "improved selection." See J. Wilson, 1851.

[14]Widely grown in Colonial America.

[15]The name is derived from an English farmer's selection of a stray stalk in 1788 in an Essex potato field so its association with a particular landrace has not been established, and some speculate that it was a continental transplant.

[16]J. Wilson (1851) records that Hopetoun originated from an English Potato oat selection about 1830.

[17]According to agronomist F. A. Coffman (1977), "…practically all oats grown from the Central states southward as well as along the Pacific Coast now trace" to five varieties which he dates from their appearance in North America: White Russian (c. 1850), Green Russian (1870), Kherson (Ukraine)/Sixty-Day (1896), Markton (1904), and Victory (1908). White Russian was a late maturing, rust-resistant variety introduced early to the United States and used in many subsequent crosses. "Russian winter oats" are also mentioned in the March 19, 1874 issue of *The Willamette Farmer*. Of the ten highest yielding experimental oat varieties in the 1890s reported by Canadian plant breeder William Saunders of Canada's principal Western experimental farm at Agassiz, British Columbia (e.g., Golden Giant, Banner, Lincoln, Early Blossom, Early Gothland, Columbus), none are reported in use by Northwest American farmers or among the five mentioned by Coffman as contributing to most modern West Coast varieties (W. Saunders, 1901). Highland Chief oats were grown in Oregon in the 1890s. The Pacific Northwest's most widely grown oat varieties in 1910 were Improved American, Swedish Select, Big Four, Sixty-Day (Kherson), Black Russian, and Oregon Gray Winter (C. Warburton, 1910).

[18]Sometimes mistakenly identified as a Turkish landrace because of archaic maps used when selected for use abroad.

[19]Likely descended from a Spanish/Moorish landrace brought to the New World by Spanish conquistadors in the 1500s.

[20]Probably brought to the United States by American soldiers who fought in the Mexican War. Among Red Rustproof's prominent prodigies were Burt—possibly the first US experimental oat selection, Fulgum, winter-hardy Culbertson, smut-resistant Ferguson Navarro, and Aurora.

Appendix III:
Pacific Northwest Wheat Varieties and Prevalence (1919/1920)*
Showing Landraces/Natural "Improved Selections," Hybrid Crosses, and Classes

Wheat varieties reported by USDA based on 1919 data; acreage total (4,715,502) based on Fourteenth US Census (1920) county reports: Washington: 2,494,160 acres; Idaho: 1,141,295; Oregon: 1,080,047. (Varieties grown on approximately 4% of the region's total acreage were not reported.) Source: J. Allen Clark, John H. Martin, and Carleton Ball, *Classification of American Wheat Varieties.* USDA Bulletin 1074, Washington, D.C.: Government Printing Office, 1922:210–16. Landraces and natural "improved selections" are marked with †.

Abbreviations:

HRS: hard red spring   HRW: hard red winter   HWS: hard white spring
SWS: soft white spring   SRW: soft red winter   SWW: soft white winter
 1. Pacific Bluestem† (SWS, 883,800): 18.7%
 2. Turkey Red† (HRW, 510,800): 10.8%
 3. Goldcoin† (SWW, 473,800): 10.1%
 4. Marquis (HRS, 440,800): 9.4%
 5. Baart (HWS, 360,500): 7.7%
 6. Hybrid 128 (SWW, 289,100): 6.1%
 7. Jones Fife (SRW, 241,100): 5.1%
 8. Club†[4] (various, 215,400): 4.6%
 9. Dicklow[3] (SWS, 159,800): 3.4%
10. Red Russian (HRW, 154,700): 3.3%
    Total 10 Most Acreage: 79.2%

Varieties and production on at least 10,000 acres but less than 2% of total Northwest yield: Little Club† (75,900 acres), Jenkin (66,500), White Winter†[2] (50,700), Hybrid "Shot Club" 143[1] (49,500), Foisy[2] (41,300), Red Chaff† (40,000), Sonora† (35,400), Hybrid "White" 63 (33,200), Hybrid "Red Walla Walla" 123 (28,100), Martin (26,100), Kinney[2] (23,400), Huston[2] (22,400), Prohibition[2] (21,600), Defiance[2] (18,500), Galgalos[2] (16,500), Odessa†[3] (14,500), Rink[2] (14,400).
Varieties reported with production between 100 and 10,000 acres: Coppei, Hybrid 108, Sol (all Washington only); Cox, Dale Gloria, Wilbur (all Oregon only); Allen, Fultz, Gypsum, Lofthouse, Mediterranean†, Touse (all Idaho only); Durum[4], Eaton, Red Fife, Surprise.
Incidental varieties reported on less than 100 acres: Arcadian, Mexican Bluestem, Spring Giant, Squarehead Master (all Washington only); Bluechaff, Broadhead, Crooked Finger, Minnesota (Early) Wonder, Early Ohio, Kahla, June, Smith, Squarehead, Western Three-Mesh, White Valley (all Oregon only); Echo, McGee, Mortgage Free, Red Clawson, White Lily (all Idaho only).

[1]Washington only
[2]Oregon only
[3]Idaho only
[4]"Club" and "Durum" reported as general wheat classes rather than specific varieties.

*British Columbia wheat acreage (80,500, of which 45,000 are Peace River spring wheats) reported for 1940—Garnet (HRS, 36,800): 48.0%, Marquis (HRS, 15,700) 19.5%, Jones Fife (includes Crail Fife, SRW, 10,000): 12.4%, Red Bobs (HRS, 5,400): 6.7%, Reward (HRS, 5,200): 6.5%. Source: T. Hatcher, "The History and Regional Distribution of Wheat Production in British Columbia," M.A. Thesis, Vancouver: University of British Columbia, 1940.

Appendix IV:
Gaines Wheat Pedigree

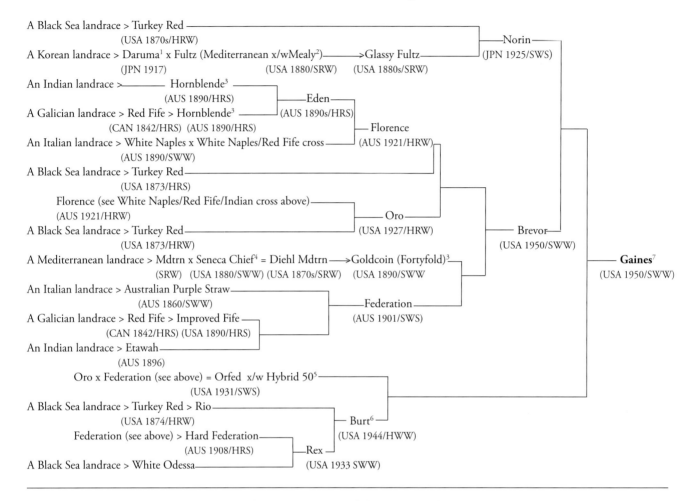

This chart is derived from agricultural histories and agronomy reports including O. A. Vogel, "Registration and History of Gaines," 1993; Melinda Smale, *Understanding Global Trends in the Uses of Wheat Diversity and International Flows of Genetic Resources,* 1999; Sanjaya Rajaram, *The Human Right to Food and Livelihoods,* 2001; Gonjiro Inazuka, "Norin 10, a Japanese Semi-Dwarf Wheat Variety," 1971, and J. Allen Clark, John H. Martin, and Carleton Ball, *Classification of American Wheat Varietie*s, 1922. Dates may refer to selection, cross, or release dates and are approximate.

Abbreviations: HRS: hard red spring HRW: hard red winter SWS: soft white spring SRW: soft red winter SWW: soft white winter

[1]Of two Daruma varieties noted at Morioka in 1946, Aka (red) and Shiro (white), the cultivar used here to cross with Fultz is believed to have been Shiro-Daruma.

[2]An 1880s New York field selection from a stand of Red Mediterranean named for the farm's owner.

[3]Hornblende was a hard red cross between Improved Fife and Scotch Fife, both hard red spring wheats.

[4]Seneca Chief and Fortyfold were both soft white field selections from red-kernel Mediterranean so may have been separate varieties.

[5]Hybrid 50 appears to have been one of a number of original Spillman hybrids that, while not commercially released, was kept for breeding stock. Documentation by Spillman on Hybrid 50's progenitors has been lost but likely included a combination of the dozen or so varieties he used to develop Hybrid 128 and others.

[6]USDA Technical Bulletin 1278 (1963:90) identifies Burt's pedigree as a cross between Rio/Rex with a Brevor selection.

[7]Among the first significant Green Revolution varieties that descended from Gaines were Pitic and Penjamo (Mexico), and Sonalika (India); soft white and other descendants widely grown in the Pacific Northwest included Nugaines (1965), Sprague (1972), Fielder (1974), and Stephens and Houser (1977). Norin-10 was also a parent of many hard red varieties introduced to American Midwest growers including Lindon (1975), Vona (1976), and Wings (1977).

Appendix V:
List of Northwest Heirloom Grains

Pacific Northwest varieties that were grown commercially before 1965 are indicated below in standard font. Others reported by U.S. and Canadian agronomists and farmers that were raised on incidental acreage, test plots, referenced as hybrid progenitors, or mentioned in other contexts are italicized.

WHEATS

Alabama
Alaska
Alaska Wonder
Alicel
Allen
Alliès-Hybride
American Banner (Gold Coin)
Amethyst
Annat
Arcadia
Arcadian
Armavir
Arnautka
Arnold's Gold Medal
Assiniboia Fife
Atlanti (Missoyen)
Australian Club
Australian Purple Straw
Baart (Early Baart)
Beaver
Beloturka
Beryl
Big Club (Oregon Club, Crooked-Neck Club)
Big Frame
Bishop Ottawa
Black Emmer
Black Prolific
Black Tea (see China Tea)
Blount's Fife (Gypsum)
Blue Democrat
Bluechaff (Calvert Club)
Boadicea
Brevor
Broadhead
Browick
Brown Squarehead
Burbank
Calvert Club (Bluechaff)
Campbell's White Chaff
Canada Club (Golden Drop)

Canadian Hybrid
Canhatch
Canus
Carosella (White Naples)
Carter's Queen
Celtic (Red Lammas)
Centennial
Chalcedony
Champaign
Charlottetown
Chattam
Chesterheaded
Childham
Chili Club (Chile Club)
China Tea (Black Tea, Java)
Chinook
Clackamas Wonder
Clawson
Colonist (Saxonka)
Columbia (Fultz)
Coppei
Cox
Crail Fife (Jones Fife)
Crimean (Turkey Red)
Crooked Finger
Crooked-Neck Club (Big Club)
Crystal Rock
Dale Gloria
Daruma
Defiance
Democrat
Diamond
Dicklow
Diehl Mediterranean (Michigan Bronze)
Dooley
Dott
Durum
Early Ohio
Early Red Clawson (Red Clawson)
Early Rice (White Polish)
Early Wilbur (Wilbur)

Early Wonder (Minnesota Wonder)
Eaton
Echo
Eden
Einkorn
Elgin
Elmar
Emerald
Emmer
Emporium
English Rivet (Poulard)
Etawah
Farquahar
Farro
Federation
Fielder
Fife (Red Fife)
Finley
Fishpole
Florence
Foisy (Red Chaff, Oregon Red Chaff)
Fortyfold (Gold Coin)
French Imperial
Fultz (Columbia)
Gaines
Galgalos (Red Russian)
Galicia (Red Fife)
Garnet
Genesee Giant
German Amber (Valley)
German Emperor
German Red
Ghirka (Red Fife)
Glassy Fultz
Gold Coin (Fortyfold, American Banner)
Golden Amber
Golden Cross
Golden Drop (Canada Club)
Goose (see Kubanka)

Gypsum (Blount's Fife)
Hallett's Golden Drop
Halychanka (Red Fife)
Hard Federation
Harvest King
Harvest Queen
Hindustan
Hornblende
Houser
Hudson Bay (White Winter)
Huston
Hybrid 50
Hybrid 60
Hybrid 63 (White)
Hybrid 108
Hybrid 123 (Red Walla Walla)
Hybrid 128
Hybrid 143 (Shot Club)
Improved Fife
Iumillo
Irish Cone (Poulard)
Jasper
Java (China Tea)
Jenkin (Jenkin's Club)
Jerusalem
Jones Fife (Jones Winter Fife)
June
Kahla
Kanred
Karmont
Kharkov
Khorasan
Kinney
Klondike
Kubanka (Pererodka, Goose)
Ladoga
Lancaster Red (Red Mediterranean)
Landreth
Lindon
Lofthouse
Lost Nation
Mammoth Red
Manitou
Marfed
Marquis
Martin Amber (Landreth)
May (Red May)
May King
Mayflower
Mayview

McGee (McGee's White)
McPherson
Mealy
Mediterranean (See Red Mediterranean)
Mediterranean Longberry
Mexican Bluestem
Michigan Amber (Red May)
Michigan Bronze (Diehl Mediterranean)
Michigan Club
Mindum
Minhardi
Minnesota Wonder
Missoyen
Molds
Monad
Mortgage Free
Muskingum
New York Spring
Norin
Northcotis
Norway White
Nugaines
Odessa
Old Squarehead
Omar
Onas
Ontario Wonder
Oregon Club (Big Club)
Oregon Red Chaff (Foisy)
Oregon Sonora
Oregon Spring
Oregon Winter (White Winter)
Orfed
Oro
Pacific Bluestem (White Australian, Palouse Bluestem)
Pansar
Pellisier
Penjamo
Pererodka (Kubanka)
Pitic
Poulard (English Rivet, Irish Cone)
Prairie du Chien
Prelude
Preston
Pride of Butte
Purple Straw

Red Allen
Red Bobs
Red Calcutta
Red Chaff (Foisy)
Red Fife (*Galicia, Ghirka, Halychanka*)
Red Lammas (Firewheat)
Red May (Yellow Lammas, Michigan Amber)
Red Mediterranean
Red Rock Chaff
Red Russian
Red Straw
Red Walla Walla (Hybrid 123)
Red Wave
Regenerated Fife
Requa
Reward
Rex
Riga
Rink
Rio
Rocky Mountain
Rosario
Ruby
Rudy Weibul
Russian Red (Galagos, Velvet Chaff, Russian Velvet)
Salt Lake Club
Sandomir
Sapphire
Sardonyx
Sari-Bugda
Saunders
Saxon Fife
Saxonka (Colonist)
Scotch Fife (Red Fife)
Seneca Chief
Shirreff's Squarehead
Shot Club (Hybrid 143)
Shumaker
Siberian
Sibley's Hybrid
Silver Chaff (Red Clawson)
Smith
Smith's Improved
Sol
Sonalika
Sonora
Spalding

Spring Giant
Squarehead Master
Stocium
Sunset
Surprise (Pringle's Surprise)
Sweetbread
Talavera
Tasmanian Red
Theiss
Titanic
Touse (Touselle)
Touselle (Touzelle, Touse)
Tracy
Triplet
Turkey Red (Crimean)
Tuscan Island
Valley
Velvet Chaff (Russian Red)
Velvet Cone (Poulard)
Vermillion
Victoria
Virginia White
Vona
Washington Sun
Western Three-Mesh
White (Hybrid 63)
White Australian (Pacific
    Bluestem)
White Bennett
White Chaff (Mammoth)
White Clawson
White Chili (Chili Club)
White Elliot
White Emmer (Vernal)
White Federation
White Lammas (Hudson Bay)
White Lily
White Mennonite
White Naples (Carosella)
White Odessa (Odessa)
White Russian
White Tuscan
White Valley
White Velvet
White Winter (Hudson Bay,
    Oregon Winter, Wold's White
    Wonder)
Wilbur
Wilhemina
Wings

Winter Alaska
Wolf Hybrid
Wysor Eureka
Yandilla
Yaroslav
Zeeuwse Witte
Zimmerman

BARLEYS

Advance
Alpine
Ambler's Rustproof
Andre
Bay Brewing (California Coast)
Beaver
Benyon
Bethge (Viktoria)
Blazer
Blue
Boyer
Burbank (Hulless)
California Coast (Coast, Bay
    Brewing)
Carter's Prize Prolific
Charlottetown
Chevalier (Hallett's Chevalier)
Chinese (Manshury)
Coast (California Coast)
Common (Ellis)
Danish Island
Egyptian Hulless
Ellis (Common)
Golden Promise
Golden Queen
Haggett's
Hanna
Harper's
Highland Chief
Kamiak
Luther
Manshury (Manchurian, Chinese)
Moravian
Northumberland
Oderbrucher
Odessa
Old Island Two-Rowed
Purple Hulless
Scotch Two-Row
Scotch Six-Row (Scots Bere)
Showin

Silver King
Silvermine
Stavropol
Steptoe
Texas Red
Trebi
Tennessee
Viktoria (*Bethge*)
Wharton
White Holland
White Hulless
White Smyrna

OATS

Ambler's Rustproof
Angus (Scotch)
Appaloosa
Anthony
Aurora
Banner
Big Four
Black Russian (Black Tartarian,
    Siberian)
Black Tartarian (Black Russian)
Blainslie
Bothrie
Brown Winter
Brunker
Burt
Cayuse
Carleton (Markton)
Colbert
Columbia
Common White
Culbertson
Danish Island
Egyptian
English Gray
English Side
Essex
Excelsior
Ferguson Navarro
Forkedeer
Fulgum
Golden Giant
Green Russian
Haggett's
Halkerton
Harper's
Highland Chief

Hopetoun
Hopkinton
Hungarian (White Tartarian)
Improved American
Irish (Strathallen)
Kherson (see Sixty-Day)
Kildrummie
Lancashire
Ligowa (Swedish Select)
Lincoln
Markton (Carleton)
Oregon Gray
Palouse Wonder
Pentagon
Potato
Red Mexican
Red Rustproof
Saxon Fife
Scotch Dunn
Scottish Chief
Seger
Siberian (Black Russian)
Side (English Side)
Silvermine (Swedish Select)
Sixty-Day (Kherson)
Sommerset
Strathallen (Irish)
Surprise
Swedish Select (Silverrmine)
Teshkin
Texas Red
Tobolsk (Early Siberian)
Trojan
Tver
Victory
Virginia Gray
Waterloo
White Holland
White Norway
White Probsteier
White Russian (White Tartarian)
White Tartarian (White Russian,
　Hungarian)
White Wonder
White Zealand
Winter Alaska
Winter Turf (Oregon Gray)

RYES AND TRITICALES

Abruzzi
Bailey
Beal
Common (Winter Common)
German Giant White
Hudson
Kodiak
Probsteier
Roberts
Rosen
Sangeste
St. John's Day (Midsummer)
Shugan
Sisolsk (Vologda)
Vyatka
Vyborg
White Russian
Winter Common
Willits
Zhelanni

Endnotes

Chapter I: Fur Trade Farming

1. For a comprehensive account of Spanish exploration of the Pacific, see Warren Cook, *Flood Tide of Empire: Spain and the Pacific Northwest, 1543–1819* (1973). On Santa Cruz de Nuca grain at Nootka Sound, see I. Wilson [José Mariano Moziño], 1970 [1790]:7–8. The Northwest's oldest potato variety, the fingerling Ozette native to Chile, came direct from Spanish plantings at Núñez Gaona where it was introduced to the Makah Indians. For Astor's American Fur Company, see James Rhonda, *Astoria & Empire* (1990). Also see Peter C. Newman, *Company of Adventurers* (1985) on Hudson's Bay Company history, and Marjorie W. Campbell, *The North West Company* (1957).

2. B. Belyea, 1994 [1807–08]:77, 105. Canada's first wheat was raised in 1605 at the French settlement of Port Royal in present Nova Scotia, and barley was likely introduced by the governor of New France, Samuel de Champlain, in 1608. The first wheat in the present US was grown in Virginia in 1611. In 1617 English oats were first grown in Quebec City, followed by plantings in Newfoundland in 1622. Thompson's fellow Nor'Wester, Daniel Harmon, planted barley and potatoes in 1811 when establishing Ft. James on Stuart Lake in present British Columbia but the grain did not flourish.

3. C. Kingston (1923) 1981:163–64; "Spanish cattle" described in E. Meeker, 1905:481. In August 1812 Astorians John Clarke, Ross Cox, and others had traveled up from the lower Columbia and Snake rivers to the mouth of the Palouse. They were welcomed by the "small and friendly tribe" inhabiting forty large tule-mat lodges, and the group moved overland with a contingent of horses to Spokane House.

4. J. Raffan, 2007:187–92; G. Simpson [F. Merk], 1931:xii–xiii; B. Barker, 1948:334–35. Possible original Selkirk wheat varieties in B. McCallum, 2008; and F. Dickinson, 1976. Wheat was grown to a limited extent as early as 1754 at the French settlement of Ft. St. Louis near Nipawin east of present Prince Albert, see B. McCallum, 2008:655. The normal schedule for the annual round-trip Columbia Express commenced westbound from York Factory as soon as weather permitted, usually in late March. The plan was to reach Ft. Vancouver via Athabasca Pass and Boat Encampment in early June and begin the return trip by month's end or early July in order to return in time to load the furs for transport to London. Furs from New Caledonia above Ft. Kamloops were taken south on the 1,500 mile "Brigade Trail" from Ft. St. James on Stuart's Lake in May and arrived at Ft. Vancouver in mid-June. The northern third of the route to Ft. Okanogan was a winding overland packhorse course. The express canoe used east of the Rockies was the voyageurs' lighter "north canoe" made of birch bark sewn together with spruce root threads. The flat-bottomed western vessels were clinker-built of yellow pine or red cedar boards gummed with a mixture of boiled pitch and salmon oil, and tied with spruce-root withes. The colorful if arduous brigades typically numbered fifty to sixty individuals with crews of seven to ten per vessel, which carried up to one and one-half tons of cargo, or about five hundred bushels of grain.

5. J. McLoughlin, 1880:46 on first delivery of grain, quoted in J. Gibson, 1985:33; J. Jackson, 1996:144–45. Simpson quotation in G. Simpson, [1824]1968:50. The Russo-American Treaty of 1824 also established 54°40'as the line south of which Russia would not colonize and ceded its interests in the Oregon Country to the United States. Early grain culture in R. Buller, 1919:1–5; G. Paulson (2008); and J. Handley, 1963:204–6.

6. J. Townshend, [1839] 1978: 171–72.

7. The North West Company established its Willamette Trading Post in 1814 on French Prairie about three miles north of present St. Paul. Father F. N. Blanchet claimed that French Canadian subsistence farmers had cultivated fields in the Willamette Valley as early as 1824. See C. Landerholm, *Notices and Voyages of the Famed Quebec Mission to the Pacific Northwest*, 1956:218. Columbia Department self-sufficiency is reported in G. Simpson to William Smith, November 17, 1828 (F. Merck, 1968:299–301).

8. J. Ball letter quoted in J. Hussey, 1967:64. Ball's original farm is believed to have been directly east of present Champoeg State Park. After considerable voyaging, Ball returned to New York and eventually made his way to Michigan where he remained for the rest of his life. John Sinclair relocated to San Francisco. Hauxhurst and his mill described in J. Hussey, 1967:74–75.

9. D. Douglas [1826] 1914:152–54; E. Walker quoted in W. Lewis, [1834]1920. For the valued assistance McLoughlin provided Douglas, he was awarded a silver medallion by London's Royal Horticultural Society in 1826.

10. G. Simpson, 1968:49–50; J. Gibson, 1985:22–23; Ft. Nez Perces Post Journal, April-September 1831, T.

Stern Papers. A Northwest Sahaptin word for wheat, *àytalú*, refers to the mountain *Calamagrosis* pinegrass and reedgrass species that resemble the grain. Yakama Sahaptin *lakamíim*, a flour soup traditionally made with salmon, is from Chinook Jargon *lakamin*, "soup, stew," which may be from *la gamelle*, French for a soup or stew pot. French origins of some Columbia Plateau Indian names for vegetables and grains is based from anthropologist Bruce Rigsby's studies of Sahaptin and Interior Salish languages with tribal elders Sam Sturgis (Nez Perce, 1964), Tom Andrews (Palouse, 1964), Jim Alexander (Yakama, 1971), and others.

11. T. Taylor, Appendix X: Criteria for Restoring Historic Vegetation (1992). Oregon Experiment Station (Corvallis) Director J. Withycombe on Hudson's Bay Company introduction of White Winter in H. Snyder, 1905:12. Oregon journalist-historian George Himes (1889:58-59) identified its source as the Red River Selkirk Settlement. A single 1916 selection of White Winter collected in Oregon kept vital this important heritage grain.

12. G. Roberts, [1847–51] 1962:197. Recent genetic analysis of Scottish and Scandinavian barley races indicates separate origins in antiquity which suggests that early Viking settlers likely found Norman barley growing in Scotland. Scotch barley reference in *The Willamette Farmer*, October 22, 1879. Scots Bere is the only European barley landrace still raised commercially though other relic landraces still survive in remote areas of Italy, Serbia, Russia, Ukraine, and Turkey. The name perpetuates the ancient northern European Latin term *bar* for bearded grain, or barley, from which the English words barb, beer, and barn are also derived.

Chapter II: The British-Russian Contract

1. J. Handley, 1963:204–6; *American Agriculturalist*, 39 (November 1880):486. The ancient European landraces began to be gradually replaced from the beginning of the nineteenth century after "improved selection" for yield and quality in Great Britain led to such varieties as Archer and Chevalier and the emergence of seed firms like Gordon, Forsythe in England and Vilmorin in France. Scottish landraces largely remained apart from the development of modern cultivars since the principal nineteenth- and twentieth-century European grain breeding centers (Cambridge, England; Svalöf, Sweden; Abed, Denmark; Weihenstephan, Germany; and St. Petersburg, Russia) often undertook cooperative trials and shared samples of their own regional varieties. The predominant nineteenth-century British durum wheat was the Poulard, known as Rivet, or Velvet Cone, a tetraploid descendant of ancient emmer with a cone-shaped head. The Northwest brewing industry involved a host of enterprising German immigrants including Henry Weinhard, a native of Württemberg, who operated breweries at Ft. Vancouver and Portland in the 1850s.

2. J. Williams, 1996:65–68; M. Maclachan, 1998:112–14. Burrs are the stone sections cemented together to form the round millstone enclosed with an iron band that contracted after heating to secure the assembly. A set of granite millstones at Spokane's Northwest Museum of Arts & Culture are believed to be from the Ft. Colvile gristmill. Ft. Vancouver's mills described in T. Farnham, II, 1843:266. One hundred pounds of milled hard red wheat yields approximately seventy-two pounds of flour, eleven pounds bran and shorts each, and six pounds of red dog from the kernel's outer aleurone layer. Specific amounts of these products depend on grain variety, test weight, and method of milling.

3. L. Hastings, 1845:46.

4. G. Simpson [1830], 1931:113–14; B. Barker, 1948:346.

5. J. Gibson, 1985:86; Simpson quote in E. Rich, 1947:85.

6. B. Barker, 1948:341; J. Radosevich, 1997/1998. The brigantine-rigged *Beaver*, the first steamship to operate in the Pacific Northwest, was built in 1835 of English oak, elm, and teak at London's Blackwall Yards along with the Hudson's Bay Company barque *Columbia*. The vessels sailed together to the Pacific via Cape Horn and arrived in the spring of 1836. Simpson on Whidbey Island and area settlement prospects in G. Simpson to Sir John Henry Pelly and Andrew Colvile, November 25, 1841 (G. Williams, 1973:92–101). Etholén's remarks on Columbia grain in J. Gibson, 1976:205. Grain yields in Russian Alaska were very poor due to the short growing season and introduction of varieties unsuited to the region. The Russian-American Company encouraged agricultural development and farming was attempted on Kodiak Island, at Sitka (New Archangel), and elsewhere, but with limited success. The Russian Banana fingerling potato, probably of Baltic origin, was likely introduced to the Pacific Northwest through British Columbia by Russian-American traders. Hudson's Bay Company shipments to Russian America from the Oregon Country in the 1840s included wheat and flour as well as substantial quantities of peas, apples, pork, and beef.

7. W. Tolmie, 1963:256, 388. The fort was relocated inland in 1843 to Nisqually Plain at present DuPont. The Factor's House and Granary were moved to Tacoma's Point Defiance Park in the 1930s to form the nucleus of the Ft. Nisqually Living History Museum and National Historic Landmark.

8. J. Gibson, 1985:123–34; W. Tolmie, 1963:387; B. McBride, 2011. Smaller Ft. Nisqually grain farming stations where sheep were also periodically folded included Ashland, Elk Plain, Gilhogwas, Tutatchee, Sastuk, Kukuleh, and Molock Plain. The entire Ft. Nisqually area of farming and ranching operations covered some 220 square miles.

9. G. Simpson [1841] 1973:92–93; C. Wilkes, IV, 1845:315.

10. Cowlitz Farm operations and productivity are recorded in G. Simpson, [1841] 1973:92–93; G. Roberts [1847–51] 1962:112–74; A. Anderson, c. 1864; and E. Huggins, 1900. Stone-ground flour by Cowlitz Indians in C. Quick and J. Zander, 2008:127–28.

11. E. Huggins, 1900; G. Dickey, 1994:3; G. Roberts [1878], 1962. Hudson's Bay "Old White Winter" wheat described in G. Roberts, 1962 (1847):120ff, and mentioned in *Willamette Farmer*, February 4, 1881 and August 28, 1881; *Portland Oregonian*, October 29, 1905; *Harper's Monthly*, October, 1882. Roberts reference to "Anent wheat" is in a letter to historian Francis Victor, see [George] Roberts to F. I. Victor, November 28, 1878, in G. Roberts, 1962:181. The continental European three-year rotation sequence was likely introduced in northeastern France as early as the ninth century AD. This approach expanded production acreage to two-thirds from the traditional medieval regime that used only half with biennially alternated fallow land. The newer sequence generally included grain (wheat, barley, or oats) > green manure legume (peas, beans, or lentils) > summer fallow. Wheat increasingly predominated after the twelfth century. The two-year rotation model (e.g., wheat>fallow>barley/rye/oats>fallow) remained in use across Mediterranean Europe due to soil and climate conditions. Extensive information on farming operations at Cowlitz and Ft. Nisqually—likely the region's most documented Hudson's Bay Company site, is due to a great extent to the preservation and literary contributions of longtime employee Edward E. Huggins (1832–1907). According to farmer-politician Leslie Scott, white clover was first brought to the Willamette Valley by Methodist missionary J. L. Parrish in 1840; red clover was introduced to the region in 1854. Fruit trees likely planted by company workers—including a Yellow Bellflower apple and Winter Nellis pear, are still bearing at Tlithlow's substantially undisturbed location near the head of Murray Creek on Joint Base Lewis-McChord near Tacoma. The company's "Spanueh Station" on the south shore of Spanaway Lake was first named "Montgomery's Place" for HBC herder John Montgomery, who relocated in 1853 to a half-section donation land claim several miles northeast along the Naches Trail in present Frederickson.

12. See John Hussey, *Champoeg: Place of Transition* (1967) for an excellent chronology of events leading to Oregon's provisional government. Meek, Griffin, and Rocky Mountain Retreat in L. Hafen, 1982:361. Probate records for the settlement of Ewing Young's estate included a detailed list of his transactions at Ft. Vancouver, providing insight to pioneer necessities. These included Hudson's Bay red bar blankets, claret brown cloth, blue flannel, purple merino, and red baize; Hyson, Congo, and Twankey tea, coffee, Cavendish tobacco, sugar, and port wine. See F. Young, 1920:270–75.

13. G. Simpson, in J. Gibson, 1985:92; J. Applegate, 1931 [1851]:141. Virgil quotation in *Puget Sound* [Steilacoom] *Courier*, May 19, 1855. Oregon Trail pioneer and Puget Sound booster Ezra Meeker also tells of early Northwest harvesting techniques in his popular memoir, *Seventy Years of Progress*. The use of grain as a medium of trade was commonplace well into the twentieth century.

14. See John C. Jackson, *Children of the Fur Trade*, for a complete account of the Red River colonists' migration to the Northwest.

15. John Flett eventually settled in the Lakeview area and served as the government farmer for the Puyallup Indian Reservation from 1862–1878, and George Roberts resided at Cowlitz Farm from 1859 to 1871.

16. E. Owens, 2009:51–54; G. Reese, 1984:1–2; S. Dolan, 2007:291. San Juan Island's scenic Friday Harbor was named for one of the company's Hawaiian shepherds, Joseph Poalie Friday. Some of the region's oldest pear trees that date from the late 1800s still survive on the island including a Flemish Beauty, White Doyenne, Belle Angevine (Pound), and Belgian. The White Doyenne is an ancient variety introduced to France in the 1550s from Italy and identified as the old Roman pear "Sementinum."

17. F. Laing, 1938:329–31.

18. J. Deans, "Rustic Rhyms by a Rural Rhymster: Poetry and Recollections of Life at Craigflower [1853]," Royal British Columbia Archives, Provincial Museum, Victoria, MS-2431, and D. Pethick, 1968:89–90 9.

19. R. Melrose, "A Royal Emigrant's Almanack Concerning Five Years Servitude under the Hudson's Bay Company on Vancouver Island [August 1852-July 1857]," Royal British Columbia Archives; Vancouver Island grains described in *British Colonist*, February 5, 1861. Victoria area farming and milling in D. Pethick, 1968:99–100; L. Robinson, 1948:49–83; and *British Colonist*, May 12, 1860; February 5, 1861; and February 24, 1864. English agronomist Henry Evershed identified various "Essex" wheats including White Essex, Red Essex (Kessingland), "and four other sorts" (H. Evershed, 1889:240). Ethnobotanist Sharon Rempel of Victoria's Vancouver Island Wheat Project and Jennifer Iredale, curator of Craigflower Living History Farm, have documented many vegetable and fruit varieties grown there which they have propagated in recent years. Apple varieties include Red Astrachan (Abe Lincoln), Esopus Spitzenberg, Yellow Newtown, Rhode Island Greening, Blenheim Orange, Canada Rienette, Golden Russett, and Adams Pearmain. Nineteenth-century garden vegetables raised there included the Long Red Surrey, White Belgium, and Large Weise carrot, Maple pea, Early York and Early Drumhead cabbage, Early London cauliflower, White Globe Pomeranian and Yellow Aberdeen turnips, Ban-

holm ("Swede") rutabaga, and White Welsh onion, and Ashleaf potato. See J. Iredale, 1995. Following the Tolmies' relocation to Vancouver Island, Edward Huggins assumed oversight of Ft. Nisqually and PSAC properties in the vicinity for which the company was compensated in 1869, and in the following year the farms were opened to public entry. The company had marginally economic success with dividend payments distributed to shareholders only seven times in thirty years.

Chapter III: Missions and Migrations

1. Discussion on the Whitman–Spalding party's rumored jar of wheat from the East is in Cyrus Walker, *Portland Oregonian*, September 3, 1905. Walker attended school at the mission during the winter of 1845–46. The Snake River Indians' seed grain probably came from Henry Spalding at the Nez Perce Mission near Lapwai; see J. Mullan, 1863:88. Sorghum was also listed among the Snake River Indians' production; see *Willamette Farmer*, February 4, 1881. The original granite mill stones used near Alpowa are now in the collection of the Washington State Historical Society in Tacoma. N. Whitman quotation in J. Gibson, 1985:182; Rev. Walker in J. Cole, 1979:188. F. I. Trotter [C. Miller], 1938 (2):14–41 on Chief Red Wolf's Snake River apple orchard; E. Walker quote (April 15, 1839) in C. Drury, 1940:123.

2. A. Splawn, 1917:15–16; W. Brown, 1961:76–77; A. Waller letter, April 1845, quoted in Boyd, 1996:151. Indian crops at present Douglas, Ephrata, and Palisades from Madeline Covington interview with Verne Ray, October 1956. F. Chenowith in *Oregonian*, July 12 and 15, 1851; J. Muir [1889], 1992:973. French-Canadian frontiersman and army scout Ned Chambreau also comments on Chief Moses' crops in Moses Coulee during the late 1870s.

3. J. Cole, 1979:202; L. Palladino, 1922:58–60.

4. E. Laveille, 1981:136–41, 171; The Kalispel (Pend d'Oreille) St. Francis Borgia and St. Ignatius missions were merged in 1854 under the latter, which is located on the Flathead Indian Reservation. Catholic missionaries first arrived at Ft. Vancouver in 1838 when Fathers Francis Norbert Blanchet and Modeste Demers came to minister to French Canadian employees of the Hudson's Bay Company.

5. C. Wilkes, IV, 1845:315, 460–61; J. Ayer, 1916:40–41; W. Tolmie, "History of Puget Sound and the Northwest Coast," n. d.:10–11, Royal British Columbia Archives, Victoria, BC. On the Simmons-Bush family settlement south of Puget Sound, see M. Morgan, 1979:70–75. The group traveled over the Oregon Trail in the company of prominent Oregon pioneer John Minto, who remembered that Bush told him one day when they were riding together that if he could not procure "free man's rights"

in the Northwest he would go to California and seek protection under Mexican law (J. Minto, 1901:212). Legislation passed in June 1844 by the Oregon Provisional Government excluded Blacks from residing in the territory. On George W. Bush's 1820 expedition to the Pacific Northwest, see Belle Bush Twohy oral history (1963–65) in P. Thomas, 1965:81–83.

6. W. Tolmie, 1963:388–89. In an era when barter was commonplace, millers like Simmons usually kept one-eighth of the grist as commission. Books on agriculture included Henry Stephens' *The Book of the Farm* and four-volume *Rural Cyclopedia*. See Steven A. Anderson, *The William Tolmie Library*, Tacoma: The Fort Nisqually Foundation, 2005. The region's first public library was the Multnomah Circulating Library established at Oregon City during the winter of 1842–43 and consisted of some three hundred volumes assembled.

7. On the Lewelling's historic trek on the Oregon Trail, see Alfred Lewelling, *Proceedings and Papers of the Quarter Century Celebration of the Oregon State Historical Society*, 1910; and S. Dolan, 2007:104–05, T. McClintock, 1967:157–60; and J. Cardwell, 1906:32–38. Seth Lewelling also introduced Italian and Golden prunes, Lincoln and Willamette cherries, the Lewelling grape, and Sweet Alice apple. A Yellow Bellflower still growing in the Henry Dorch orchard in southeast Portland is an original planting from the Lewelling–Meek nursery. The Northwest's oldest pear tree may be one planted by Mukilteo's first settler, Jacob Fowler, in 1863. The tree is probably a Seckel and grows today in the Washington city's Dobro Park. Heirloom fruit cultivars are maintained by the USDA at the National Clonal Germplasm Repositories at Cornell University in Geneva, New York (apple, cherry, grape); and at Oregon State University in Corvallis (pears, berries, hops).

8. G. Hines, 1868:318–20; *Oregon Statesman* editorial from October 4, 1853. The first agricultural newspaper published north of California, Portland's *Oregon Farmer*, remained in circulation from 1858 to 1863. State fairs were organized in Washington in 1894 (Yakima) and Idaho in 1897 (Boise).

9. G. Kellogg, 2002:17–20; and V. Farrar [Mrs. I. N. Ebey], 1917 [1853]. Challenges of early Whidbey farmers in R. White (1980):46–47. Winfield letter quoted in M. Libbey, 1995:4. Northwest viticulturists Kathleen and Gerald Hill speculate that the original Ft. Vancouver grapes were the Black Prince (Cinsault) and Black (Muscat) Hamburg; see K. Hill and G. Hill, 2004: 223. Popular nineteenth-century varieties in the Roseburg-Grants Pass area of southern Oregon included the *vinifera* Mission and White Sweetwater, and native American Concord, Catawba, Isabella, and Pocklington.

10. *The Columbian*, February 2, 1852; *Puget Sound Mail*, August 19, 1882; H. Trexler, 1918:6–7; and L. Huff-

stetler, 2011. Father Blanchet observed Chief Netlam's potato patch on Whidbey Island in 1840. A Skagit tribal elder later told anthropologist Wayne Suttles they had first come from the Seechelt, a Canadian Salish tribe. Vegetables closely identified with Whidbey Island include the Hungarian Piros Feher "Rockwell" bean introduced in the late 1800s, and the early twentieth-century Sugar Hubbard, a hybrid Blue Hubbard x Sweetmeat cross. Ebey family experiences and Robertson Mill in V. Farrar [Isaac and Rebecca Ebey (1852–53)] 1917:130–35; F. Engle, 1928; and J. Cook, 1972:60–78. Wilson & Co. tide-powered mill described in *Puget Sound Mail*, December 18, 1879. Coupeville farmer A. J. Comstock claimed the 1898 world wheat yield record of 117½ bushels per acre for his stand of Red Russian, a soft red winter variety widely grown in the Pacific Northwest at the time. See L. McKinley (1993) for a comprehensive history of Ebey's Landing National Historic Reserve, a 17,000-acre tract on central Whidbey Island where much of the nineteenth-century small farm landscape and architecture remains.

11. Colorful John Owen, a native of Wheatfield, Pennsylvania, came west in 1849 as a civilian sutler with a rifle regiment from Ft. Leavenworth. See S. Dunbar, 1927. Mullan Road packing in J. Watt, 1971:41–43, and *Walla Walla Statesman,* May 20, 1864.

12. H. Stevens, 1900:400–403. Americans Lloyd Brook, George Bumford, and John Noble formed a partnership in 1852 to establish a store at the abandoned Waiilatpu Mission and raise cattle. The men were forced to abandon their operation after the outbreak of hostilities with area tribes in 1855; see R. Scheuerman and M. Finley, *Finding Chief Kamiakin: The Life and Legacy of a Northwest Patriot* (2008).

13. MacMurray's visits to Columbia Plateau tribal leaders are chronicled in C. Trafzer and R. Scheuerman, *The Palouse Indians and the Invasion of the Inland Pacific Northwest* (1986). He visited the Yakama Reservation in July 1884 on behalf of regional commander General O. O. Howard, and conferred with Chief Kamiakin's nephew, the *twáti* ("medicine man") Kotaiaqan, who sought to reconcile his people's traditional way of life with the new order. Kotaiaqan told the officer that his band was now raising crops while continuing to honor the sacred foods—roots like camas, kouse and bitterroot, berries, and salmon. Chief Cleveland Kamiakin—the legendary chief's son who relocated from the Palouse Country to the Colville Reservation in the 1880s—spoke of the matter many years later to a group of Ephrata farmers: "We must live together on the same land; one people to another, face to face. We have families, communities, in friendship on this land. I will not tell [you] how to manage the land, but my food is also here and I hope we can continue to gather it. You use this land for your needs

as we have ours. May we live together…maintaining a sacred relationship with the land, and all creatures, so all of us can dwell here." Text of Cleveland Kamiakin speech in R. Scheuerman and M. Finley, 2009/2010:25–26. The 1956 recording of Kamiakin's words, entirely in Sahaptin, surfaced in 2008 at the Ellensburg Public Library.

14. Carl Sandburg, *Abraham Lincoln: The Prairie Years* (I) 1926:49; E. Ross, 1929:57. The Homestead Act provided 160 acres from the public domain to any American or prospective citizen who was the head of a family or over twenty-one years old. Title was issued after residence of five years and improvements were made. The 1862 Pacific Railway Act provided grants of public land and monies to fund construction of the Union Pacific-Central Pacific, the nation's first transcontinental line, which was completed in 1869. Similar subsequent legislation authorized construction of the Northern Pacific and Southern Pacific railroads. The Land-Grant College Act donated 30,000 acres from the public domain within the state of each member of Congress to support education in agriculture and the mechanical arts.

15. Lincoln's Wisconsin speech, annual addresses to Congress, and letter quotations from Roy P. Basler, *The Collected Works of Abraham Lincoln* (8 volumes), 1953; also see W. Rasmussen, 1972. In his first annual report, Commissioner Newton wrote that the Department's major goals would include collecting, organizing, and publishing statistical and other useful agricultural information; introducing useful plants and animals; chemical analyses of soils, grains, vegetables, fruits, and manures; and establishing a national agricultural library and museum.

Chapter IV: Frontier Farming to Global Trade

1. Qualities of (Red) May wheat, also known as Firewheat in eighteenth century England, reported in the *Puget Sound* [Steilacoom] *Herald*, November 11, 1859; Rev. David Blaine letter on Duwamish Chili wheat, Sieber [1854] 1978:119; J. Mullan, 1863:14–15. For original Northwest grain varieties and subsequent sales in Europe see M. Carleton, 1900; and *The Willamette Farmer*, August 22, 1979, and February 4, 1881. Samples of heritage grains are presently available in limited amounts from Seed Savers Exchange, Peters Seeds and Research, and the USDA National Small Grains Collection Germplasm Research Facility in Aberdeen, Idaho, the country's principal custodian of over 56,000 accessions from 120 countries. The world's largest "Noah's Ark" of seeds is Svalbard Global Seed Vault which houses more than two million food plants on the Norwegian Island of Spitsbergen. Seed kept frozen at 12 percent or less moisture can remain vital for decades. Soft white Little Club from Spanish American in J. Clark, 1935:131. A soft

red cultivar also known as Little Club was raised in the eastern United States in the nineteenth century.

2. J. Mullan, 1863:27–30; 40–41; *Missoula Pioneer*, October 13, 1870; February 9, 1871. Father De Smet also mentions Rocky Mountain mission production of parsnips, turnips, beets, yams, and carrots. See P. De Smet, 1905 (IV):572, 757.

3. J. Minto letter in *The Willamette Farmer*, December 18, 1874; J. Patterson in F. Loutzenhiser, 1937/38 (I):192–93. Spelt in Germany is known as *Dinkel* wheat. Testimonials on Norway oats in *The Oregon Sentinel*, October 22, 1870. See R. Nisbet, 1979:3–6. German Giant White rye described in *Willamette Farmer*, July 28, 1876.

4. M. Bailey [1854], 1986:189–91.

5. *The Willamette Farmer*, February 4, 1881. Maria Cutting quotation in "After Thoughts," n.d., in G. Roberts, 1962:241. Aspects of frontier cooking are from J. Williams, 1995:65, 92; E. Reich, 2003; and M. Lautensleger 2007. Northwest pioneer accounts of grain coffee milling and drinks (W. Boatman, Puyallup; C. Houser, Ellensburg; M. Givens, Chehalis; J. Harder, Kahlotus; M. Hunter, Thurston County, et al.) in F. H. Loutzenhiser, 1937/1938. On Ravalli and Mengarini see P. De Smet [H. Chittenden], 1905 (IV):572; E. Laveille, 1981:195; and L. Palladino, 1884:5. Grain coffees were manufactured in the Northeast in late nineteenth century under such brand names as Golden Grain, Grain-O, Old Grist Mill ("made from California wheat"), and Battle Creek, Michigan, cereal magnate C. W. Post's enduring Postum. Washington's utopian community of Equality, established in the Skagit Valley in the 1890s, sold "Equality Cereal Coffee" that was made from grain raised on their commune near Edison. Barley teas like Portland brewer Henry Weinhart's Malt Tea were popularly regarded to aid in digestion, while oat tea benefited the nervous system. See C. Woods and T. Merrill, 1900:103–05; and J. Brown, *Early American Beverages*, 1966:88–90.

6. Similar versions of Anne Clarke's original 1883 cookbook were published in Canada and the United States until the early 1900s in many editions under such titles as *The People's Cook Book*, *The Ideal Cook Book*, *The Eclipse Cook Book*, *The White Cook Book*, and *Ye Old Miller's Household Book*.

7. Kinneys and grain in *Daily Astorian*, September 12, 1877, and April 9, 1879.

8. W. Carleton, 1881:117.

9. J. Williams, 1996:66–68; E. Isaacs, 1908:165–66; *British Columbian*, November 14, 1866; W. Brent, n.d. H. Pierce, 1883:6–7. The middling purifier was introduced in 1870 to separate the outer hull of bran and produce whiter flour. Owen Hutchinson's North Star Mill at Thorp, Washington, was among the first in the region

to install steel rollers with a corrugated surface to further remove the bran and germ from the kernel and grind harder varieties of wheat. Flat rollers then pulverized the endosperm into fine white flour. Other Washington mills still in operating condition include the Pataha (Houser) Mill near Pomeroy, Waitsburg Flour Mill on the Touchet River, Oakesdale's Barron Mill, and Cedar Creek Mill near Woodland. Martin Schweikert's two-story gristmill at Havillah northeast of Tonasket, since converted to a home, was built in 1903. The German immigrant farmer milled wheat from Colville Reservation and other area growers under the "Gold Sheaf" label, appropriate for the tiny rural community's Hebrew namesake, "…where the gold of that land is good" (Genesis 2:12). Frank Howard produced "Nespelem Chief Fancy Family Flour" at his mill on Nespelem Creek, while Indian and white farmers in the reservation's eastern Inchelium–Kewa district joined together to purchase a portable, horse-powered Foos grain mill that remained in operation until the 1930s. Oregon's original mills include Thompson's (Boston) Mill on the Calapooia River at Shedd, and Butte Creek Mill in Eagle Point near Medford. British Columbia's Keremeos Grist Mill was built in 1877 near the site of the 1860s Hudson Bay Company Similkameen Trading Post and is operated by the British Columbia Heritage Trust. According to Okanagan tribal elder Ned Louis (see S. Louis, 2002:123), some of the mill's grinding equipment came from a unit originally purchased by a prominent Okanagan Indian farmer, Kemitiken (Louie Jim), from the HBC post in Kamloops. Flour "bleaching" with chlorine gas was introduced in the early 1900s to remove any trace of color. See Florence Sherfey, *Eastern Washington's Vanished Gristmills* (1978) for a detailed explanation of the pioneer milling process. The drier Unifine milling method was originally developed in England during the 1930s but inventor John Wright came to the US to perfect the process after his equipment was destroyed during World War II. Several Unifine mills were built by Washington State College engineers at Pullman and installed at facilities in Fairfield, Oakesdale, and Pullman. Some are operated today in Dufur, Oregon, by Azure Standard to process organic grains grown on the family company's nearby farmland. The mill is ideal for whole wheat products as the grain is blown into a high-speed flywheel to be pulverized against the rough surface of the outside container. This method reduces the moisture present in conventional rolling operations to preserve more nutrients and reduce rancidity. See L. Clark, 2011/12:19–20.

10. R. Delong, 1980; R. Scheuerman, 2003:55–56, 78. Bailey poem in *Wind and Weather* (1919:71). An 1881 issue of the *Willamette Farmer* (February 4) reported the most popular Northwest apple varieties were Red Astrachan, Gravenstein, Rambo, Swaar, Baldwin, White

Pearmain, Ortley, Jenneting, Red Cheek [Monmouth] Pippin, Esopus Sptizenberg, Winesap, Lady, Newtown Pippin, Gloria Mundi, and [Yellow] Bellflower. Washington's first Board of Horticulture report issued in 1893 listed most of these same varieties in production as well as Early Harvest, Rhode Island Greening, Roxbury Russet, Peck's Pleasant, and Westfield. A Northwest variety, the yellow and crimson Palouse apple, was introduced in the early 1890s by George Ruedy of Colfax, Washington. Pears included Clapp Favorite, Bartlett, Anjou, Fall Butter, Seckel, Brandywine, Clairgeau, Onondaga, Flemish Beauty, Duchesse, Burré, and Winter Nellis. Recommended peach varieties were Hale's Early, Foster, Crawford, Malta, Indian, Salway, Coxe's Cling, and Late October. See D. Fisher and W. Upshall, 1976:146. On Palouse orchards and irrigation see A. McGregor, 1982:219–226.

11. R. Scheuerman, 2003:158–59, 196–98; 1979:37–39. Saxonka wheat described in William Saunders, 1889: 110–111; and M. Carleton, 1920:42. Saunders partnered with other Canadian crop scientists in the 1880s to undertake trials with Russian Saxonka (*T. a. erythrospermum*) and other wheats in Manitoba and the North West Territories. A. N. Minkh and other nineteenth century Volga German historians identify "*Vymolocheno*" as a wheat originally distributed to the colonists in the 1760s. However, the Russian word is a generic expression for "flailed wheat" so does not likely refer to a specific variety. Egyptian Hulless barley was also raised on the drier steppes east of the Volga. Russian-German immigrant farmers also introduced White Russian, a soft white spring wheat, to Manitoba in the 1870s.

12. "The Palouse" poem in H. Helm, 1962:19.

13. John Jantz quoted in *Spokane Chronicle*, December 21, 1955. On Northwest Russian-German history see R. Scheuerman and C. Trafzer, *The Volga Germans: Pioneers of the Pacific Northwest* (1980). Wiley's Odessa wheat reported in the *Puget Sound Mail*, December 13, 1879.

14. Northwest Touse wheat described in J. Clark, 1922:19. Wait's work was reported in the *Willamette Farmer*, February 3, 1881. Oregon, Brown Winter, Hopkinton, Scotch Dun, Surprise, and Waterloo oats are also mentioned in Northwest newspaper accounts of the era. On the improved selection process and nineteenth century leading figures in European grain breeding, see M. Carleton, 1920:191–95, and N. Kingsbury, 2009:178–82. Mendel's two articles of plant hybrids had been published in the 1860s in *Verhandlungen des Naturforschenden Vereins in Brünn*.

15. M. Carleton, 1904:190–91.

16. H. Vilmorin, 1889; L. Vilmorin, 1850. Three generations of nineteenth-century Vilmorins contributed over 250 articles on plants for proceedings of agricultural,

horticultural, and botanical societies. Henri de Vilmorin's 1889 *Catalogue* is also remarkable for the provenance of period varieties listed. In addition to the Northwest varieties, the Vilmorin-Andrieux seed company obtained many others from the United States, primarily from the Ohio and New York departments of agriculture and Philadelphia's David Landreth and Sons, including Chattam, English Red, Genesee Red, Stoicum, Virginia White (1852); Arnold's Gold Medal, Clawson, Dott, Muskingum, Shumaker (1876); Silver Chaff (1877), Diamond (1879), Alabama (1882); Big Frame, Democrat, Early Rice, Finley, Mammoth Red, Martin's Amber, Smith's Improved, Sibley's Hybrid, White Chaff, Wysor Eureka (1884); Crystal Rock, McGee's White, Surprise, White Bennett, White Mennonite, and White Velvet (1887). Henri de Vilmorin's son, scientist and businessman Philippe de Vilmorin (1872–1917), published a sixty-page *Supplément Aux Meilleurs Blés*, in 1909 with descriptions and illustrations of twenty-seven company hybrids. The USDA's most notable color lithographs of grains from this period were from paintings by botanical artist Deborah G. Passmore (1840–1911).

17. *The Willamette Farmer*, July 8, 1881; (Salem) *Evening Capital Journal,* September 20, 1889; T. Kiesselbach and W. Lyness, 1924:33. Reed and Henri de Vilmorin in *Yakima Herald*, August 8, 1889; and February 9, 1893; promotion of Pacific Bluestem in J. Clark, et al., 1922:65. See Dan Morgan, *Merchants of Grain* (1979) for a study of world grain trade intrigue and finance. Some agricultural historians consider Cyrus Pringle's Champaign to be the first American hybrid wheat, while others date hybridization to the 1840s.

18. In comparison, Washington and Oregon's combined total wheat production in 2000 was approximately 195,000,000 bushels.

19. D. Meissner, 2003; P. Kaiser, 1989. The first direct shipment of Northwest grain to Europe took place in 1869 with the bark *Helen Angier*'s five-month voyage from Portland via the Atlantic to Liverpool. In 1894 the Northern Pacific Railroad sold its extensive inland wheat district network of thirty-nine elevators and 750,000-bushel capacity Tacoma Terminal Elevator to the recently incorporated Tacoma Grain Company. The new firm, headed by Frank Cardin and John Bibb, manufactured the flour brands Pyramid, Sperry's Drifted Snow, and Seattle Whole Wheat. A partnership led by German immigrant Moritz Thomsen founded Spokane's Centennial Mill in 1889 which expanded operations to Seattle in 1898. Centennial acquired Balfour, Guthrie's Tacoma Grain and Portland's Crown Mill in 1948 and moved its headquarters to Seattle in 1958. Archer Daniels Midland (ADM) acquired Centennial in 1980 and continues operations in the Spokane Valley and in Cheney at the former F. M. Martin (later National

Biscuit Company) Mill. Seattle's Fisher Flouring Mills Company established the area's largest mill in 1910 on Harbor Island, which was subsequently acquired by Pendleton Mills of Oregon and closed in 2002. Several independent flour mills have emerged in the Northwest in recent years including Seattle's Stone Ground Milling, Fairhaven in Burlington, and Bob's Red Mill in Milwaukee, Oregon.

20. *St. Paul Globe*, August 26, 1899; H. Price, 1922:1–5. According to USDA agronomists B. B. Bayles and J. Allen Clark (1954), Red Russian was the name used in the Pacific Northwest for English Squarehead. Barley grades were also introduced by the nation's boards of trade at this time to include fancy, choice, medium, low, and feed. Each grade varied in price from two to three cents per bushel at this time. The Pacific Northwest is the only region today that markets three sub-classes of soft white wheat—soft (common), club, and Western white.

    No. 1 Brewing Barley: Blue or white barley that is sound, bright, plump, and dry; reasonably free from broken and skinned kernels and other grains.

    No. 1 Feed Barley: Blue or white barley that is sound and sweet, plump and dry, and does not exceed 20 percent of other grains.

    No. 2 Feed Barley: Shriveled and tight barley or mixed more than 20 percent with other grains.

21. W. Hunt, 1951:50-51; M. Rothstein, 1963:400-412. Alexander Baillie was also instrumental in establishing the first golf course in the western US, Tacoma Golf & Country Club, located near his palatial Italianate estate Waloma on American Lake near Tacoma. The Balfour, Guthrie Warehouse is the only surviving structure of Tacoma's original "Mile-Long Warehouse," and has served since 2008 as the Foss Waterway Seaport Maritime Museum. Construction of the Snake River dam and lock system below Lewiston, Idaho, in the 1950s and '60s and improvements to lower Columbia River navigation facilitated substantial delivery of grain by barge since then from the Inland Northwest to shipping terminals in Portland and Kalama.

22. Donald Meinig's comprehensive economic history of the region, *The Great Columbia Plain: A Historical Geography, 1860–1912* (1968), chronicles the history of Dorsey Baker's regional enterprises and early Northwest agricultural trading networks. Wilcox's rise to prominence in regional grain storage and trading is recounted in Daniel Meissner's, "Theodore B. Wilcox: Captain of Industry and Magnate of the China Flour Trade, 1884–1918," *Oregon Historical Quarterly* (2003).

23. E. Holmes, 1902:567–78; L. Reitz, 1976:572. West Coast bulk wheat and flour exports in bushel equivalents for 1900 were from San Francisco (15.5 million),

Portland (12.5), and Puget Sound (8.2). SS *Minnesota's* completion reported in the *New York Times*, August 21, 1904. See *Proceedings of the Convention of Producers, Shippers, and Millers, Otherwise Known as the Wheat Convention*, 1906:17–18; hereafter cited as *Wheat Convention Proceedings*, 1906.

Chapter V: Cradles to Combines

1. F. Clemens quote in A. McGregor, 1982:16. On draft horses see T. Keith, 1976:37–47; mules in C. Penner, oral history, 1973, Penrose Library Archives, Whitman College.

2. M. Ochs interview, 1991; W. Snyder quote in A. McGregor, 1982:156–57.

3. *The Ranch*, July 1, 1904. On the 1893 Sandberg and Leiberg expedition, see R. Mack, 1988:118–28.

4. R. W. Thatcher, 1912; B. Hunter, 1907; Campbell system described in *The Ranch*, September 1, 1904.

5. B. Hunter, 1907:25–27 and 1927:13–22; Spillman's theories on Palouse soil and conservation in *The Ranch*, April 1, 1904; and USDA Farmers Bulletin 406 (1910). Country Life Commission quote in T. Salutos and J. Hicks, 1951:20.

6. Pope's thresher described in *American Farmer*, April 11, 1823; and P. Bidwell, 1941:215. Fanning mills and Buffalo-Pitts operation in H. Hines, 1894:294; and *Oregon Spectator*, September 17, 1847.

7. W. Carleton, 1881:114.

8. T. Galloway and B. Galloway, 1969:3; G. Hunt, 1908:160–63. C. L. Best served from 1925 to 1951 as Caterpillar's first board chairman. The Gilbert Hunt Co. also manufactured portable burr and rolling mills.

9. Descriptions of the horse and steam-powered harvest era are based on A. McGregor, 1982:178–85; K. Brumfield, 1986, and interviews with Northwest farmers including Marlo Ochs (1991) of Endicott, Washington, and Don Schmick of Colfax, Washington (2008). The Fort Walla Walla Museum agriculture exhibit features a 1919 Harris Hillside combine with a full-scale, thirty-three mule team in complete harness.

10. Don Schmick (2008) recalled that the Moore brothers, Russian–German immigrants from the Volga region who settled in the Palouse, used a single header to thresh nearly a thousand sacks of grain in one day in 1911.

11. *Palouse Republic*, August 12, 1983; K. Brumfield, 1968:32; *Wheat Convention Proceedings*, 1906:13–14.

12. Okanogan Valley farmer Harry Sherling took part in the unusual McDowell–Johnston threshing bee and recounted the story in B. Wilson, 1990:169.

13. Zane Grey (1872–1939) authored dozens of best-selling adventure novels including *Riders of the Purple Sage*,

Light of Western Stars, and *Rogue River Feud.* Several of his books depict aspects of rural farm life in the waning years of draft horses and steam-power, but few rival *The Desert of Wheat* for attention to agrarian detail.

14. *Palouse Republic,* April 14, 1911.

15. V. Carstensen, 1975:12; M. McGregor, 1932 Daybook, McGregor Land and Livestock Company Records, WSU; M. McGregor to J. L. Day, March 24, 1936, in McGregor Ranch Records, McGregor Company Archives, Colfax, Washington; O. Camp and P. McGrew, 1969:3–6; D. Roe and R. Riehle, 2003.

Chapter VI: Hybridization at Home and Abroad

1. Progress at the NPRR Oregon Improvement Company's Walla Walla farm reported in *East Oregonian,* October 8, 1900. Jones Fife was a hybrid variety developed in the late 1880s by New York breeder A. N. Jones using a cross of Mediterranean Longberry, Fultz, and Russian Velvet. Spillman's son, Dr. Ramsey Spillman, wrote an extensive biography of his father in 1939. The manuscript is at the National Agricultural Library in Beltsville, Maryland, and includes a colorful account of his years in Pullman and previous teaching experience at the Monmouth, Oregon, Normal School from 1891 to 1894. Following Spillman's death in 1931, Ramsey traveled to Pullman to spread his father's ashes in an experiment station plot where the distinguished scientist and educator had launched his career. Further information on Spillman's hybridization research is from J. Shepherd, 1980; S. Jones and M. Cadle, 1996:25–29; W. Schillinger and R. Papendick, 2008:175–80; and *Wheat Convention Proceedings,* 1906:67–69.

2. Spillman quote in *Proceedings of the 15th Annual Convention of the Association of American Agricultural Experiment Stations Official Report,* 1901:88–98. The paper he delivered was titled "Quantitative Studies in the Transmission of Parental Qualities of Hybrid Offspring." On Inland Northwest wheats of the 1890s, see E. Gaines, 1915:8. According to a USDA report, wheat varieties grown in the Inland Pacific Northwest at the turn of the century included Arcadian, Australian Club, Canadian Hybrid, Chili Club, Early Wilbur, Fortyfold, Genesee Giant, German Red, Goldcoin, Jenkin, Jones Fife, Klondike, May King, Mediterranean Red, Red Allen, Red Russian, Rosaro, Scotch Fife, Turkey Red, Sonora, White (Martin) Amber, White Elliot, White Tuscan, Wolf Hybrid, and "several durum wheats" (B. Hunter, 1907:22).

3. *Colfax Gazette,* Jun 14, 1901; *Ranch and Range,* June 20, 1901. Spillman also developed improved spelt varieties and a wheat-spelt progeny in order to strengthen wheat straw through hybridization. He also sought to introduce Turkestan alfalfa from Central Asia in order

to give Northwest dryland farmers a commercially viable rotation crop.

4. Northwest and other 1893 Chicago World's Fair grains described in H. Wiley, *Analysis of Cereals at the World Columbia Exhibition,* USDA Bulletin 45, 1895:14–47; and *Victoria Colonist,* February 25, 1893. "Best quality" specifications of the period included protein ("albumens") content of approximately 12.25 percent and 26.50 percent moist gluten determined by cold water kneading treatments. Lifelong consumer advocate Harvey Wiley went on to establish the Good Housekeeping "Seal of Approval." W. O. Bush also garnered gold medals for his cereal grains exhibitions at the 1901 World's Fair in Buffalo and the 1905 Pan-American Exhibition in St. Louis. Bush was also part of the group that introduced Washington legislation (House Bill 90) to create Washington State College.

5. *Portland Oregonian,* October 29, 1905.

6. W. Spillman, 1902:88–98; 1903:343–43; H. Roberts, 1929:276–83. Spillman quote on predictability of types in C. Hurst, 1925:110, and on creating a hybrid in S. Jones and M. Cadle, 1996:27. In his 1904 *USDA Yearbook* article, "A Model Farm," Spillman analyzed the careful and profitable management of a Pennsylvania farmer's fifteen-acre dairy farm that included rotations of corn, rye, grasses, peas, oats, and millet. Spillman observed that "methodical manners" on smaller acreages "cause land to yield two or three times as much as the present average." For Spillman's contributions to twentieth-century farm management and his USDA career, see L. Carlson, *William Spillman and the Birth of Agricultural Economics* (2005).

7. Process of hybridization described in M. Carleton, 1920:216. Dutch plant breeder L. Broekema pioneered scientific hybridization in Europe with his 1901 release of Wilhemina, a cross of the popular red winter club English Squarehead with the Dutch landrace selection Zeeuwse Witte. Idaho red wheat production in J. Jones, 1911:21–22. The popular nineteenth century Midwest wheat Red Clawson was developed in 1881 by crossing Gold Cross, a red semi-hard, with White Clawson, a 1860s stubble field selection from New York.

8. Commercial miller grain preferences in M. Martin, 1956:10. Grain variety prices reflected milling qualities as well as inspection standards. Portland and Tacoma No. 1 grade wheat prices in January 1910 indicate these values: Pacific Bluestem: $1.20; Little Club: $1.20; Red Fife: $1.13; Turkey Red: $1.10; Forty-Fold: $1.10; Red Russian: $1.08; Valley: $1.08. USDA and University of Idaho officials joined together in 1911 to establish the Aberdeen Experiment Station to better address the needs of southeastern Idaho farmers of irrigable lands. In 1988 the USDA relocated its National Small Grains

Collection from Beltsville, Maryland to Aberdeen where it remains to this day and safeguards the only samples of many Northwest and other American heritage grains in its collection. USDA's Plant and Seed Introduction Section, established in 1898 in Washington, DC, with test plots first located on the National Mall, was the forerunner of Beltsville and Aberdeen collections.

9. On the relative contribution of biological and labor-mechanical innovations to US wheat yields since 1865, see A. Olmstead and P. Rhode, "The Red Queen and Hard Reds," 2002.

10. D. Fairchild, 1906:19–22; R. Wahl, 1906:255–57. Fairchild credited Moravian plant scientist Ritter von Proskowetz with development of the two-row improved selection Hanna, and also mentioned Franken and Saale as brewing barleys being raised in the United States. Northwest hulless varieties reported in *The Morning Capital Journal*, March 28, 1891; *Yakima Herald*, June 10, 1902; and *The Ranch*, February 15, 1906. Brewing barley from local sources made possible the territory's first breweries which included German immigrant Martin Schmieg and Joseph Butterfield's Puget Sound Brewery in Steilacoom in 1858, and one operated by Joseph Helmeth and Emil Meyer in Walla Walla by 1860 (*Walla Walla Statesman*, December 20, 1860). Regional booster Ezra Meeker planted the area's first substantial hop field in 1865 on his Puyallup farm and production soon spread to the Fraser, Okanagan, and Yakima valleys. Early hop varieties included Kentish Golding from England and German Spalt (E. Meeker, 1883:25–26).

11. On Mark Carleton's remarkable life and travels see T. Isern, 2000. M. Carleton, 1900:79; O. F. Cook, 1899:5–15; and J. Smith, 1900:10–14.

12. M. Carleton, 1904:18–22

13. Carleton identified the "original home" of the Russian hard red winter wheats as the Crimean, Don, and Kuban territories "just east and north of the Black Sea and north of the Caucasus Mountains" (M. Carleton in J. Clark, 1922:14). Svalöf "place-based breeding" approaches reported in *Pacific Rural Press* 72:17 (October 1906). Carleton drew considerably from his experiences in Russia for his seminal work, *The Basis for the Improvement of American Wheats* (1900), which appeared soon after his return from Europe and contained tabular analyses of 245 different world varieties. USDA agronomists recommended red beardless Ghirka, a major nineteenth-century Russian export from the Volga and Black Sea regions, for its drought resistance. This spring wheat matured early but was slightly softer than Red Fife and most other Russian bread wheats; see J. Clark, 1916:2–3. The introduction of Kubanka from Russia's Kirghiz Steppe significantly boosted durum wheat production on America's Northern Plains in the early

twentieth century. Karmont described in B. Bayles and J. Clark, 1954:127. On Carleton and Black Emmer see J. Clark, et al., 1922:195 and J. Martin, 1938:5–6. The Italian word *farro* may refer to emmer, einkorn, or spelt. On Northwest oat varieties see USDA publications M. Carleton, 1900; and T. R. Stanton, 1929.

14. Grain breeding during this period increasingly focused on the development of specific varieties for the distinct soil and climatic conditions of Columbia Plateau precipitation districts, which ranged from eight-to-twelve inches per year to over eighteen inches per year. Mayview Tram described in J. Crithfield, 1964:52–62. Origins of Mayview, Coppei, and white spring wheat field selections made by farmers on the Columbia Plateau in the early 1900s like Bluechaff, Jenkin, Red Chaff, and Wilbur are discussed in J. Clark, et al., 1922:178–80.

15. Körnicke's 1889 article was published in *Verhandlungen des Naturhistorichen Vereins der Preussischen Rheinlande, Westfalesn, und des Regierungs-Bezirks Onnabrük*. His authoritative two-volume work on world cereal grains, *Handbuch des Getreidebaues: Die Arten und Varietätan des Getreides* (1885), was coauthored with Hugo Werner. The specimen of emmer he saw in the Vienna herbarium had been found in 1855 by German botanist Theodor Kotchy in the foothills of Mt. Hermon. Aaronsohn's account of his discovery of wild emmer appeared in Bulletin 180 of the USDA Bureau of Plant Industry, "Agricultural and Botanical Explorations in Palestine," 1910:39–42.

16. On the Ithaca Congress see J. Crow, 1992; Vavilov letters quoted in M. Popovsky, 1968:119–20, 140. An English translation of Vavilov's 1920 paper on hereditary variation can be found in *Journal of Genetics* 12 (1922):47–89, and "Center of Origins of Cultivated Plants" appears in a compilation of his major works, *Origin and Geography of Cultivated Plants* (Cambridge University Press, 1992). At the time he met with the Gainses in Pullman, Vavilov also served as president of the Soviet Geographical Society and chief editor of the monumental *Teoreticheskiye Osnovy Selekskii (Theoretical Foundations of Plant Breeding)* 3 vols. (Moscow and Leningrad: *Gosudarstvennoye izdatelstvo selskokohozyiastvennoi I kolkhoznoi literatury*, 1935). Vavilov was selected to serve as chair for the VIII Congress to be held in Russia in 1939 but impending clouds of war prevented the conclave from being held. He was arrested by the NKVD in 1941 and condemned to death for promoting ideas inconsistent with Trofim Lysenko's pseudo-scientific views favored by Stalin regarding socio-cultural influences on inheritance. Vavilov refused to disavow his research and starved to death in a Saratov prison in 1943 after composing several other major works on world crops while in confinement. Soviet authorities rescinded the verdict in 1955 and in 1966 the All-Union Society of Geneticists and Plant Breeders was

named in his honor. Vavilov's profound legacy endures today in Russia's principal cereal germplasm repository which is also the world's oldest and largest. The Vavilov All-Russian Scientific Research Industry of Plant Industry in St. Petersburg safeguards approximately 320,000 accessions representing 155 botanical families.

17. H. French, 1891:62–872; 1892: F. Coffman, 1977:66–67; J. Mahoffy, 2013. Six-row spring Blue barley, also likely of North African origin, was raised to a limited extent in the Inland Pacific Northwest from about 1910 to 1920. Formaldehyde solutions were also marketed as a cheaper alternative to copper sulfate for combating seed-borne smut fungi, and in the 1920s carbon carbonate dusts and mercury solutions were found to be more effective. WSU's Spillman Agronomy Farm was initially established in 1955 on 222 acres southwest of the Pullman campus, and the Wilke Research and Extension Farm near Davenport in the late 1980s; see S. Lyon, 2010:10–11. Trebi barley described in G. Wiebe, 1958:137–38.

18. Most of the initial Corvallis wheat accessions were from experiment stations and seed suppliers in Indiana, Illinois, and Colorado. French and Coote also grew a series of wheat-rye crosses (triticale, first hybridized in Scotland in the 1870s), obtained from James M. Thornburn in New York—Willits, Roberts, Bailey, Stewart, Beal, and Hudson. Smut research in D. Stephens, 1922:30–31. Farmer selections in *Ranch and Range*, October 12, 1899 and *Colfax Gazette*, August 3, 1900; Jenkin and Bluechaff history in J. Clark, 1922:11–15. A rare natural cross between Turkey Red and Goldcoin noticed by Pomeroy area farmer Edward Requa in 1926 led to distribution of the soft white winter wheat Requa.

19. J. Martin (1923):4–7; *USDA Weekly Newsletter* 45:3 (July 14, 1916). Lewis County hop grower Herman Klaber of Boitsfort also booked passage on *Titanic* after marketing his crop in London but perished in the disaster.

20. On Marquis wheat and the work of agronomist William Saunders and son, see Stephan Symko, *From a Single Seed: Tracing the Marquis Success Story in Canada to Its Roots in the Ukraine* (1999). Seager Wheeler's career is profiled in Jim Shilliday, *Canada's Wheat King: The Life and Times of Seager Wheeler* (2007). Canadian varieties in T. Hatcher, 1940:35–36, B. Bayles and J. Clark, 1954:84–86, and Sharon Rempel, personal communication, April 8, 2012. Considerable controversy arose in the 1920s over grading methods used by some marketers and others in the Canadian grain industry to promote Garnet wheat. See Jim Blanchard, "The Garnet Wheat Controversy," *Manitoba History* 19 (Spring 1990). Twentieth- century White Winter production in K. Kephart, 1993.

21. C. Swanson and N. Giles, 1987:373–85; K. Sax, 1918:309–27; 1921:280–83; 1922:513–52; 1924:552–560. Japanese geneticist Tetsu Sakamura had first proposed wheat polyploidy in 1918 while conducting research at the University of Heidelberg. The pioneering work of Sax and Sakamura was widely shared among plant geneticists and enabled Russian wheat taxonomist K. A. Flaksberger (1939) to formulate the modern classification of the genus *Triticum* in the diploid, tetraploid, and hexaploid chromosome series. This approach was adopted soon afterward by USDA researchers J. Allen Clark and B. B. Bayles and remains in use today with minor changes in nomenclature.

22. K. Sax, 1938:494–516. Vavilov was closely accompanied during his 1932 visit to the United States by a Soviet trade official and "interpreter," Vladimir Saenko, though the acclaimed scientist was fluent in English. Sax later became an outspoken critic of the oppressive treatment of Vavilov and other scientists by the Soviets.

23. J. Martin, 1935:5–8. USDA agronomist Cecil Salmon (1934:147) estimated that about three hundred varieties of wheat were commercially grown in the US by 1930. Rosen was named for Joseph A. Rosen, Jewish agronomist from Russia who undertook extensive studies of American agriculture for the new Soviet government as Chief of the American Agriculture Bureau of the Ekaterinoslav Zemstvo in present Ukraine.

24. H. Kübar, 2012:1–3. The improved Sangeste cultivar Kodiak was developed at the University of Alberta in Edmonton and released in the 1970s. It was shorter, more resistant to lodging and was grown widely throughout Canada until the 1990s.

Chapter VII: Grasses, Gaines, and the Green Revolution

1. The remarkable range and productivity of Suksdorf's work is legendary among historians of Northwest botanical studies. Although a highly introverted individual, he had studied with Asa Gray at Harvard and maintained an extensive correspondence with the country's leading botanists throughout his long life, among them Cyrus Pringle. At the time of his death in 1932, Suksdorf had accumulated one hundred fifty thousand pressed specimens at his small Bingen home. Botanist Curtis Bjork (2004) notes that his collections dating back to years when many areas still hosted native climax vegetation make possible the identification of species unique to Northwest locales. Through Suksdorf's painstaking documentation, a number of Spokane area species are known to have been extirpated including *Carex aqualitilis* and *Trifolium douglassii* (Latah Creek), *Carex echinata* (Newman Lake), *Carex interior* and *Lotus pinnatus* (Spangle), *Heteranthera dubia* (Marshall), and *Pyrrocoma liatriformis* (Philleo Lake).

2. In addition, some forty varieties of grass-like sedges, rushes, and reeds grew primarily in wetland areas. The sedge known as wool grass, however, preferred the drier areas of the western Palouse and would become a notorious pioneer plow-breaker.

3. B. R. Bertramson, n.d.: 3–7; L. Henderson, 1903:199–200.

4. M. Schneidmiller, 1995. Roy Goss and Charles Gould at WSU's Puyallup Agricultural Experiment Station conducted extensive research in the 1950s and '60s on turf grass varieties suited to areas west of the Cascades. By 2000, Idaho, Washington, and Oregon produced 90 percent of the nation's Kentucky bluegrass seed.

5. J. Weber, 1980.

6. For Grand Coulee Dam and Columbia Basin Project history, see Paul E. Fitzer, *Grand Coulee Dam: Harnessing a Dream* (1994), and Robert E. Ficken, *Rufus Woods, the Columbia River, and the Building of Modern Washington* (1995).

7. L. Briggle and L. Reitz, 1963:64, 117–18. Soft white winter Martin, also known as Martin Amber and Landreth, descended from a New York farmer's 1875 field selection in a stand of Clawson.

8. O. Vogel, "Winter Wheat Improvement in Washington to 1982," n.d., Folder 245, Box 7, O. Vogel Papers (CN 524, 2nd Accession), Terrell Library Archives, Washington State University, Pullman; D. Nagamitsu, 2012; L. Briggle and L. Reitz, 1963:88. The authors became well acquainted with Dr. Vogel and Dr. Bertramson in the 1970s and our conversations have informed this account. Robert Zimmerman's contributions to the John Deere HZ drill in W. Shillinger and R. Papendick, 2008:13. Vogel 1948 field notebook quote in S. Jones and M. Cadle, 1996:31. Soft white spring Idaed descended from a 1920 cross between the Australian varieties Sunset and Boadicea which was improved in the 1930s at the Idaho Agricultural Experiment Station in Moscow. For a report by one of the Japanese agronomists involved in the original selections of Norin-10, see G. Inazuka, 1971:25–30. Salmon's 1946 report is *The Agricultural Experiment Stations of Japan*. Daruma, derived the name from its ability to withstand lodging and "to not tumble down." A description of the variety appears in Mark Carleton's 1900 USDA Bulletin, *The Basis for the Improvement of American Wheats*, and is one of only five among nearly 250 cultivars from around the world that Carleton identified as "small." WSU crop breeder Stephen Jones named the soft white winter wheat Masami, released in 2004, in honor of agronomist Masami "Dick" Nagamitsu.

9. A. McGregor, 1982:306–12. Jacquot released extensive annual "Agronomy Reports" throughout his long career with the McGregors (1951–1973), and his research was featured in a *Farm Journal* article by Glenn Lorang, "How to Grow 10 bu. More Wheat Per Acre" (February 1958). Gaines wheat pilfering in R. Allan, personal correspondence with the authors, October 25, 2012.

10. O. Vogel, et al., 1951; D. Dalrymple, 1980:30–35; R. Gibbs, 1962:88. Vogel developed Nugaines for superior milling qualities and greater resistance to stripe rust than Gaines. The hard red winter variety Oro is also cited in secondary crosses of Brevor and Norin offspring that eventually produced Gaines, but Oro was also a "pure Turkey selection" made at the Oregon Agricultural Experiment Station in Moro and released to growers in 1927; see D. E. Stephens, et al., 1932. The 1965 Lind releases Wanser and McCall revived regional farmer interest in hard red winters. Vogel collaborated widely with prominent scientists including Oklahoma State University archaeobotanist and geneticist Jack Harlan—son of legendary USDA "barley explorer" H. V. Harlan. The younger Harlan's indefatigable efforts to safeguard landrace crops for future genetic potential included his retrieval on a mountain slope of eastern Turkey in 1948 of "a miserable wheat" that lodged and yielded poorly. The unimpressive specimen was shared with ARS wheat geneticist Robert Metzger and other researchers at Corvallis and Pullman who found over a decade later that it was resistant to forty-five races of bunt and four of stripe rust. When these diseases threated Northwest grain yields in the 1960s, the variety still bearing the humble designation P. I. 178383 was extensively used in hybridization of Northwest wheats, and provided significant vindication of the Harlans' lifetime commitment to preserving landrace grains. Hard red Khorasan landrace seed found by an American serviceman in Egypt in 1949 was grown by Ft. Benton, Montana, farmers in the 1950s and is presently marketed nationwide under the trademark name Kamut.

11. R. Bertamson, 1986:156–59; *Walla Walla Union Bulletin*, June 5, 1952. Smith authored an important summary of the college's initial decade of radiobiological research as *"Cytology and Genetics of Barley" The Botanical Review* XVII:1 (January 1951) which also appeared that year as Washington Agricultural Experiment Station Scientific Paper 903.

12. R. Nilan and C. Konzak, 1961:437–60; S. Stephens, 1961:505–508; R. Bertramson, 1986; 160–65. Nilan's work in the 1970s with Andris Kleinhofs and Wajih Owais at WSU led to the identification of sodium azide as the source of one of the most widely used chemical mutagens for biotechnological research worldwide.

13. C. Little, 1987:50–55; R. Veseth, 1986. By 2000, most earlier models of direct seed drills were approaching structural fatigue and no longer being manufactured. In 2012, The McGregor Company of Colfax, Washington, introduced lead designer Paul Buchholtz's deep fur-

row MD 1610 Drill. The innovative implement helped growers in the drier portions of the Columbia Plateau better conserve moisture and produce higher yields by seeding into heavier residue.

14. R. J. Cook, 2001:119–26; D. Marsh and D. Huggins, 2010; J. Cook and R. Veseth, 1991:iv–v. Recent USDA-ARS studies on significant moisture retention through direct seed farming points to further advantages of this approach in the Northwest; see D. Huggins, 2012:8. Conventional Northwest crop rotations and experiments with alternative crops like yellow mustard (*Brassica hirta*) and safflower (*Carthamus tinctorius*) discussed in W. Schillinger and R. Papendick, 2008:16.

Epilogue: Swords into Plowshares

1. R. Scheuerman, 2011:29–31; Lewis Townshend (Fund for Democracy and Development) to US Non-Governmental Organization Providers, October 4, 1992; and V(ictor) Andreev to Yuri Sabotnikov, February 2, 1994, Center for Global Curriculum Studies International Correspondence File, Seattle Pacific University, hereafter cited as CGCS/SPU. The Northwest companies providing substantial quantities of seed included Charles Lily, Ed Hume Seeds, and Northrup-King.

2. A. Deyneka, 2007. On the role of Alaska Airlines and Bruce Kennedy in Russia see *New York Times*, March 30, 1997; and *Seattle Times*, June 30, 2007.

3. Mikhail Morgulis and Constantine Lubenchenko to Ralph Munro, Russian Parliament Center, Moscow, February 15, 1992; Michelle Burkheimer to Vladimir Prudki and Sergei Savinskii, Olympia, Washington, February 27, 1992; Ralph Munro to Interested Citizens of Washington State, Washington Secretary of State Memorandum, February 21, 1992; Heather Bomberger, "Humanitarian Aid to Russia," US Senate Memorandum, Washington, DC, March 31, 1992; David Cannon, "[FESCO] Humanitarian Delivery and Dispersal of Cargo," February 27, 1992; Operation KareLift File, CGCS/SPU. Origins and impact of the KareLift project in the *Spokesman-Review* feature edition by journalist Eric Sorensen, "Feeding a Dream," April 26, 1992. For his contributions in promoting Russian-American diplomatic and business relationships and KareLift relief efforts, Munro was presented the Russian Medal of Friendship by President Yeltsin in 1998.

4. Michael Dobbs, "Yeltsin Appeals for American Aid," *The Washington Post*, June 18, 1992; Imbert Matthee, "Visit Here a Sign," *Seattle Post-Intelligencer*, September 29, 1994; Arthur Gorlick and Karen West, "Yeltsin's Pitch: Let's Trade, Missile Era Behind Us," *Seattle Post-Intelligencer*, September 30, 1994; Mike Lowry, 2007. Among other partnerships that emerged through KareLift associations has been the USAID "Modern Technologies in Grain Production" initiative to improve farming and marketing operations in Eastern Europe and Central Asia. As a primary consultant for this work, Thornton, Washington, area farmer Lee McGuire made ten trips to Russia, Kazakhstan, and Azerbaijan and provided WSU crop breeder Fred Muehlbauer with chickpeas (garbanzos) that have contributed to improved hybrid varieties for Northwest growers. See ACDI/VOCA, 2000.

5. S. Jones, 2012:74–77; G. De Pasquale, 2012; A. So, 2012:63. In Pearl S. Buck's preface to *Whole Grain Cookery* (1951), the famed anthropologist-gourmand explained the special qualities of whole grains: "Rain and sun, the strong sweet properties of minerals and the hidden magic of growth are contained only in the whole grains. They flavor the dishes which they make with that divine touch which man can only weakly imitate. There is a natural affinity between natural foods and the human body. They share the earth as source, and the body so fed holds energies to be found in no other way. We call it health" (S. Standard, 1951:vii–viii).

6. Valerie Sivertson, 2012. A group of dedicated Columbia Basin heritage-minded residents successfully lobbied the National Association of Wheat Growers in the early 1960s to designate Ritzville, Washington, as the site of a National Wheat Museum. In spite of organizational and funding challenges, the persevering rural community and Adams County Historical Society has promoted the idea for over fifty years. With recent support from the Ritzville-based Washington Wheat Foundation, Washington Association of Wheat Growers, and area farmers and businesses, the concept of a "Wheat Interpretive Center" reached the design phase in a 2011 partnership with the WSU-Spokane Interdisciplinary Design Institute. Plans call for an education and exhibition center with adjacent crop plots to promote public awareness of regional agriculture, commodity processing, and local food products. See *Spokesman-Review*, January 30, 1965; February 6, 2012; *Ritzville-Journal Times*, January 27, 2011.

7. J. Mercer, 2003:12-14; J. Feldman, 2013. Philips acquired 1500 acres on central Whidbey Island from the Northern Pacific Railroad and named the area for his birthplace, Greenbank, Delaware. Greenbank Farm became a model of self-sufficiency with a substantial herd of Holstein dairy cattle, Tamworth and Jersey swine, potatoes, and grain fields. The property was sold in the 1930s to German immigrant John Molz who eventually planted 125 acres of loganberries and launched Greenbank's popular Pommerelle Loganberry Wine with fruit from the trellised canes. By the 1950s, Greenbank was the nation's largest loganberry farm and Molz went on to help found Ste. Michelle Vintners, forerunner of Woodinville's Chateau Ste. Michelle Winery.

8. L. Scott, 1917:67–68; E. Wilson, 2002:xxiii–xxiv,118; M. Smale, 1996:27–28. On evolutionary participatory breeding and perennial grains see J. Glover, et al., 2010 and K. Murphy, et al., 2005. Jones quote in S. Jones and M. Cadle, 1996:34. R. Allan quote in H. Scott, 2012:12.

9. Gates remarks reported in *Farm Futures*, October 15, 2009.

10. O. Winther, 1950:78.

Bibliography

Published Works

Aaronsohn, Aaron. *Agricultural and Botanical Explorations in Palestine*. USDA Bureau of Plant Industry Bulletin 180. Washington, DC: Government Printing Office, 1910.

Åberg, Ewert. *Classification of Barley Varieties Grown in the United States and Canada*. USDA Technical Bulletin 907. Washington, DC: Government Printing Office, 1946.

ACDI/VOCA. *Farmer-to-Farmer Russia: Report to USAID*. Washington, DC: Russia Program Consortium, 2000.

Adler, Jerry. "An Amber Wave." *Smithsonian Magazine* (December 2011).

Anderson, Alexander C. "Cowlitz Farm in 1840." Unpublished manuscript. Folder 5, Hudson's Bay Collection. Lewis County Historical Museum Archives, Centralia, Washington.

Anderson, Steven A. "Steilacoom Farm: The British Colonization of Puget Sound, 1841-1849. *Occurrences* XVIII:4 (Fall 2000).

Anderson, Steven A. "The Forgetting of John Montgomery: Spanaway's First White Settler, 1845–1885." *Pacific Northwest Historical Quarterly* 101:2 (Spring 2010).

Anderson, Steven A. "Ouvre's River." *Renton Historical Society & Museum Quarterly* 33:4 (November 2002).

Anderson, Steven A. *The William Tolmie Library*. Tacoma, Washington: The Fort Nisqually Foundation, 2005.

Aoki, Keith. "Malthus, Mendel, and Monsanto: Intellectual Property and the Law and Politics of Global Food Supply." *Journal of Environmental Law and Litigation* 19:2 (2004).

Applegate, Jesse. "Umpqua Agriculture, 1851." *Oregon Historical Quarterly, Oregon Historical Quarterly* XXXII (June 1931).

Aubry, Carol, Robin Shoal, and Vicky Erickson. *Grass Cultivars: Their Origins, Development, and use on the National Forests and Grasslands in the Pacific Northwest*. Olympia, Washington: USDA Forest Service, 2005.

Ayer, John E. "George Bush, Voyageur." *Washington Historical Quarterly* VII:1 (January 1916).

Bailey, Liberty H. *Wind and Weather*. Ithaca, New York: Comstock Publishing, 1919.

Bailey, Margaret Jewett. *The Grains or Passages in the Life of Ruth Rover, with Occasional Pictures of Oregon, Natural and Moral*. Corvallis: Oregon State University Press, [1854]1986.

Ball, Carleton. "The History of Wheat Improvement." *Agricultural History* 4:2 (April 1930).

Barker, Burt B. *Letters of John McLoughlin, 1829–1832*. Portland: Oregon Historical Society, 1948.

Barrett, C. A. "Early Farming in Umatilla County." *Oregon Historical Quarterly* XVI (March-December 1915).

Barry, Neilson J. "Agriculture in the Oregon Country, 1795–1844." *Oregon Historical Quarterly* XXX (June 1929).

Barry, Nielson, J. "Site of Historic Granary of the Methodist Mission." *Oregon Historical Quarterly* XLIII (September 1942).

Basler, Roy P., ed. *The Collected Works of Abraham Lincoln*. 8 vols. New Brunswick, New Jersey: Rutgers University Press, 1953.

Bayles, B. B. "New Varieties of Wheat." *1943–1947 USDA Yearbook of Agriculture*. Washington, DC: Government Printing Office, 1947.

Bayles, B. B., and J. Allen Clark. *Classification of Wheat Varieties Grown in the United States in 1949*. USDA Technical Bulletin 1083. Washington, DC: Government Printing Office, 1954.

Beckwith, T. D., A. F. Vass, and R. H. Robinson. *Ammonification and Nitrification Studies of Certain Types of Oregon Soils*. OAES Bulletin 118. Corvallis: Oregon State College, 1914.

Belyea, Barbara, ed. *Columbia Journals: David Thompson*. Buffalo: McGill-Queen's University Press, 1994.

Berry, Wendell. *The Unsettling of America: Culture & Agriculture*. San Francisco: Sierra Club Books, 1977.

Bertramson, B. Rodney. "History of the WSU Department of Agronomy and Soils, 1889–1984." Unpublished manuscript, 1986. Folder 1, Box 91, CN 458, B. R. Bertramson Papers, WSU.

Bertramson, B. Rodney. "The History of the Forage Program at WSU." Unpublished manuscript, n.d. Folder 3, Box 91, CN 458. B. R. Bertramson Papers, WSU.

Bidwell, Percy W., and John I. Falconer. *History of Agriculture in the Northern United States, 1620–1860*. New York: Peter Smith, 1941.

Bjork, Curtis R. "The Extirpated Flora of Spokane County, Washington." *Botanical Electronic News* 330 (May 2004).

Blanchard, Jim. "The Garnet Wheat Controversy, 1923-1938." *Manitoba History* 19 (Spring 1990).

Blanchet, Francis Norbert. *Historical Sketches of the Catholic Church in Oregon*. Portland, Oregon: n. p., 1878.

Blank, Steven C. *The End of Agriculture in the American Portfolio*. Westport Books: Quorum Books, 1998.

Bloomfield, Robert. *The Farmer's Boy: A Rural Poem* [1800]. Cambridge: Lark Books, 1986.

Boyd, Robert. *People of The Dalles: The Indians of the Wascopam Mission*. Lincoln: University of Nebraska Press, 1996.

Brent, William. "History of the Okanagan." Unpublished manuscript, n. d., Box 1, M. H. Brent Collection, Greater Vernon Museum & Archives, Vernon, British Columbia.

Briggle, L. W., and L. P. Reitz. *Classification of Triticum Species and of Wheat Varieties Grown in the United States*. USDA Technical Bulletin 1278. Washington, DC: Government Printing Office, 1963.

Brown, John Hull. *Early American Beverages*. Rutland, Vermont: Charles E. Tuttle Company, 1966.

Brown, William C. *The Indian Side of the Story*. Spokane: C. W. Hill Printing Company, 1961.

Brumfield, Kirby. *This Was Wheat Farming: A Pictorial History of the Farms and Farmers of the Northwest Who Grow the Nation's Bread*. New York: Bonanza Books, 1968.

Buller, H. Reginald. *Essays on Wheat*. New York: The McMillan Co., 1919.

Cahail, Alice Kellogg. "Sea Captains of Whidby Island." *Whidbey Island Farm Bureau News,* March 9–April 27, 1939.

Camp, Oscar A. and Paul C. McGrew. *History of Washington's Soil and Water Conservation Districts*. Pullman: Washington Association of Soil and Water Conservation Districts, 1969.

Campbell, Marjorie Wilkins. *The North West Company*. New York: St. Martin's Press, 1957.

Cardwell, James R. "The First Fruits of the Land: A Brief History of Horticulture in Oregon." *Oregon Historical Quarterly* VII:1 (March 1906).

Carleton, Mark. *The Basis for the Improvement of American Wheats*. USDA Division of Vegetable Physiology and Pathology. Washington, DC: Government Printing Office, 1900.

Carleton, Mark, and Joseph S. Chamberlain. *The Commercial Status of the Durum Wheats*. USDA Plant Industry Bulletin 70. Washington, DC: Government Printing Office, 1904.

Carleton, Mark. "Hard Wheats Winning Their Way." *Yearbook of the United States Department of Agriculture, 1914*. Washington, DC: Government Printing Office, 1915.

Carleton, Mark. *Russian Cereals Adapted for Cultivation in the United States*. USDA Botany Bulletin 23. Washington, DC: Government Printing Office, 1900.

Carleton, Mark. *The Small Grains*. New York: The Macmillan Company, 1920.

Carleton, Will. *Farm Festivals*. New York: Harper & Row, 1881.

Carlson, Laurie W. "The Cattle Battle: Livestock Ownership and the Settlement of the Pacific Northwest." *Columbia Magazine* (Winter 2001–02).

Carlson, Laurie W. *William Spillman and the Birth of Agricultural Economics*. Columbia: University of Missouri Press, 2005.

Carabelli, Angelina J. *Abraham Lincoln: His Legacy to American Agriculture*. Beltsville, Maryland: Associates of the National Library of American Agriculture Library, 1972.

Carstensen, Vernon. "The Land of Plenty." *American Issues* 1:2 (July 1975).

Clark, Anne. *The Dominion Cook Book*. Winnipeg: The Hudson's Bay Company, 1899.

Clark, J. Allen, John H. Martin, and Carleton Ball. *Classification of American Wheats*. USDA Bulletin 1074. Washington, DC: Government Printing Office, 1922.

Clark, J. Allen. *Improvement of Ghirka Spring Wheat in Yield and Quality*. USDA Bulletin 450. Washington, DC: Government Printing Office, 1916.

Clark, J. Allen, and B. B. Bayles. *Classification of Wheat Varieties Grown in the United States*. Washington, DC: US Government Printing Office, 1935.

Clark, J. D. "Manshury Barley." *Fourth Annual Report of the Wisconsin Agricultural Experiment Station Association*. Madison: WAESA, 1906.

Clark, Larry. "The Lost and Found Flour Mill." *Washington State Magazine* (Winter 2011/12).

Coffman, F. A. *Oat History, Identification, and Classification*. Washington, DC: US Government Printing Office, 1977.

Cole, Jean M. *Exile in the Wilderness: The Life of Chief Factor Archibald McDonald, 1790–1853*. Seattle: University of Washington Press, 1979.

Cook, Jimmie J. *"A Particular Friend, Penn's Cove": A History of the Settlers, Claims, and Buildings of Central Whidbey Island*. Coupeville, Washington: Island County Historical Society, 1873.

Cook, O. F. *Foreign Seeds and Plants Imported by the USDA*. Division of Botany Inventory No. 2. Washington, DC: Government Printing Office, 1899.

Cook, R. James. "Management of Wheat and Barley Root Diseases in Modern Farming Systems." *Australasian Plant Pathology* 30:2 (2001): 119–26.

Cook, R. James, and Roger Veseth. *Wheat Health Management.* St. Paul, Minnesota: APS Press, 1991.

Cook, Warren L. *Flood Tide of Empire: Spain and the Pacific Northwest, 1543–1819.* New Haven: Yale University Press, 1973.

Cox, Ross. *Adventures of the First Settlers on the Oregon or Columbia River.* London: 1831.

Crithfield, June. *Of Yesterday and the River.* Pullman, Washington: WSU Extension Services, 1973.

Crooks, Drew. "The Farming Outstations of Fort Nisqually." *Occurrences* XVII:3 (Summer 1999).

Crow, James. "Sixty Years Ago: The 1932 International Congress of Genetics." *Genetics* 131 (August 1992).

Curtiss, Daniel L. *Wheat Culture: How to Double the Yield and Increase the Profits.* New York: Orange Judd Company, 1888.

Dalrymple, Dana G. "Changes in Wheat Varieties and Yields in the United States, 1919–1984." *Agricultural History* 62:4 (Fall 1968).

Dalrymple, Dana G. *Development and Spread of Semi-Dwarf Varieties of Wheat and Rice in the United States: An International Perspective.* USDA Agricultural Economics Bulletin 455. Washington, DC: Government Printing Office, 1980.

Davis, Ellen. *Scripture, Culture, and Agriculture: An Agrarian Reading of the Bible.* Cambridge: Cambridge University Press, 2008.

De Smet, Fr. Pierre. *The Life, Letters, and Travels of Father Pierre Jean De Smet, S. J., 1801–1873.* Hiram M. Chittenden and Alfred T. Richardson, eds. New York: Francis T. Harper, 1905.

Deans, James. "Rustic Rhyms by a Rural Rhymster: Poetry and Recollections of Life at Craigflower [1853]." Royal British Columbia Archives, Provincial Museum, Victoria.

Dickey, George. *Journal of Occurrences at Fort Nisqually, 1831–1859.* Tacoma, Washington: Ft. Nisqually Historic Site, 2002.

Dickey, George. "Tlithlow Journals, 1851, 1856–1857." Tacoma, Washington: Fort Nisqually Historic Site, n. d.

Dickey, George. *Journal of Occurrences at Muck Station, 1858–1959.* Tacoma, Washington: Fort Nisqually Historic Site, n. d.

Dickey, George. "The Outstations." *Occurrences* XII:1 (Spring 1994).

Dickey, George. "The Puget Sound Agricultural Company." *Occurrences* XI:2 (Fall 1993).

Dickinson, F. L. *Prairie Wheat: Three Centuries of Wheat Varieties in Western Canada.* Winnipeg: Canada Grains Council, 1976.

Dixon, Jack, ed., *Unifine Flour: Milling, Baking, and Consumer Acceptance Tests.* Washington State Institute of Technology Bulletin 206 (April 1950).

Dolan, Susan A. *A Fruitful Legacy: A Historic Context of Fruit Trees and Orchards in the United States, 1600 to the Present.* Seattle: National Park Service Pacific West Regional Office, 2007.

Dondlinger, Peter T. *The Book of Wheat: An Economic History and Practical Manual of the Wheat Industry.* New York: Orange Judd, 1908.

Douglas, David. *Journal Kept by David Douglas During His Travels in North America, 1823–1827.* London: The Royal Horticultural Society, 1914.

Drury, Clifford M. *Elkanah and Mary Walker: Pioneers Among the Spokanes.* Caldwell, Idaho: The Caxton Printers, 1940.

Dunbar, Seymor. *The Journals and Letters of Major John Owen, Pioneer of the Northwest.* New York: Edward Eberstadt, 1927.

Edgar, William C. *The Story of a Grain of Wheat.* New York: D. Appleton and Company, 1920.

Edwards, Everett E., ed. *Washington, Jefferson, Lincoln and Agriculture.* Washington, DC: USDA Bureau of Agricultural Economics, 1937.

Elliott, T. C., ed. "The Journal of Captain Charles Bishop of the 'Ruby' in 1795." *Oregon Historical Quarterly* XXIX:4 (December 1928).

Ellis, William. *The Modern Husbandman, or the Practical Art of Farming.* 4 vols. London: Osborne and Cooper, 1772.

England, Olive S. *Ceres, A Harvest Home Festival.* Salem, Oregon: The E. M. Waite Printing Company, 1893.

Engle, Flora A. P. *Recollection of Early Days on Whidbey Island.* Coupeville, Washington: Island County Times, 1928.

Esquinas-Alcázar, J. T. "Plant Genetic Resources." M. D. Hayward ed., *Plant Breeding: Principles and Prospects.* London: Chapman & Hall.

Evans, George Ewart. *The Farm and the Village.* London: Faber and Faber, 1969.

Evershed, Henry. "Varieties of Wheat and Methods of Improving Them." *Journal of the Royal Agricultural Society of England* XXV (1889).

Fairchild, David. "Pure Races of Brewing Barley." *American Brewers Review* 20 (January 1906).

Farnham, Thomas J. *Travels in the Great Western Prairies.* 2 Vols. London: Richard Bentley, 1843.

Farrar, Victor J., ed. "Diary Kept by Colonel and Mrs. I. N. Ebey." *Washington Historical Quarterly* VIII:1 & 2 (January & April 1917).

Ficken, Robert E. *Rufus Woods, the Columbia River, and the Building of Modern Washington.* Pullman: Washington State University Press, 1995.

Fifield, C. C., C. E. Bode, and H. C. Fellows. *Milling and Baking Experiments with Wheat Varieties Grown in the Western United States, 1936–1945.* USDA Technical Bulletin 1014. Washington, DC: Government Printing Office, 1950.

Fisher, D. V., and W. H. Upshall. *History of Fruit Growing and Handling in the United States of America and Canada.* University Park, Pennsylvania: American Pomological Society, 1976.

Flaksberger, K. A. *Key to the True Cereals: Wheat, Barley, Rye, Oats.* Moscow: All-Union Academy of Agricultural Science, USSR People's Commissariat of Agriculture, 1939.

Flint, Charles. *Grasses and Forage Plants.* 1859.

Foote, Wilson H. *Small Grains for Oregon.* AES Circular 621. Corvalis: Oregon State University, 1964.

French, H. T. *Notes on Varieties of Wheat and Flax.* OAES Bulletin 8. Corvallis: Oregon State College, 1891.

French, H. T. *Notes and Varieties and Yield of Wheat.* OAES Bulletin 16. Corvallis: Oregon State College, 1892.

Gaines, E. F. *Washington Wheats.* WAES Bulletin 121. Pullman: Washington State College, 1915.

Galbraith, John S. "The Early History of the Puget's Sound Agricultural Company." *Oregon Historical Quarterly* LV:3 (September 1954).

Galloway, Terry R., and Brent D. Galloway. "Daniel Best Biography." *Engineers & Engines Magazine* 14:6 (March-April 1969).

Gerhard, Peter. "A Black Conquistador in Mexico." *Hispanic American Historical Review* 58:3 (August 1978).

Gibbs, Rafe. *Beacon for Mountain and Plain: The Story of the University of Idaho.* Caldwell, Idaho: The Caxton Printers, 1962.

Gibson, James R. *Farming the Frontier: The Agricultural Opening of the Oregon Country, 1786–1846.* Seattle: University of Washington Press, 1985.

Gibson, James R. *The Lifeline of the Oregon Country: The Fraser Columbia Brigade System, 1811–47.* Vancouver: University of British Columbia Press, 1997.

Gibson, James R. *Imperial Russia in Frontier America: The Changing Geography of Supply of Russia America, 1784–1867.* New York: Oxford University Press, 1976.

Glen, Julia Veazie. "John Lyle and Lyle Farm." *Oregon Historical Quarterly* XXVI:2 (June 1925).

Glover, Jerry, Stephen S. Jones, Wes Jackson, et al. "Increased Food Security via Perennial Grains." *Science* 328 (June 2010).

Grey, Zane. *The Desert of Wheat.* New York: Harper & Brothers, 1919.

Grigg, David. *English Agriculture: An Historical Perspective.* Oxford: Basil Blackwell, 1989.

Hafen, LeRoy R., and Harvey L. Carter, eds. *Mountain Men and Fur Traders of the Far West.* Lincoln: University of Nebraska Press, 1982.

Haller, Granville. "Whidbey Island Farm Journal." Charles M. Gates, *Readings in Pacific Northwest History: Washington, 1790–1895.* Seattle: University of Washington Bookstore, 1941.

Handley, James E. *Scottish Farming in the Eighteenth Century.* London: Faber and Faber, 1963.

Hanus, Mark and Midori. "The 'Russian Contract,'" *Occurrences* XVI:1 (Winter 1997/1998).

Harlan, H. V. *Barley: Culture, Uses, Varieties.* USDA Farmers Bulletin 1464. Washington, DC: Government Printing Office, 1925.

Harlan, Jack R. *The Living Fields: Our Agricultural Heritage.* London: Cambridge University Press, 1998.

Hart, Jeff. *Montana Native Plants and Early Peoples.* Helena: Montana Historical Society Press, 1976.

Hastings, Lansford. *The Emigrant's Guide to Oregon and California.* Cincinnati: George Comclin, 1845.

Hatcher, Temple. "The History and Regional Distribution of Wheat Production in British Columbia." M. A. Thesis. Vancouver: University of British Columbia, 1940.

Heath, Joseph. *Memoirs of Nisqually* [1845–49]. Fairfield, Washington: Ye Galleon Press, 1979.

Helm, Harry. *Love Singer in Paradise.* Portland: Metropolitan Press, 1962.

Henderson, L. F. *Grasses and Forage Plants in Idaho.* AES Bulletin 38. Moscow: University of Idaho, 1903.

Hill, D. D., and E. R. Jackman. *They Broke the Trail.* Corvallis: Oregon Wheat Commission, 1960.

Hill, Kathleen T., and Gerald N. Hill. *Northwest Wine Country: Wine's New Frontier.* Guilford, Connecticut: Globe Pequot Press, 2004.

Himes, George, ed. *Transactions of the Oregon Pioneer Association for 1888.* Portland: Himes Printing, 1889.

Hines, Gustavus. *Oregon and its Institutions.* New York: Carlton & Porter, 1868.

Hines, H. K. *An Illustrated History of the State of Washington.* Chicago: The Lewis Publishing Company, 1894.

Holmes, Edwin S. "Wheat Ports of the Pacific Coast." *1901 USDA Yearbook of Agriculture.* Washington, DC: Government Printing Office, 1902.

Huggins, David. "No-Till and Snow Can Help Crops Grow." *Agricultural Research* 60:7 (August 2012):8.

Huggins, E. E. "Reminiscences of Puget Sound." *Sunday [Portland] Oregonian,* August 26, 1900.

Hungerford, C. W., ed. *Highlights in Agricultural Research in Idaho.* AES Bulletin 229. Moscow: University of Idaho, 1939.

Hunt, Gilbert. "Manufacturers of Walla Walla." *The Coast* XV:2 (February 1908).

Hunt, Thomas F. *The Cereals in America.* New York: Orange Judd Company, 1907.

Hunt, Wallis. *Heirs of Great Adventure: A History of Balfour, Williamson & Company.* 2 vols. London: Jarold & Sons, 1951.

Hunter, Byron. *Dry Farming and Practices in Wheat Growing in the Columbia and Snake River Basins.* USDA Farmers Bulletin 1545. Washington, DC: Government Printing Office, 1927.

Hunter, Bryon. *Farm Practices in the Columbia Basin Uplands.* USDA Farmers Bulletin 294. Washington, DC: Government Printing Office, 1907.

Hurst, Charles Chamberlain. *Experiments in Genetics.* London: Cambridge University Press, 1925.

Hussey, John A. *Champoeg: Place of Transition.* Portland: Oregon Historical Society, 1967.

Hussey, John A. *The Fort Vancouver Farm.* Vancouver, Washington: Fort Vancouver National Historic Site, n. d.

Inazuka, Gonjiro. *Norin 10, A Japanese Semi-Dwarf Wheat Variety.* Wheat Information Service Bulletin 32 (March 1971).

Iredale, Jennifer. *Creating a Puget Sound Agricultural Company Garden.* Victoria: Craigflower Living History Farm, 1995.

Irvine, Ronald, and Walter J. Clore. *The Wine Project: Washington's Winemaking History.* Vashon, Washington: Sketch Publications, 1997.

Irwin, Judith. "The Life of Simon Plamondon." *Cowlitz Historical Quarterly* XXIV:3 (1982).

Isern, Thomas. "Wheat Explorer the World Over: Mark Carleton of Kansas." *Kansas History* 23 (Spring/Summer 2000).

Isaacs, E. S. "Walla Walla County Flour Milling." *The Coast* XV:3 (March 1908).

Jackson, John C. *Children of the Fur Trade: Forgotten Métis of the Pacific Northwest.* Missoula, Montana: Mountain Press Publishing Company, 1995.

Jackson, Lee. *Wheat Cultivars for California.* Davis: University of California-Davis: Department of Plant Sciences, 2011.

Jacobs, H. E., and Peter Reinhart. *Six Thousand Years of Bread: Its Holy and Unholy History.* New York: Doubleday Books, 1944.

Jaradat, Abdullah A. *Wheat Landraces: Genetic Resources for Sustenance and Sustainability.* Morris, Minnesota: USDA-ARS, 2011.

Johnson, Cuthbert W. *The Farmer's Encyclopædia and Dictionary of Rural Affairs.* Philadelphia: Carey and Hart, 1848.

Jones, J. S., H. P. Fishburn, and C. W. Clover. *A Report on the Milling Properties of Idaho Wheat.* IAES Bulletin 72. Moscow: University of Idaho, 1911.

Jones, Stephen S. "Kicking the Commodity Habit: On Being Grown Out of Place." *Gastronomica* 12:3 (Fall 2012).

Jones, Stephen S., and Molly M. Cadle. "Spillman, Gaines, and Vogel—Building a Foundation." *Wheat Life* (February 1996).

Kaiser, Phyllis. "Tacoma's Floury Past." *Tacoma: Voices of the Past.* Tacoma: Pierce County Washington State Centennial Committee, 1989.

Kaiser, Verle. "A Rough and 'Bready' Land: An Agricultural History of the Palouse Region of Southeastern Washington and Adjacent North Idaho." Unpublished manuscript, 1981. V. Kaiser Papers, WSU.

Keith, Thomas B. *The Horse Interlude: A Pictorial History of Horse and Man in the Inland Northwest.* Moscow: University of Idaho, 1976.

Kellogg, George A. *A History of Whidbey's Island.* Coupeville, Washington: Island County Historical Society, 2002.

Kephart, Kenneth D. *USDA Soft White Wheat Records.* Columbia: University of Missouri, 1993.

Kiesselbach, T. A., and W. E. Lyness. *Spring Small Grains.* AES Bulletin 201. Lincoln: University of Nebraska College of Agriculture, 1924.

Kilian, Benjamin, Hakan Özkan, Carlo Pozzi, and Francesco Salamini. "Domestication of the *Triticeae* in the Fertile Crescent." *Genetics and Genomics of the* Triticeae. New York: Springer, 2009.

Kingsbury, Noel. *Hybrid: The Science of Plant Breeding.* Chicago: University of Chicago Press, 2009.

Kingston, C. S. "Introduction of Cattle to the Pacific Northwest." *Washington Historical Quarterly* XIV:3 (July 1923).

Kingston, Ceylon S. *The Inland Empire of the Pacific Northwest: The Historical Essays and Sketches of Ceylon S. Kingston.* Glen Adams, ed. Fairfield, Washington: Ye Galleon Press, 1981.

Klippart, John. *The Wheat Plant: Its Origins, Culture, Growth, Development, Composition, Varieties, and Diseases.* Cincinnati: Moore, Wilstach, Keys & Co., 1860.

Körnicke, Friedrich, and Hugo Werner. *Handbuch des Getreidebaues: Die Arten und Varietätan des Getreides.* Bonn: Emil Strauss, 1885.

Kosinski, Dorothy. *Van Gogh's Sheaves of Wheat.* Dallas: Dallas Museum of Art, 2006.

Kübar, Harri. *Sangaste Rye: The Life's Work of Estonia's Last Count-Farmer.* Lossiküla, Estonia: Sangaste Loss, 2012.

Laing, F. W. "Hudson's Bay Company Lands and Colonial Farm Settlement on the Mainland of British Columbia." *Pacific Historical Quarterly* VII:4 (December 1938).

Landerholm, Carl. *Notices and Voyages of the Famed Quebec Mission to the Pacific Northwest.* Portland: Oregon Historical Society, 1956.

Laveille, E. *The Life of Father De Smet, S. J.* Chicago: Loyola University Press, 1981.

Lawson, Peter. *The Agriculturalist's Manual of the Agricultural Plants Cultivated in Europe and a Report of Lawson's Agricultural Museum in Edinburgh.* Edinburgh: William Blackwood & Sons, 1886.

Lee, Norman E. *Harvests & Harvesting Through the Ages.* Cambridge University Press, 1960.

Lewelling, Alfred. *Proceedings and Papers of the Quarter Century Celebration of the Oregon State Historical Society.* Portland: Oregon Historical Society, 1910.

Lewis, William S. "Archibald MacDonald: Biography and Genealogy." *Washington Historical Quarterly* 9:1 (January 1918).

Libbey, Marilyn. *Bow to Plow: Timber, Tillage, and Taters: Agriculture and Logging in Island County, 1850–1920.* Coupeville, Washington: Island County Historical Society, 1995.

Little, Charles E. *Green Fields Forever: The Conservation Tillage Revolution in America.* Washington, DC: Island Press, 1987.

Loudon, J. C. *Encyclopedia of Agriculture,* 1831.

Louis, Shirley, ed. *Q'sapi: A History of Okanagan People as Told by Okanagan Families.* Penticton: Theytus Books, 2002.

Lyon, Steve. "Farm Overviews and Variety History." *2010 Dryland Field Day Abstracts: Highlights of Research Progress.* Technical Report 10-2. Pullman: Washington State University Extension Service, 2010.

MacEwan, Grant. *Harvest of Bread.* Saskatoon, Saskatchewan: Western Producers Prairie Books,

Mack, Richard N. "First Comprehensive Botanical Survey of the Columbia Plateau, Washington: The Sandberg and Leiberg Expedition of 1893." *Northwest Science* 62:3 (1988).

Maclachan, Morang. *The Fort Langley Journals, 1827–30.* Vancouver: University of British Columbia Press, 1998.

Malenbaum, Wilfred. *The World Wheat Economy: 1885–1939.* Cambridge, Massachusetts: Harvard University Press, 1953.

Malle, A. Dureaude de la. "De l'Origine et de le Patrie des Céréales." *Annales de Sciences Naturelles* 1:9. Paris, 1826.

Marsh, Debra and David Huggins, eds. *Dryland Farming Field Day Abstracts: Highlights of Research Progress.* Technical Report 10 2. Pullman, Washington: WSU Extension Service, 2010.

Martin, John H. and Clyde E. Leighty. *Emmer and Spelt.* USDA Farmers Bulletin 1429. Washington, DC: Government Printing Office, 1938.

Martin, John H. *Growing Rye in the Western Half of the United States.* USDA Bulletin 1358. Washington, DC: Government Printing Office, 1935.

Martin, John H. *Polish and Poulard Wheats.* USDA Bulletin 1340. Washington, DC: Government Printing Office, 1923.

Martin, Michael, Hans D. Ratke, and Harold E. Hollands. *Pacific Northwest Wheat.* OAES Bulletin 556. Corvallis: Oregon State College, 1956.

McCallum, Brent D. and Ronald M. DePauw. "A Review of Wheat Cultivation in the Canadian Prairies." *Canadian Journal of Plant Science* 4 (July 2008):649–77.

McClelland, Peter D. *Sowing Modernity: America's First Agricultural Revolution.* Ithaca, New York: Cornell University Press, 1997.

McClintock, Thomas. "Henderson Lewelling, Seth Lewelling, and the Birth of the Pacific Coast Fruit Industry." *Oregon Historical Quarterly,* LXII:2 (June 1967).

McDonald, Archibald. *The Ft. Langley Journals, 1827–1830.* Morag McLatchlan, ed. Vancouver: University of British Columbia Press, 1993.

McGregor, Alexander C. *Counting Sheep: From Open Range to Agribusiness on the Columbia Plateau.* Seattle: University of Washington Press, 1982.

McGregor, Alexander C. "From Sheep Range to Agribusiness: A Case Study of Agricultural Transformation on the Columbia Plateau." *Agricultural History* 54:1 (January 1980).

McGregor, Alexander C. "'A Love for the Land, the Farm, and Hard Work': Hall of Fame Farm Families and the Road Ahead for Inland Northwest Agriculture." Mid-Columbia Agricultural Hall of Fame Keynote Address. Pasco, Washington; January 2013.

McGregor, Alexander C. "Unraveling Secrets through Hard Work in the Trenches: Reflections about Northwest Agricultural Research and Its Finest Practitioner." Unpublished manuscript, 2011. A. McGregor Collection, WSU.

McKinley, Laura. *An Unbroken Record: Ebey's Landing National Historical Reserve*. Seattle: National Park Service, Pacific Northwest Region, 1993.

McLoughlin, John. "Copy of a Document Found Among the Private Papers of the late Dr. John McLoughlin." *Transactions of the Oregon Pioneer Association, 1880*.

Meeker, Ezra. *Hop Culture in the United States, Being a Treatise on Hop Growing in Washington Territory*. Puyallup, Washington: Ezra Meeker & Company, 1883.

Meeker, Ezra. *Pioneer Reminiscences of Puget Sound*. Seattle: Lowman & Handford, 1905.

Meeker, Ezra. *Seventy Years of Progress*. Seattle: Allstrum Printing, 1921.

Meinig, Donald. *On the Margins of the Good Earth: The South Australian Wheat Frontier, 1869–1884*. Chicago: Rand McNally,1962.

Meinig, Donald. *The Great Columbia Plain: A Historical Geography, 1860–1910*. Seattle: University of Washington Press, 1968.

Meissner, Daniel. "Theodore B. Wilcox: Captain of Industry and Magnate of the China Flour Trade, 1884–1918." *Oregon Historical Quarterly* 104:4 (Winter 2003).

Melrose, Robert. "The Diary of Robert Melrose: A Royal Emigrant's Almanack Concerning Five Years Servitude under the Hudson's Bay Company on Vancouver Island, 1852–1857." *British Columbia Historical Quarterly* VII:2,3,4 (April, July, October 1943).

Mercer, Jerry. *One Hundred Years at Greenbank*. Greenbank, Washington: Saratoga Design, 2003.

Minto, John. "Reminiscences of Experiences on the Oregon Trail." *Oregon Historical Quarterly* II:2 (April 1901).

Morgan, Dan. *Merchants of Grain*. New York: Viking Press, 1979.

Morgan, Murray. *Puget's Sound: A Narrative of Early Tacoma and the Southern Sound*. Seattle: University of Washington Press, 1979.

Morrison, Dorothy N. *Outpost: John McLoughlin and the Far Northwest*. Portland: Oregon Historical Society Press, 1999.

Muir, John. *The Eight Wilderness Discovery Books*. Seattle: Diadem Books, 1992.

Mullan, John. *Report on the Construction of a Wagon Road from Fort Walla-Walla to Fort Benton*. Washington, DC: US Government Printing Office, 1863. Published separately as S.E.D. 43, 37th Cong., 3rd Sess., Serial 1149.

Murphy, Kevin, Steve Lyon, Stephen S. Jones, et. al. "Breeding for Organic and Low-Input Farming Systems: An Evolutionary Participatory Breeding Method for Inbred Cereal Grains." *Renewable Agriculture and Food Systems* 20:1 (2005).

Nazarea, Virginia D. *Heirloom Seeds and Their Keepers: Marginality and Memory in the Conservation of Biological Diversity*. Tucson: University of Arizona Press, 2005.

Negro, Maria Vittoria, ed. *Terra Madre—1200 World Food Communities*. Bra, Italy: Slow Food Editore, 2004.

Nesbit, Robert C. and Charles M. Gates. "Agriculture in Eastern Washington, 1890–1910." *Oregon Historical Quarterly* 37:4 (October 1946).

Newman, L. H., J. G. C. Fraser, and A. G. O. Whiteside, *Handbook of Canadian Spring Wheat Varieties*. DOA Farmers Bulletin 18. Ottawa, Canada: Cereal Division Experimental Farms Service, 1946.

Newman, Peter C. *Company of Adventurers*. Ontario, Canada: Penguin Books, 1986.

Nilan, R. A., and C. F. Konzak. "Increasing the Efficiency of Mutation Induction." *National Academy of Sciences Symposium on Mutation and Plant Breeding*. Raleigh: North Carolina State College, 1961.

Nisbet, Jack. *Sources of the River: Tracking David Thompson Across Western North America*. Seattle: Sasquatch Books, 1994.

Nisbet, Robert A. "Early Horticulture in Oregon: Nurserymen and Pleasure Gardens." Unpublished manuscript, 1979. Oregon Historical Society Archives, Portland.

Olmstead, Alan L., and Paul W. Rhode. "The Red Queen and Hard Reds: Productivity Growth in American Wheat, 1800–1940." *The Journal of Economic History*. 62:4 (December 2002).

Ormsby, Margaret A. "Agricultural Development in British Columbia." *Agricultural History* 19:1 (January 1945).

Owens, Erica. *Sandwith Homestead Cultural Landscape Survey*. San Juan Island National Historic Park, 2009.

Palladino, Lawrence. B. *Anthony Ravalli, S. J.: Forty Years a Missionary in the Rocky Mountains*. Helena, 1884.

Palladino, Lawrence B. *Indian and White in the Northwest*. Lancaster, Pennsylvania: Wickersham Publishing Company, 1922.

Palmer, Gary. "Indian Pioneers: The Settlement of Ni'lukhwalqw (Upper Hangman Creek, Idaho) by the Schitsu'umsh." *Oregon Historical Quarterly* 102:1 (Spring 2001).

Pambrum, Sam. *Who Was Joseph Laroque?* Walla Walla Frenchtown Historical Foundation, 2012.

Paulson, Gary M. and James P. Shroyer. "The Early History of Wheat Improvement in the Great Plains," *Agronomy Journal* (2008).

Percival, John. *The Wheat Plant.* New York: E. P. Dutton & Company, 1921.

Perkins, John H. *Geopolitics and the Green Revolution: Wheat, Genes, and the Cold War.* Oxford: Oxford University Press, 1997.

Pethick, Derek. *Victoria: The Fort.* Vancouver: Mitchell Press, 1968.

Pierce, Henry H. *Report of an Expedition from Ft. Colville to Puget Sound.* Washington, DC: Government Printing Office, 1883.

Pitzer, Paul C. *Grand Coulee Dam: Harnessing a Dream.* Pullman: Washington State University Press, 1994.

Popovsky, M. A. *Nado Speshit* (We Must Hurry). Moscow: Detskaya literatura, 1968.

Price, H. Bruce. *Private Exchange and State Grain Inspection.* Chicago: American Institute of Agriculture, 1922.

Proceedings of the Convention of Producers, Shippers, and Millers, Otherwise Known as the Wheat Convention. Colfax: Commoner Printing Company, 1906.

Proceedings of the 15th Annual Convention of the Association of American Agricultural Experiment Stations Official Report. Experiment Station Bulletin 115. Washington, DC: Government Printing Office, 1901.

Quick, Cindy, and Julie M. Zander, eds. *The Toledo Community Story.* Chehalis, Washington: Lewis County Historical Museum, 2008.

Quick, Graeme, and Wesley Buchele. *The Grain Harvesters.* St. Joseph, Michigan: American Society of Agricultural Engineers, 1978.

Radosevich, Jean. "The Origins of the Russian America Company," *Occurrences* XVI:1 (Winter 1997/1998).

Raffan, James. *Emperor of the North: Sir George Simpson and the Remarkable Story of the Hudson's Bay Company.* Ontario: HarperCollins Publishers, 2007.

Rajaram, Sanjaya. *The Human Right to Food and Livelihoods: The Role of Global Wheat Research.* Canberra: ATSE Crawford Fund and Australian Institute of Agricultural Science and Technology, 2001.

Rasmussen, Wayne. *Abraham Lincoln: His Legacy to American Agriculture.* Beltsville, Maryland: Associates of the National Agricultural Library, 1972.

Reed, Norman. "Grist for the Mill: A Brief History of Flour Milling in Washington." *Columbia Magazine* 22:4 (Winter 2008–09).

Reed, Norman. "Implements of Change: Selling Agricultural Evolution in the Pacific Northwest." *Columbia Magazine* 26:4 (Winter 2012–13).

Reese, Gary F. *A Documentary History of Fort Steilacoom.* Tacoma: Tacoma Public Library, 1984.

Reganold, John P. "Planting the Seeds for Perennials." *Wheat Life* 54:1 (January 2011).

Reitz, L. P. *Wheat in the United States.* USDA Information Bulletin 386. Washington, DC: Government Printing Office, 1976.

Rempel, Sharon. *Growing Local Food and Community with Traditional Wisdom and Heritage Wheat.* Victoria: Grassroots Solutions, 2008.

Rhonda, James. *Astoria & Empire.* Lincoln: University of Nebraska Press, 1990.

Rich, E. E. *Part of Dispatch from George Simpson Esq. Governor of Ruperts Land to the Governor & Committee of the Hudson's Bay Company London.* Toronto: The Champlain Society, 1947.

Roberts, George. "The Round Hand of George Roberts: The Cowlitz Farm Journal, 1847–51." *Oregon Historical Quarterly* 63:2 & 3 (June-September 1962).

Roberts, H. F. *Plant Hybridization before Mendel.* Princeton: Princeton University Press, 1929.

Robinson, Leigh Burpee. *Esquimalt: "Place of Shoaling Waters."* Victoria: Quality Press, 1948.

Robison, Ken. *Ft. Benton.* San Francisco: Arcadia Publishing Company, 2009.

Ross, Earle D. "Lincoln and Agriculture." *Agricultural History* III:2 (April 1929).

Rothstein, Martin. "A British Firm on the American West Coast, 1869–1914." *The Business History Review* 37:4 (Winter 1963).

Salmon, S. Cecil. *The Agricultural Experiment Stations of Japan.* Natural Resources Section Report No. 59. Tokyo: General Headquarters, Supreme Commander for Allied Forces, 1946.

Salmon, S. Cecil. "300 Varieties of Wheat Grown on United States Farms." *1933 USDA Yearbook of Agriculture.* Washington, DC: Government Printing Office, 1934.

Salutos, Theodore, and John D. Hicks. *Agricultural Discontent in the Middle West, 1900–1939.* Madison: University of Wisconsin Press, 1951.

Sambasivan, M. S. "The Evergreen Revolution." *Crop Science* 46:5 (September 2006).

Saunders, William. *Report of the Dominion Experimental Farms* CEFS Bulletin 4. Ottawa: Canada Department of Agriculture, 1889.

Sax, Karl. "The Behavior of the Chromosomes in Fertilization." *Genetics* 3:4 (July 1918).

Sax, Karl. "Sterility in Wheat Hybrids I: Sterility Relationships and Endosperm Development." *Genetics* 6:4 (July 1921).

Sax, Karl. "Sterility in Wheat Hybrids II: Chromosome Behavior in Partially Sterile Hybrids." *Genetics* 7:6 (November 1922).

Sax, Karl, and E. F. Gaines. "A Genetic and Cytological Study of Certain Hybrids of Wheat." *Journal of Agricultural Research* 28:6 (May 1924).

Sax, Karl. "Chromosome Aberrations Induced by X-rays." *Genetics* 23:5 (September 1938).

Schaffer, E. C. *Wheat Varieties in Washington*. WAES Bulletin 207. Pullman: Washington State College, 1926.

Scheuerman, Richard D. "Wagon Trails to Iron Rails: Russian German Immigration to the Pacific Northwest." *American Historical Society of Germans from Russia Journal* 2:2 (Fall 1979).

Scheuerman, Richard D. *Palouse Country: A Land and Its People*. Walla Walla: Color Press, 2003.

Scheuerman, Richard D. "Streams in the Desert: A Centennial Tribute to Russian-German Pioneering in Central Washington." *Journal of the American Historical Society of Germans from Russia* 8:3 (Fall 1985).

Scheuerman, Richard D. *Telling, Sharing, Doing: Deyneka Russian Ministries and Eastern European Education Initiatives, 1990–2010*. Seattle: SPU Center for Global Curriculum Studies, 2011.

Scheuerman, Richard D., and Clifford E. Trafzer. *The Volga Germans: Pioneers of the Pacific Northwest*. Moscow: University of Idaho Press, 1980.

Scheuerman, Richard D. and Michael O. Finley. "Chief Cleveland Kamiakin and 20th Century Political Change on the Colville Reservation." *Pacific Northwest Historical Quarterly* 101:1 (Winter 2009/2010).

Schillinger, William F., and Robert I. Papendick. "Then and Now: 125 Years of Dryland Wheat Farming in the Inland Pacific Northwest." *Agronomy Journal* "Celebrate the Centennial" Supplement. Madison, Wisconsin: American Society of Agronomy, 2008.

Schlebecker, John T. *Whereby We Thrive: A History of American Farming, 1607–1972*. Ames: Iowa State University Press, 1975.

Scofield, Carl S. *A Description of Wheat Varieties*. USDA Plant Industry Bulletin 47. Washington, DC: Government Printing Office, 1903.

Scott, Heidi. "A Little Bit of History: The Journey of White Wheat to Eastern Washington." *Wheat Life* (May 2012).

Scott, Heidi. "Money in the Bank: Institutions Provide a Safe Deposit for World's Seeds." *Wheat Life* (August/September 2012).

Scott, Leslie M. "Soil Repair Lessons in the Willamette Valley." *Oregon Historical Quarterly* XVIII (March 1917).

Scott, William Bell. *A Poet's Harvest Home: Being One Hundred Short Poems*. London: Elkin Mathews & John Lane, 1893.

Shaver, F. A. *An Illustrated History of Southeastern Washington*. Spokane: Western Historical Publishing, 1906.

Shepherd, James F. "The Development of New Wheat Varieties in the Pacific Northwest." *Agricultural History* 54:1 (January 1980).

Shepherd, James F., "The Development of Wheat Production in the Pacific Northwest." *Agricultural History* 49:1 (January 1975).

Sherfey, Florence. *Eastern Washington's Vanished Grist Mills and the Men Who Ran Them*. Fairfield, Washington: Ye Galleon Press, 1978.

Shilliday, Jim. *Canada's Wheat King: The Life and Times of Seager Wheeler*. Regina: University of Saskatoon Press, 2007.

Shillinger, William F., and Robert I. Papendick. *Then and Now: 125 Years of Dryland Wheat Farming in the Inland Pacific Northwest*. Pullman, Washington: Washington State University Extension Service, 2009.

Shirreff, Patrick. *Improvement of the Cereals*. London: William Blackwood and Sons, 1873.

Sieber, Richard, ed. *Memoirs of Puget Sound, Early Seattle 1853–1856: The Letters of David & Catherine Blaine*. Fairfield: Ye Galleon Press, 1978.

Simpson, George. *Fur Trade and Empire: George Simpson's Journal, 1824–25*. Frederick J. Merk, ed. Cambridge: Harvard University Press, 1968.

Simpson, George. *London Correspondence Inward from Sir George Simpson, 1841–42*. Glyndwr Williams, ed. London: The Hudson's Bay Record Society, 1973.

Smale, Melinda. *Understanding Global Trends in the Uses of Wheat Diversity and International Flows of Wheat Genetic Resources*. Economics Working Paper 96-02. Mexico City: CIMMYT, 1996.

Smekalova, Tamara. "Cultivated Plant Inventory of Russia," in M. Veteläinen, V. Negri, and N. Maxted, eds. *European Landraces: On-Farm Conservation, Management, and Use*. Biodiversity Bulletin No. 15. Rome, Italy: Biodiversity International, 2009.

Smith, Bruce D. *The Emergence of Agriculture*. New York: Scientific American Library, 1995.

Smith, Jared G. *Foreign Seeds and Plants Imported by the USDA*. Division of Plant Botany Inventory No. 7. Washington, DC: Government Printing Office, 1900.

Smith, Luther. "Cystology and Genetics in Barley." *The Botanical Review* XVII:1 (January 1951).

Snyder, Harry. *Studies on the Digestibility and Nutritive Value of Bread*. USDA Bulletin 156. Washington, DC: Government Printing Office, 1905.

So, Adrienne. "The Business of Being Green." *Beer West Magazine* 5:3 (Summer 2012).

Sokolov, Raymond. "Barley's Ghost." *Natural History* 102:6 (June 1993).

Sorensen, Eric. "Wheat: A 10,000-Year Relationship." *Washington State Magazine* 11:1 (Winter 2011/12).

Splawn, A. J. *Ka-Mi-Akin: Last Hero of the Yakimas*. Portland: Kilham, 1917.

Spillman, William J. *The Hybrid Wheats*. Agricultural Experiment Station Bulletin 89. Pullman, Washington: State College of Washington, 1909.

Spillman, William J. "Mendel's Laws in Relation to Animal Breeding." *Proceedings of the American Breeders Association*. Vol.1. Washington, DC, 1905.

Spillman, William. "Quantitative Studies on the Transmission of Parental Characters of Hybrid Offspring." *Proceedings of the 15th Annual Convention of the Association of American Agricultural Colleges and Experiment Stations Official Report*. USDA Bulletin 115. Washington, DC: Government Printing Office, 1902.

Spillman, William J. "Soil Conservation." *USDA Farmers Bulletin 406*. Washington, DC: Government Printing Office, 1910.

Spillman, William J. "Systems of Farm Management in the United States." *Yearbook of the United States Department of Agriculture*. Washington, DC: Government Printing Office, 1903.

Spillman, William J. "Theoretical Studies in Breeding." *Proceedings of the American Breeders Association*. Vol. 1. Washington, DC, 1905.

Spillman, William. J. "A Model Farm." *1904 USDA Yearbook*. Washington, DC: Government Printing Office, 1905.

Stallknecht, G. F., K. M. Gilbertson, and J. E. Ranney. "Alternative Wheat Cereals as Food Grains: Einkorn, Emmer, Spelt, Kamut, and Triticale." J. Janick, ed., *Progress in New Crops*. Alexandria, VA: ASHA Press, 1996.

Standard, Stella. *Whole Grain Cookery: A Gourmet Guide for Glowing Health*. New York: The John Day Company, 1951.

Stanton, T. R. *Oats in the Western Half of the United States*. USDA Farmers Bulletin 1611. Washington, DC: Government Printing Office, 1929.

Stern, Theodore. *Chiefs and Chief Traders: Indian Relations at Fort Nez Percés, 1818–1855*. Corvallis: Oregon State University Press, 1996.

Stephens, D. E, and C. E. Hill. *Dry Farming Investigations at the Sherman County Branch Experiment Station, Moro, Oregon*. Station Bulletin 144. Moro: Oregon Agricultural Experiment Station, 1917.

Stephens, D. E., and H. M. Woolman. *Wheat Bunt Problems in Oregon*. OES Bulletin 188. Corvallis: Oregon State College, 1922.

Stephens, D. E., R. B. Webb, and J. F. Martin. *Wheat Varieties for the Columbia Basin of Oregon*. OES Bulletin 308. Corvallis: Oregon State College, 1932.

Stephens, S. C. "Resume of the Symposium." *National Academy of Sciences Symposium on Mutation and Plant Breeding*. Raleigh: North Carolina State College, 1961.

Steury, Tim. "How Washington Tastes—The Apple Meets Cougar Gold." *Washington State Magazine* 12:2 (Spring 2013).

Stevens, Hazard. *The Life of Isaac Ingalls Stevens*. 2 vols. New York: Houghton, Mifflin, and Company, 1901.

Swanson, Carl P. and Norman H. Giles. "Karl Sax." *Biographical Memoirs*. V. 7. Washington, DC: National Academy of Sciences, 1987.

Symko, Stephan. *From a Single Seed: Tracing the Marquis Success Story from Canada to Its Roots in the Ukraine*. Ottawa: Agri-Foods Canada, 1999.

Taylor, Terri A. *Ft. Vancouver: Cultural Landscape Report*. Seattle: National Park Service, 1992.

Thatcher, R. W. *The Nitrogen and Humus Problem in Dry Farming*. WAES Bulletin 105. Pullman: Washington State College, 1912.

Thatcher, R. W. *Wheat and Flour Investigations (Crop of 1905)*. AES Bulletin 84. Pullman: Washington State College, 1907.

Thomas, Paul F. "George Bush." M. A. Thesis. Seattle: University of Washington, 1965.

Thoreau, Henry David, and Bradley P. Dean, ed. *Wild Fruits: Thoreau's Rediscovered Last Manuscript*. New York: W. W. Norton, 2000.

Thorness, Bill. *Edible Heirlooms: Heritage Vegetables for the Maritime Garden*. Seattle: Skipstone, 2009.

Thorpe, I. J. *The Origins of Agriculture in Europe*. London: Routledge, 1999.

Tolmie, William Fraser. *The Journals of William Fraser Tolmie: Physician and Fur Trader*. Vancouver, British Columbia: Mitchell Press, 1963.

Townshend, John Kirk. *Narrative of a Journey Across the Rocky Mountains to the Columbia River*. Lincoln: University of Nebraska Press, 1978.

Trexler, Harrison A. *Flour and Wheat in the Montana Gold Camps, 1862-1870*. Missoula: Dunstan Printing, 1918.

Trotter, F. I., and F. H. Loutzenhiser. *Told by the Pioneers: Tales of Frontier Life as Told by Those Who Remember the Days*. 3 Vols. Olympia: Washington Works Progress Administration, 1937–38.

True, A. C. *A History of Agricultural Experimentation and Research in the United States, 1607–1925*. USDA Miscellaneous Publication 251. Washington, DC: Government Printing Office, 1937.

Varlo, Charles. *A New System of Husbandry*. 3 vols. New York: N. Nickson, 1770.

Vavilov, Nicholai I. *Origin and Geography of Cultivated Plants*. Cambridge University Press, 1992.

Veseth, Roger. "Perceptions of No-Till in the Palouse," *Pacific Northwest Tillage Handbook No. 2*. Moscow: University of Idaho Extension Service, 1986.

Vilmorin, Henri de. *Les Meilleurs Blés: Description et Culture des Principales Variétés de Froments*. Paris: Vilmorin-Andrieux, 1880.

Vilmorin, Henri de. *Catalogue Mèthodique et Synonymique des Froments qui Composent la Collection de H. Vilmorin*. Paris: Vilmorin-Andrieux, 1889.

Vilmorin, Louis de. *Essai d'un Catalogue Mèthodique et Synonymique des Froments qui Composent la Collection de L. Vilmorin*. Paris: Vilmorin-Andrieux, 1850.

Vilmorin, Philippe de. *Supplément Aux Meilleurs Blés: Description et Culture des Principales Variétés de Froments*. Paris: Vilmorin Andrieux,1909.

Vogel, O. A., S. P. Swenson, and C. S. Holton. *Brevor and Elmar Two New Washington Winter Wheats*. State College of Washington Bulletin 525 (May 1951).

Vogel, O. A. "Registration and History of Gaines Wheat." *USDA Soft White Wheat Records*. Columbia: University of Missouri, 1993.

Vogel, O. A. "Winter Wheat Improvement in Washington to 1982." Unpublished manuscript, n.d. Folder 245, Box 7, CN 524. O. A. Vogel Papers, WSU.

Wadham, Samuel. *Australian Farming, 1788–1965*. Melbourne: F. W. Cheshire, 1967.

Wahl, Robert. "Something on Barley Variation and Pure Races." *American Brewers Review* 20 (May 1906).

Warburton, C. *Sixty-Day and Kherson Oats*. USDA Farmers' Bulletin 395. Washington, DC: Government Printing Office, 1910.

Watt, James W. *Journal of Mule Train Packing in Eastern Washington in the 1860's*. Fairfield: Ye Galleon Press, 1971.

Weatherford, Marion. "Fields of Amber Grain," *The Western Shore: Oregon Country Essays Honoring the American Revolution*. Thomas Vaughn, ed. Portland: Oregon Historical Society, 1976.

Weaver, John C. *American Barley Production: A Study in Agricultural Geography*. Minneapolis: Burgess Publishing Company, 1950.

White, Richard. *Land Use, Environment, and Social Change: The Shaping of Island County, Washington*. Seattle: University of Washington Press, 1980.

White, William Allen. "The Business of a Wheat Farm." *Scribner's Magazine XXII* (November 1897).

Whitley, Andrew. *Bread Matters: The State of Modern Bread*. Fourth Estate, 2006.

Wiebe, Gustav A., and David Alexander. *Classification of Barley Varieties Grown in the United States and Canada*. USDA Technical Bulletin 1224. Washington, DC: Government Printing Office, 1958.

Wiley, Harvey W. *Analysis of Cereals Collected at the [1893] World's Columbian Exposition*. USDA Bulletin 45. Washington, DC: Government Printing Office, 1895.

Wilkes, Charles. *Narrative of the United States Exploring Expedition in the Years 1838, 1839, 1840, 1841, and 1842*. 5 vols. Philadelphia: Lea and Blanchard, 1845.

Williams, Jacqueline B. *The Way We Ate: Pacific Northwest Cooking, 1843–1900*. Pullman: Washington State University Press, 1996.

Wilson, Bruce. *Late Frontier: A History of Okanogan County, Washington (1800–1941)*. Okanogan, Washington: Okanogan County Historical Society, 1990.

Wilson, Edward O. *The Future of Life*. New York: Alfred A. Knopf, 2002.

Wilson, Iris. H. *Noticias de Nutka: An Account of Nootka Sound in 1792 by José Mariano Moziño*. Seattle: University of Washington Press, 1970.

Wilson, John M. *The Rural Cyclopedia*. Edinburgh: A. Fuller & Co., 1851.

Wilson, A. Stephen. *A Bushel of Corn*. Edinburgh: David Douglas, 1883.

Winther, Oscar O. *The Old Oregon Country: A History of Frontier Trade, Transportation, and Travel*. Stanford: Stanford University Press, 1950.

Woods, Charles D., and T. H. Merrill. "Coffee Substitutes," *Maine Agricultural Experiment Station Annual Report*. Orono, Maine, 1900.

Young, F. G. "Ewing Young and His Estate with Documentary Records." *Oregon Historical Quarterly* XXI:3 (September 1920).

Zaharia, Heléne. "Bread of Life." *Seedling* (April 2007).

Zeven, Anton C. "Classification of Landraces and Improved Cultivars of Rivet Wheat and Bread Wheat from Great Britain as Described in 1934." *Euphytica* 47:1 (1990).

Zeven, Anton. "Classification of Landraces." *Euphytica* 59:1 (1991).

Zeven, Anton C., and Theo J. L. Hintum. "Classification of Landraces and Improved Cultivars of Hexaploid Wheats Grown in the USA and Described in 1922." *Euphytica* 59:1 (1992).

Oral Histories

De Pasquale, George. Seattle, Washington. September 14, 2012.

Delong, Ray. St. John, Washington. July 19, 1980.

Deyneka, Anita. Wheaton, Illinois. August 8, 2007.

Eggert, Chuck. Tualatin, Oregon. September 18, 2012.

Feldman, Judy. Greenbank, Washington. July 7, 2013.

Fisher, Gordon. Lapwai, Idaho. July 24, 2008.

Frank, Jr., Billy. Seattle, Washington. March 10, 1989.

Henrich, Thomas. Woodland, Washington (Cedar Creek Mill). May 7, 2011.

Huffstetler, Lillian. Coupeville, Washington. September 25, 2011.

Jones, Stephen. Mt. Vernon, Washington. October 12, 2010.

Joseph, Andrew. Sr. Elmer City, Washington. May 9, 2011.

Kamiakin, Cleveland (with Nat Washington). Ephrata, Washington. October 1956.

Lautensleger, Mildred. Vancouver, Washington. April 20, 2007.

Lowry, Mike. Seattle, Washington. December 3, 2007.

McBride, Bud. Tacoma, Washington. February 17, 2011.

McGuire, Lee. Thorton, Washington. January 19, 2013.

McGuire, Mike. Tacoma, Washington (Ft. Nisqually Living History Museum). July 10, 2009.

Mahoffy, JoAnn. Tacoma, Washington. January 14, 2013.

Munro, Ralph. Olympia, Washington. March 20, 1996.

Nagamitsu, Masami "Dick." Lind, Washington. April 18, 2012.

Ochs, Marlo. Endicott, Washington. October 8, 1991.

Putnam, Karl. Inchelium, Washington. April 26, 2013.

Redthunder, Keith. Elmer City, Washington. April 12, 2013.

Reich, Evelyn. Colfax, Washington. May 7, 2003.

Riehle, Rich. Colfax, Washington, May 16, 2003.

Rhind, Bill. Tacoma, Washington (Ft. Nisqually). July 10, 2009.

Rigsby, Bruce. Brisbane, Queensland. September 13, 2011.

Robison, Ken. Ft. Benton, Montana. May 21, 2010.

Roe, Dennis. Colfax, Washington. June 12, 2003.

Schmick, Donald. Colfax, Washington. April 14, 2008.

Schneidmiller, Gary. Coeur d'Alene, Idaho. July 19, 2012.

Schneidmiller, Manuel. Post Falls, Idaho. June 21, 1995.

Schultz, Fred. Woodland, Washington (Cedar Creek Mill). May 7, 2011.

Sivertson, Valerie. Eatonville, Washington (Pioneer Living History Museum). September 19, 2012.

Thomas, Jeffrey. Puyallup, Washington. June 3, 2011.

Vogel, Orville. Pullman, Washington. October 5, 1972.

Weber, Jacob. Quincy, Washington. April 17, 1980.

Manuscript Collections

Ft. Nisqually History Museum Archives, Tacoma, Washington (Ft. Nisqually Journals of Occurrences, 1833–1860 [Edward Huggins, William Tolmie, and William G. Young Folders]).

Gonzaga University, Foley Library Archives, Spokane (Verne Ray Collection, 1930–1975 [Madeline Covington and Nellie Friedlander Interviews, 1956]).

Greater Vernon Museum & Archives, Vernon, British Columbia (Marie H. Brent Fonds, 1908–66. MS 303/2000.060).

Lewis County Historical Museum, Chehalis, Washington (Cowlitz Farm & Hudson's Bay Company Files).

Princeton University Archives, Mudd Manuscript Library, Princeton, New Jersey (J. V. A. MacMurray Papers, 1715–1960. MC 094 [J. W MacMurray Diary]).

Royal British Columbia Archives, Provincial Museum, Victoria (McKenzie Family Fonds, 1779–1943. MS-2431; Robert Melrose Papers, 1852–1857. E/B/M49.1; William Fraser Tolmie Records, 1830–1883. MS-0557 [Tolmie Letterbook, 1844–74; Botanical Notebooks, 1832–47]).

Seattle Pacific University, School of Education, Seattle, Washington (Center for Global Curriculum Studies, International Correspondence and Trip Note Files).

University of Oregon Archives, Eugene (Theodore Stern Papers, 1949–1999; 2000-51 [Fort Nez Perces Post Journal, 1831–1832].

University of Washington, Suzzallo Library Archives, Seattle (Puget Sound Agricultural Company Records, 1834–1905, MC 5033).

USDA National Agricultural Library, Beltsville, Maryland (Ramsey Spillman Manuscript, 1939, CN 160; Harry V. Harlan Manuscript, 1957, CN 87).

Washington State University, Terrell Library Archives, Pullman (McGregor Land and Livestock Company Records, 1887–1949, MS 1982-04; Orville A. Vogel Papers, 1931–1988, CN 524; Richard Scheuerman Papers, 1978–1995, MS 2010-17 [Cleveland Kamiakin Recordings, 1956]); Verle Kaiser Papers, 1932–1982, CN 527; William Jasper Spillman Papers, 1891–1940, CN 250).

Whitman College, Penrose Library Archives, Walla Walla, Washington (Vance Orchard Horse Era Oral History Recordings).

Newspapers and Periodicals

American Farmer
American Agriculturalist
British Colonist (Victoria)
British Columbian
The Coast
Evening Capital Journal (Salem)
Farm Futures
Farm Journal
The Good Fruit Grower
Missoula Pioneer
Morning Capital Journal (Salem)
Northwestern Miller
New York Times
Oregon Spectator
Oregonian
Oregon Farmer
Pacific Rural Press
Palouse (Colfax) *Gazette*
Puget Sound (Steilacoom) *Courier*
Puget Sound (Port Townsend) *Mail*
Ranche and Range (Yakima)
The Ranch (Seattle)
Seattle Times
Spokane Chronicle
Spokane Times
St. Paul Globe
Tacoma Ledger
USDA Weekly Newsletter
Walla Walla Statesman
Walla-Walla Union Bulletin
Weekly News Letter (USDA)
Wheat Life
Willamette (Salem) *Farmer*
The Working Farmer (New York)
Yakima Herald

Index